Praise for *Yoga Bitch*

"Thoughtful, honest, and hilarious."   —*Publishers Weekly*

"Brings the higher path down to earth with refreshing honesty."
                                         —*Kirkus Reviews*

"I love this book. In an era of so much truth telling and blogging and reality shows, we forget how well true stories can be told when they're in the right hands. *Yoga Bitch* has sucked me in and made me laugh and made me think about my own spiritual fucked-up state. You had me at 'Do they make you eat your own poop?'"
                         —Lauren Weedman, author of *A Woman Trapped in a Woman's Body* and former *Daily Show* correspondent

"Suzanne Morrison's memoir is a glorious mash-up of a book. It's all at once a gimlet-eyed look at the ridiculousness of yoga culture, a somewhat reluctant spiritual journey, and a beautifully observed travelogue. But at its core (to use a very yoga-ish word), *Yoga Bitch* is a love story. Like Austen's heroines, Suzanne Morrison has to figure out who she loves in order to know who she is. The result is an unabashedly romantic book, in the very best way—like watching your funniest, most sardonic friend realize that she's head-over-heels in love."
                                    —Claire Dederer, author of *Poser: My Life in Twenty-Three Poses*

"A smart, funny, and keenly observed travelogue of a modern yogini's quest for awakening. *Yoga Bitch* flows like a quirky vinyasa, with each pose just twisted enough to be hilarious."
                —Anne Cushman, author of *Enlightenment for Idiots: A Novel*

"Suzanne Morrison has been through the yoga wars, she has the literal scars to prove it, and she's produced a hilarious and thoughtful memoir."   —Neal Pollack, author of *Stretch*

YOGA *Bitch*

ONE WOMAN'S QUEST *to* CONQUER SKEPTICISM,
CYNICISM, *and* CIGARETTES *on the* PATH *to*
ENLIGHTENMENT

Suzanne **MORRISON**

THREE RIVERS PRESS
NEW YORK

Published in the United States by Three Rivers Press,
an imprint of the Crown Publishing Group,
a division of Random House, Inc., New York.
www.crownpublishing.com

Three Rivers Press and the Tugboat design are registered
trademarks of Random House, Inc.

Library of Congress Cataloging-in-Publication Data
Morrison, Suzanne.
   Yoga bitch : one woman's quest to conquer skepticism, cynicism, and
cigarettes on the path to enlightenment / Suzanne Morrison.—1st ed.
      p. cm.
   1. Morrison, Suzanne.   2. Spiritual biography.   3. Yoga. I. Title.
   BL73.M667A3 2011
   204'.36092—dc22
   [B]

                                                              2010041940

      ISBN 978-0-307-71744-3
      eISBN 978-0-307-71745-0

PRINTED IN THE UNITED STATES OF AMERICA

Cover design by Jessie Sayward Bright

10   9   8

First Edition

for

KURT ANDERSON

Contents

YOGA *Bitch*

1. *Indrasana*

...and before Kitty knew where she was, she found herself not merely under Anna's influence, but in love with
her, as young girls do fall in love with older and married
women...

— LEO TOLSTOY, *Anna Karenina*

Today I found myself strangely moved by a yoga teacher
who spoke like a cross between a phone-sex operator and a
poetry slam contestant. At the start of class, she asked us to
pretend we were floating on a cloud. As she put it, "You're
oh-pening your heart to that cloud, you're floating, you're
blossoming out and tuning in, you're evanescing, yeah,
that's right, you're evanescing."

I briefly contemplated giving the teacher my yoga finger
and walking out. I've been practicing yoga for close to a

decade now, and at thirty-four I'm too old for that airy-fairy horseshit. As far as I'm concerned, floating on a cloud sounds less like a pleasant spiritual exercise and more like what you think you're doing when you're on LSD while falling out of an airplane. But I tuned out her mellifluous, yogier-than-thou voice and soon enough found myself really meditating. Of course, I was meditating on punching this yoga teacher in the face, but still.

At the end of class, she asked us to join her in a chant: *gate, gate, paragate, parasamgate*…which means, she said, her voice shedding its yogabot tones, *gone, gone, gone beyond*. She was young, a little cupcake of a yoga teacher in her black and gray yoga outfit. Maybe she was twenty-five. Maybe younger. She said her grandmother had recently passed away, and she wanted to chant for her and for all of our beloveds who had already gone beyond. In that moment, I forgave her everything, wanted to button up her sweater and give her a cup of cocoa. I chanted *gone, gone, gone beyond* for her beloveds and for mine, and for the twenty-five-year-old I once was.

I turned twenty-five the month after September eleventh, when the stories of those who had gone beyond that day were fresh and ubiquitous. I was working three jobs to save money to move from Seattle to New York, and whether I was at the law firm, at the pub, or taking care of my grandparents' bills, the news was on, and it was all bad. So many people looking for the remains of the people they loved. So many images of the planes hitting the towers, the smoke, the ash.

I had never really been afraid of death before that year. I thought I had worked all that out by the age of seventeen, when I concluded that so long as one lives authentically, one dies without fear or regret. As a teenager, it seemed so simple: if I lived my life as my authentic self wished to live, then death would become something to be curious about; one more adventure I would experience on my own terms.

Religion was an obstacle to authenticity, I figured, especially if you were only confirming in the Catholic Church so that your mother wouldn't give you the stink-eye for the rest of your life. So, at seventeen, I told my mother I wouldn't be confirming. That Kierkegaard said each must come to faith alone, and I hadn't come to faith—*and she couldn't make me.*

This was all well and good for a teenager who secretly believed herself to be immortal, as my countless speeding tickets suggested I did. But by twenty-five the idea of death as an adventure struck me as idiotic. As callous, heartless, and, most of all, clueless. Death wasn't an adventure; it was a near and ever-present void. It was the reason my throat ached when I watched my grandfather try to get up out of his chair. It was the reason we all watched the news with our hands over our mouths.

I had recently graduated from college, having postponed my studies until I was twenty-one in order to follow my authentic self to Europe after high school. Now I was supposed to leave for New York by the following summer. Before the attack on lower Manhattan, I had been nervous about moving to New York, but now what was supposed to be a difficult but necessary rite of passage felt more like courting my own annihilation.

Everywhere I looked, I saw death. My move to New York was the death of my life in Seattle, of a life shared with my family and friends. Given the precariousness of our national security, it seemed as if moving away could mean never seeing them again. I remember wondering how long it would take me to walk home from New York should there be an apocalypse. I figured it would take a while. This worried me.

Even when I wasn't filling my head with postapocalyptic paranoid fantasies, death was out to get me. Once we got to New York, my boyfriend, Jonah, and I would move in together, and I knew what that meant. That meant marriage was coming, and after marriage, babies. And only one thing comes after babies. Death.

I came down with cancer all the time. Brain cancer, stomach cancer, bone cancer. Even trimming my fingernails reminded me that time was passing, and death was coming. Those little boomerangs of used-up life showed up in the sink week after week.

I measured out my life in toenail clippings.

"Stop thinking like that!" my sister said.

"I can't."

"Just try. You haven't even tried."

My sister, Jill, has always been the wisest, the most grounded, of my three siblings. But she couldn't teach me how to live in the face of death, not then. But Indra could.

Indra was a woman, a yoga teacher, a god. Indra taught me how to stand on my head, how to quit smoking, and then lifted me off this Judeo-Christian continent, to fly over miles and miles of indifferent ocean, before dropping me down on a Hindu island in the middle of a Muslim archipelago at the onset of the War on Terror. Indra was my first yoga teacher and I loved her. I loved her with the kind of ambivalence I've only ever had about God, and every man I've ever left.

Indra introduced me to the concept of *union*. That's what hatha yoga is all about, uniting mind and body, masculine and feminine, and, most of all, the individual self with the indivisible Self—who some call God.

When I was seventeen, I was proud that I had chosen not to confirm into the Catholic Church. I figured everybody I told—all those sane people in the world who did not share my crazypants DNA—would agree with me. I was right; most of them, especially my artist friends, did. But one teacher, my drama teacher, said something I've never forgotten. After rehearsal one day, she listened indulgently while I bragged about my lack of faith, a half-smile on her face. Then she said, "It's okay to fall away from the Church when you're young. You'll come back when people start dying."

People were starting to die. And as if my drama teacher had seen something in the prop room's crystal ball, spiritual

memoirs started accumulating on the floor beside my bed.
I told no one what books I was reading. If I had, I wouldn't
have said that I was reading them in the hopes of finding
God. I would have said that they were works of fiction,
really, redemption narratives dressed up in the styles and
mores of different times and places. I would never have
admitted that what kept me reading was the liberating
expansion I felt in my lungs as narrator after narrator was
transformed from lost into found.

Maybe that's what led me to Indra. I don't know. All
I know is that one night in the fall of 2001, I walked in
off the street to my first real yoga class. I had done yoga
in acting classes, and once or twice at the gym where my
sister worked, so I knew the postures already. I had never
been especially attracted to the idea of a yoga practice,
but now I walked into this studio as if I had spent all day
weeping in the garden like Saint Augustine, waiting for
a disembodied voice to sing, *Pick your ass up off the lawn
furniture and go work your shit out, for the love of God.*

That night, I stepped out of the misty Seattle dusk and
into a warm, dimly lit studio. Candlelight glinted off

the hardwood floors. The low thrum of monks chanting emanated from an unseen speaker, and a stunningly beautiful woman with straight, honey-colored hair sat perfectly still in front of a low altar at the front of the room. Indra. She wore flax-colored cotton pants and a matching tank top. Tan, blonde, tall: I've never been one to worship at the altar of such physical attributes. It was more the way she sat, still and yet fluid, that attracted me, and her eyes, which were warm and brown, with friendly crow's-feet lengthening toward her hairline.

Soon we were stretching and lunging and sweating. The lights stayed low and her voice stayed soft, so that eventually it almost seemed as if her instructions were coming from inside my head. Toward the end of class, we were doing something ridiculously hard, lying on our backs with our legs hovering a foot off the ground until my abdominal muscles felt like they would burst. Without realizing it, I had folded my hands at my solar plexus. "That's a good idea," Indra said, nodding at my hands as she kneeled beside me to adjust my hips. "It always helps me to pray when I don't know what I'm doing."

I had to laugh at how baldly she acknowledged my

incompetence, but even as I laughed I wanted to point out to her that I hadn't been praying. I had been thinking, *Kill me. Please kill me.* I wouldn't *pray.* Who on earth was there to pray to? Or, for that matter, who *not* on earth?

But by the end of class I was thanking the gods for this teacher. Before I left, I wrote her a check for a month's worth of classes, and told her I'd be back soon.

Indra co-owned the little studio on Capitol Hill with her partner, Lou. Lou was older than Indra by at least ten years, but they were both the same height and weight—both tall, both strong. That was one of the first things Indra told me when I asked her about Lou, as if this were proof that she and Lou had been designed for one another. I didn't go to Lou's classes much—afterwards I always felt like my tendons had turned to rubber bands, but he was too intense and his gaze too penetrating for me. Also, his classes were full of smelly drum-circle types. But Indra's classes felt like home.

I don't know if I can fully express how bizarre a statement that was. *Indra's classes felt like home.* Not long before I met Indra, I would've mocked myself mercilessly

for saying such a thing. Before her, my idea of exercise
was walking up the hill to buy smokes. Rearranging my
bookshelves. Having sex. Maybe an especially vigorous
acting exercise. Most of the time I lived above the neck.

I'm a reader. Being a reader means I like to be in small,
warm places like beds and bathtubs, whether I'm reading
or snoozing or staring at dust motes in a shaft of sunlight.
At twenty-five, the idea of physical exertion put me in a
panic. I would actually get angry, sometimes, when I saw
people jogging, sort of in the same way I would get angry
at people who wanted me to believe in a God who requires
us to be miserable all the time if we're to get into heaven.
All joggers believed in an afterlife, I figured. They must;
why else would they be wasting so much time in this life,
which by all rational accounts is short and finite? In my
hometown the population was split. Half the people in
Seattle jogged and believed in an afterlife, and the other
half read and believed in Happy Hour.

At twenty-five I was firmly entrenched in the latter half
of Seattle's population, so it came as an absolute shock,
not just to me but to everyone who knew me, when I
found myself going to Indra's yoga studio in leggings and

tank tops four times a week, sometimes more, to sweat
and stretch and experience what it was to use my body for
something other than turning over in bed. I would arrive
at the studio feeling like I'd spent the day tied by the
ankles to Time's bumper, my fingernails scraping the earth.
I walked out upright, fluid, graceful, as if Indra herself
was the pose I needed to master. My acting teachers were
always telling us to find characters through their walks,
that if we could physically embody our characters, we
could begin to map their mental and emotional landscapes.
So, when I walked somewhere alone, I walked like Indra.
Spine erect, chin lowered, I was all straight lines when I
was Indra—tall and long, my softer curves elongating into
her ballerina sinew. My steps were deliberate and faithful.
No need to look down; Indra would trust the terrain.

In class I watched the way she eased her body into each
pose. No matter how excruciating the posture was for me,
no matter how mangled and unbalanced I felt in it, Indra's
face was always calm. She seemed to be somewhere beyond
the pose, even, as if she were only faintly aware that her
body was being sculpted into the posture by an unseen
hand, her arms pulled into perfect alignment, trunk twisted

and massaged, the arches of her feet caressed into graceful caverns. Her toes splayed out one by one like the feathers in a burlesque dancer's fan.

Indra made me want to buy things. Things like hair straighteners. Even Indra's hair expressed a certain serenity, while my wavy, fluffy hair, forever escaping its hairbands, said no such thing about me.

She made me want to buy yoga mats and books with titles like *City Karma* and *Urban Dharma* and *A Brooklyn Kama Sutra*. I left her class every morning and walked straight to Trader Joe's, as if the purchase of organic cheese and tomatoes and biodynamic bubble bath was an extension of my yoga practice.

And according to *Yoga Journal*, it was.

But the most amazing thing of all was that Indra made me want to quit smoking. After class one morning, just as I was putting on the long wool coat I had worn out to the bar the night before, she asked me if I was a smoker. I told her I was, you know, sometimes—like when I drank, or when a girlfriend was going through a breakup, or like, you know, when I was awake.

"But I'm in the process of quitting," I said.

Indra laughed, a deep, appreciative belly laugh. "I know how that goes," she said. She lowered her voice and leaned toward me as if she were about to tell me something she'd never shared with another student. "I was in the process of quitting smoking myself—for about twelve years."

"You're kidding," I whispered back.

She nodded. "But the thing about quitting smoking is, it's not really a process." She smiled. "It's an *action*."

It wasn't the last time Indra would call me on my bullshit. But beyond her words I heard something far more provocative, inspiring and terrifying all at once. *I was once you, so one day you can be me.*

I wonder, now, if that's the first time I felt ambivalent about Indra? When for a moment I saw not just my potential to be her, but her potential to be me? I don't know. All I know is that soon something happened that made me willing to follow her anywhere, if she would only teach me how to live.

It was Thanksgiving. That year my grandmother wasn't well enough to join us at my aunt and uncle's for dinner,

but my grandfather would never miss a party if he could
help it. In fact, my grandfather usually *was* the party; now
that Gram's health was failing, we all spent more and more
time hanging out at the house to keep Grandpa company.
It wasn't unusual for my sister and me to arrive at our
parents' and find our brothers mixing Scotch and waters for
Grandpa on a Friday night; all four of us often started our
weekends doing just that. This was not a chore. Even my
friends liked spending time with my grandfather.

My mom always called her father-in-law *an old shoe*,
the kind of person everybody's comfortable around, who
you can't help but love right away. My sister called him
the Swearing Teddy Bear. Six foot four, with a square head,
thick white hair, and bright blue eyes, my grandfather was
famous for saying the wrong thing at the right time. When
he met my friend Francesca for the first time, he looked her
up and down, a sly smile on his face, and said, "Well you're
a spicy little number, aren't you?" She laughed so hard she
almost spat her wine across the table.

When I told him that my best friend from the time I
was in elementary school had come out, he said, "That's

fine, but what the hell do those lesbians do together, Suzie? What do they do?"

"They do everything a man and woman do together, Grandpa."

He wagged his finger, already pleased with himself. "Ah, yes—except for *one* thing."

Politically correct, he was not.

Grandpa wasn't in the best shape. We all tried to get him to ride his exercise bike, and sometimes he would oblige us, pedaling halfheartedly for five minutes, before giving up and requesting a tin of sardines as his reward. Mostly he liked to sit in his big red chair, watching court shows and old British imports, or listening to Verdi and Wagner through his headphones, whistling along to the good parts.

After a long night of turkey and mashed potatoes, my father and older brother were helping Grandpa into the car when he started wheezing. This wasn't unusual. The mechanics of standing up and sitting down had given him difficulty for some time; twisting and bending and lowering himself all at once to get into a car was a lot for a man who hummed to hide the grunts he made when he tried to tie his shoelaces. But tonight the wheezing started even as he walked down my aunt and uncle's short driveway, flanked by his two namesakes. By the time he reached the car, the sound coming from his chest was like sucking on taut cellophane, and as he tried to lift his foot to get in, he crumpled against my father. I ran around to the other side of the car and helped guide him into place as his breathing thinned into reedy sips of air pulled through lips molded like a flute player's. His eyes were panicked. I held on to his arm and willed him to breathe, taking deep breaths to show him how it was done, how he could find his way back to my face and to the car and to another night of sleep. "Come on, Grandpa," I said, stroking his arm. I breathed deeply over and over again, *this is how it's done, just do what I'm doing*, but soon my own breath grew shallow and sharp and I could feel that my face was wet. I was sobbing. Or hyperventilating. Or both.

I don't remember what happened next, except that I was outside the car, being hugged by my cousin Gabe, who is a priest, crying furiously until my dad ordered me to get back in the car.

Grandpa's breath had deepened a little and he relaxed,

and we scrambled to get him home. On the drive, he rested limply against the seat, exhausted. He turned his head toward mine. "Well, this is no fun at all," he said.

The next day, all I had to do was think about my grandfather, and my chest and throat would constrict as if I were drowning. I tried not to think about what was coming, but it seemed as if the clock were running faster than usual, as if I could only watch as time pleated like the bellows of an accordion. I watched my grandparents die, and then, as if only a day later, there I was, guiding my father into the car, my own children paralyzed by the realization that soon they would be guiding me. I saw myself wheezing beside my panicked grandchild, creating another link in this daisy chain of family love and heartache, and I knew that it wouldn't matter if I lived an authentic life or not, if I lived for my family or my boyfriend or some idea of my truest self. None of that would help me as I peered into the void.

I went to Indra's class and did everything she told me to do. I inhaled when she said to inhale, I exhaled when she said to exhale, and by the end, when we were lying still in Corpse pose, I could finally breathe again.

It was just a few months later that I took all the money I would have spent on a year's worth of cigarettes—about twelve hundred dollars—and gave it to Indra. It was a down payment to attend a two-month yoga teacher training in Bali with Indra and her partner, Lou. But I'll be honest: it wasn't a down payment to become a yoga teacher; it was a down payment on a new me.

Not long after I sealed my fate with that check, I bought a thick, lined journal bound in teal leather, and started to write. The act of writing wasn't new; I had kept journals since my tenth birthday, when my diary had a Hello Kitty cover and a small brass lock to keep my brothers out. But this time I was vaguely aware that I was writing for someone I couldn't pinpoint. Was I writing for an older version of myself, so that I might remember who I once was? Or was it for Indra, for Jonah, for the ether? I can't say for sure. But I'm thinking of Thomas Mallon, now, who said, "No one ever kept a diary for just himself." In the case of the diary to follow, he is right.

February 17, 2002
Seattle, 3:00 a.m.

Okay. So, I'm freaking out.

I leave for my yoga retreat in Bali one week from today. I can't wait to go, and I don't want to go. It's heartbreaking to think that in one week I'll be on the other side of the globe, while Jonah starts packing his things to move to New York. When I get back, he'll be gone. I'll have a few weeks to shut down my life in Seattle before joining him there. He'll find an apartment for us in Brooklyn while I'm still in Bali.

I don't know what's more shocking to me—that Jonah and I are going to leave Seattle, or that my mother is actually *happy* that I'll be living with my boyfriend. *Living in sin.* She says she'd prefer it if we just got married already, since everybody knows that's the plan. But as she put it, "If you're not ready, you're not ready. But I feel better knowing you'll be in New York with a man in the house."

Bali. Two months away from home and family. I'm not cutting the umbilical cord, not yet. I'm just sort of perforating it.

I used to have balls, dammit. I look back on the person I was when I was fresh out of high school, and I don't even know her anymore. Back then, I did what I wanted. I didn't care what people thought of me, or if I was letting anybody down. When all of my friends went off to college, I ran away to Europe as if it were the most natural thing in the world. I hadn't even been out of the country yet, but I knew what I wanted to do, and so I saved up my money and I did it.

I wasn't afraid of anything. Now I feel like I have to apologize to my family for moving to New York. For cutting short the precious time we have together in order to pursue my own selfish dreams.

I'm even afraid of this journal. I'm terrified of being honest with myself, but I've made a promise that I won't censor myself here. Ever since the ex-boyfriend read my journal (including an unfortunate entry about how I had cheated on him with a German engineering student named Jochim. Or Johann. I couldn't remember), I haven't been able to bring myself to write about anything too risky, except in code. But this trip will be mine. No boyfriend, no family. If I write anything too damaging, I can always burn this book before I come home.

I haven't been to confession in over a decade. When I was a kid my mom would say, "Don't you feel better? A nice clean slate," after every confession. I usually felt guilty when she said that, because I knew my slate was still smudgy. I could never bring myself to do all of my penance—if the priest said to do twelve Hail Marys and ten Our Fathers, I'd do two or three of each and call it good. So I knew I hadn't really been purified.

But now I am ready for the clean slate. This trip to Bali is an exhilarating adventure when I think about spending two months with Indra, who I love. But it also represents two months of Hail Marys and Our Fathers, a purgatory of sorts, when I think about spending so much time with Lou, Indra's partner, who will be teaching alongside her.

Lou scares the crap out of me. I feel like he can read my mind. Hell, I'm writing this right now and I have the creepy sensation that he knows I'm doing it. I imagine him, already in Bali, in some womblike meditation chamber, shirtless and tan, wearing linen pants with an elastic waistband. I see him breathing deeply, communing with Babaji, when suddenly he opens his eyes, and knows. That's all he would do, just open his eyes, and know. He wouldn't know it with his mind; he would know it with his *mindbody*.

When I first began attending Indrou Yoga last fall, I quickly became aware of a certain group of slightly smelly, deeply focused yoga students who followed Lou around like he was Jesus in Spandex shorts. They showed no fear around Lou, just reverence and adoration.

Lou makes me feel very small and very weak. Maybe it's the way he calls his students "people" as if we're all more hopelessly human and flawed than he is. It might be simply that Lou reminds me of a priest. Well—a priest who smells of curry, has fingernails stained yellow from turmeric, and who chews cloves instead of breath mints. Lou's the kind of yogi who probably uses a tongue scraper. I think tongue scrapers are revolting.

Which is not to say that Lou is Indian. Actually, I think he was born and raised in Connecticut. The legend at the studio is that Lou *dropped out* in the late sixties, wore his hair long, and draped himself in East Indian getups that looked like long linen nightgowns. He rivaled Timothy Leary in hallucinogenic drug consumption, and when he was done with drugs, he spent four years consuming nothing but fruit juice.

The first time I went to one of his classes, he looked straight at me and said, "People, if you are here to study yoga in the same way you studied aerobics in the eighties, please leave. Yoga is not exercise. It's a spiritual practice. When I see you practicing, you'll get more of my attention."

I've avoided his classes since then. But now I'll be with him every day. Holy hell.

February 18

The last time I was in New York, a year or so ago, I was smoking a cigarette at a downtown Starbucks when I overheard two women chatting outside the yoga studio next door. They were gossiping, actually, but in a yogic sort of way. It was clear that they meant their cooing to suggest that they were more *concerned* than angry. They were talking about another girl in their yoga teacher training program. They both spoke in soothing tones, their vowels as round as the breasts of a Hindu goddess. Clearly this classmate of theirs had done something appalling, because their conversation went like this:

"Feather just doesn't get it."

"Mmm-hmmm. She doesn't get it. Poor Feather."

"She doesn't even get how unyogic she's being."

"I mean, I feel sorry for her, honestly. She just doesn't get it."

"I know, and I can't believe she thinks she gets it. Mmmmm. She totally doesn't get it."

"She doesn't get it at all!"

"I mean, maybe she's a young soul, you know? Right? But what troubles me is that she thinks she gets it."

"Right? And now we're upset and she's polluting the whole environment. It's like what guruji said. She's got, like, no *samtosha*."

"I had total bliss before she came in."

"I know, total bliss, right?"

"Right!"

And so on.

At first I laughed at them. I went home to Seattle and Jill and I joked about them for months. When I told her I was going to Indonesia to study yoga, she said that if Bali turned me into one of those yoga bitches she would strap me down and force-feed me steak and beer and cigarettes until I came back to life. "I've got your back," she said. I love my sister.

But ever since I bought my plane ticket I haven't been able to stop thinking about them. I don't know what I'm more afraid of—that I will become one of them, or that I'm going to a place where I'll be surrounded by them. What I keep thinking of as a yoga retreat is technically a yoga teacher training. But I'm more interested in the retreat part.

February 19

When I made these plans to be in Bali while Jonah moved to New York, it seemed like a good idea. Maybe we needed a break. We haven't been getting along well in months. But now that the date is approaching he's sweet and attentive and stays late at the pub till I get off my shift so we can go home together. It's like we've had a renaissance just knowing our time in Seattle is ending.

I've been packing very slowly, and today Jonah was hanging out while I put my toiletry bag together. I've had the same bottle of sunscreen for at least three years—I have so little need for it beneath Seattle's pewter skies—and I started to pack it, but then I had a thought.

"Does sunscreen go bad?" I asked Jonah. He looked sort of puzzled, and got up off my futon to look at the bottle I held in my hands. "This bottle's been around forever."

He took it, popped the top, and squirted a tiny bit onto his finger. Then, with a quick glance to make sure I was paying attention, he licked it off his finger and smacked his lips the way he would when testing butter to see if it's gone rancid. "Tastes fine to me," he said, shrugging. For a moment I actually thought that he knew what sunscreen was supposed to taste like when it had gone off, but then he cracked up and started wiping his tongue with his sleeve. "Blech," he sputtered. "Remind me not to do that again."

I hate the idea of coming home to find him gone.

A friend of mine, a sailor who's been around the world a million times, came to the pub last night and he and I talked about Indonesia for a long time. I've always had a bit of a secret crush on him. Last night I felt that familiar thrill—equal parts euphoria and panic—when he walked in. But today? Today I miss Jonah already.

Later

So, I know I said I wasn't going to censor myself in this journal, but in this one instance, I have to: my friend, the guy who came into the pub last night. I've been thinking about it, and I can't write his real name. It just feels wrong. So, I'll allow myself this one act of cowardice, even if it is terribly *Sex and the City* of me. He's a sailor, so that's what I'll call him. The Sailor.

He gave me a novel to bring with me to Bali. I'm looking at it right now.

Anyway, he's just a friend. I mean—sure, there was one night, before I was with Jonah, when we kissed. A lot. Without our clothes on. But that was three years ago. So there's no reason for me to feel guilty about him, even if I did get a little jolt when I opened up the book he gave me and found a card in it. It doesn't say much other than "Bon Voyage," but still.... Normally this would send me into paroxysms of guilt and I would fantasize about an alternate universe in which I live with him and we lie around in his turret reading books all day and talking about them at night. And other things. You know.

But I'm too depressed about leaving Jonah. Can't even enjoy a good fantasy.

February 20

So my yoga clothes for my yoga retreat in Indonesia were made in Indonesia. Is this a good sign? Like, my pants will get a homecoming? Or is this a terrible sign, that I will be greeted as an imperialistic capitalist neocolonialist visiting Bali to check up on my sweatshops?

Ugh. I'm pretty sure I was supposed to buy organic cotton "Definitely made by grown-ups" yoga clothes. Shit. I'm already behind the curve.

February 22

I e-mailed Indra to tell her that I don't think I can go. I'm not up for this, I'm not a brave person anymore and all I can think about is that the world is about to end—everybody says so, Nostradamus, the drunk at the pub last night who kept saying, "You think 9/11 was bad? Wait till you see 6/13!"—and I don't want to be away from my family and friends when God's other shoe drops.

Indra wrote back. She's already in Bali, and she said that if things go down she knows where she wants to be, and it isn't the U.S. She told me it's beautiful and warm and peaceful there, and that they're waiting for me.

"Everything is simpler here," she said.

Then she told me to do a visualization exercise in which I imagine everything going well. "Imagine a best-case scenario for your yoga practice, your meditation practice, and your life in this unbelievable paradise."

Okay. So, my visualization: I'm living in one of those thatched huts I saw in my travel book. There's a mud floor. I'm sitting lotus style next to a straw bed, in flowing white yoga clothes, the ones I saw in *Yoga Journal* and would buy if they didn't cost half the price of my plane ticket.

My roommate is sitting next to me, and we're eating curds and rice out of charmingly ethnic bowls. The curds are delicious. Whatever curds are.

We're reading sacred texts, and they are making us feel very sacred. When it's time to go to class, we leave with our yoga mats leaning out of our straw bags just so—like baguettes in a black-and-white photograph from France.

Hmmm. It's working, kind of.

February 23

Up in the clouds.

I am not having a panic attack. I am not having a panic attack.

Later

I just realized that I didn't bring a single novel with me, nothing fun to read whatsoever, and yet I probably tore my rotator cuff waiting in the security line at SeaTac with eighty pounds of *sacred texts* in my bag. At the forty-minute mark I cursed the terrorists for ruining international travel, and my shoulder along with it. Then I took it back. Didn't seem yogic. Also, bad luck: I've got twenty hours of flying ahead of me and I don't want to tempt fate.

That said, when I reached the hour-mark and still had a half-dozen switchbacks to go before my turn for the X-ray anal probe, I allowed myself a few unyogic epithets. *They're winning!* I wanted to cry as the TSA guy fondled my emergency underwear at the frisking station. *The terrorists are winning!*

He smiled down at me as he folded the undies and put them back. He smiled as if he could read my mind, and it was a secret joke between the two of us. It was such a funny smile I couldn't help but smile back.

Then he opened my compact of birth-control pills, presumably to make sure the pills weren't actually teensy tiny little grenades.

So, back to my books. I've brought:

> *The Yoga Sutras.* ("Threads of wisdom," it says on the back. *Sutra* means "thread." Opening randomly to a page, I read this: "The body is a disgusting place to visit, a place of blood and feces and pus. So why would you want to engage in sexual activity with one?" And now…I close the book.)
>
> *The Upanishads.* (Three different translations— two of which the teller at Elliott Bay Book Company nodded at, and the last of which made him wrinkle his nose and say, "Ew, mainstream.")
>
> *The Bhagavad Gita.* (I read it in high school, senior year, and pretended that I found it really deep and interesting. I think it's about a chariot race.)
>
> *The Autobiography of a Yogi.* (Memoirists are egomaniacs. I adore the irony!)
>
> *Trunk-in-Pond: The Illustrated Kama Sutra.* (On sale, pocket-sized, and *Hindu*, people.)

I also have a trio of New Age texts that, if put together, would be called something like *The Universe Comes of Age: God(dess) in the Age of Aquarius.* (Oh dear.)

Okay, I lied. I do have one novel. The one the Sailor gave me. Oh, but I don't even remember what it's called. Forget it.

Arrgh. Still lying. It's called *Maqroll*. Never heard of it, and frankly I don't even know why I brought it. I probably won't have time to read anything fun with all these sacred texts to get through.

February 24

I wish this pen had Technicolor ink in it. From gray, gloomy Seattle to this!

Bali.

I'm in Bali.

This has been the longest day of my life.

I got in this afternoon, bleary and buckled in the joints from twenty hours of flying. After Jonah and I said good-bye, I was so teary and freaked out, my sister gave me two cigarettes in case I should need them. I put them in the pocket of my gray wool pants, and when I got off the plane in Denpasar I realized they were both broken and my pocket was full of loose tobacco.

Which was unfortunate. I could have used one last dose of home before hopping into a stranger's Land Rover to drive north to Penestanan, a village outside of the town of Ubud, which, according to my travel guides, is Bali's spiritual and artistic center.

First impression of Bali? It's hot. Like, steam-room hot. The tiny Denpasar airport is the size of Seattle's ferry terminal, and as full of white people. These other white people were smart enough to wear linen, though. The French-woman next to me in customs eyed me in my black turtle-neck and then leaned into her husband. *"Quelle idiote,"* she said. *"Elle est surement Americaine."*

I would've been mad, except that she was right. I sifted the tobacco in my pocket.

The hour-long drive to Penestanan made me wonder if I'd survived the flight from Seattle only to die right here in the middle of Indonesia. I mean, holy sweet mother Mary, these Indonesians drive like buzzing road insects looking to reincarnate as soon as possible. I honestly believed we would be lucky if we only killed a handful before we made it to the center of the island.

(My travel books told me that the Balinese are a very sacred people, deeply reverent. There is no evidence of this on their highways.)

And Holy Christ, the dogs! We were right in the middle of the freeway when a pack of mangy-looking dogs darted right in front of us. The driver, Made—who had the sweetest face and beautiful teeth—just laughed and swerved around them.

"Puppies!" he said.

I tried to be enthusiastic. "Cute! Love, love dogs. I really do." But I was lying; this pack looked mean. They kept running alongside the Land Rover, barking hoarsely, clearly wanting nothing more than to spread fear and disease. Their backs were caked with dirt and more than one of them was missing an eye or a leg. But when we slowed down I also noted, against my will, that they were all—um. Virile. It's shocking to see balls on a dog. It made my blood run cold: if these dogs aren't fixed, then there will be ever so many more of them.

We stopped at a light, and suddenly our car was surrounded by men waving newspapers in the windows. Made clucked his tongue and shook his head.

"*Jawa,*" he said. "Never take ride from Jawanese driver."

"Why not?"

"They will screw you. You are Australian?"

"No, American."

"Oh!" His eyes lit up, and he pointed to my right. "We have your restaurants!"

A McDonald's loomed like a plastic castle against the horizon. As he pointed, he turned off the highway onto a narrow dirt road, nearly taking out three motorbikes in the process. Soon we were passing villages, thatched houses, women carrying huge piles of laundry or building materials on their heads, and more dogs.

Lots of dogs.

I am going to be here for two months. That's what I kept telling myself as I looked around and tried not to imagine what those dogs smelled like. I tried to respond to Made's chatter about McNuggets and milkshakes, but I was distracted. I was starting to wake up. I mean—until now, this had all been a fantasy. I had visualized this person, me but with better arms and clothes, in a charming National Geographic–meets-chic-import-store setting. But now all I could think was, *I am going to be here, in this sticky, stinky heat for two months.*

Spring in Bali was starting to sound about as enticing as jumping into a sauna with a wet dog. I didn't bring some *Yoga Journal* model to Bali, I brought myself here, and I couldn't help but think that my pale, comfort-addicted body was not designed for roughing it. And the prospect of arriving at some mud-floored hut that was undoubtedly crawling with island creatures made me yearn for my cushy mattress and insect-free apartment.

I was headed for a complete meltdown. Packs of rabid dogs, a mud-floored hut. I'd catch lice and ringworm and Japanese encephalitis. Come to think of it, it really hasn't been all that long since Indonesia's last civil war. Maybe they're cooking up another one right now? At least if I'd gone ahead to New York, I'd only have had to deal with cockroaches. Which reminded me that Jonah is moving to New York in seven weeks. I missed my sister. I didn't want to cry. I wanted to *smoke*.

So I sort of did this meditation thing. Well—it's not really a meditation, at least not one I've ever done in class. But it's something I used to do on long car trips when I was bored or starting to get carsick. I look around at everybody else on the road, and I imagine them without their vehicles. It's sort of like the trick of imagining everybody in the audience in their underwear, but it's actually effective for calming me down. So all of us on the road, we're still in our seated positions, holding invisible steering wheels or resting an arm on the door. The motorbikes are still packed two to a bike. But there is no bike. And there are no cars. All the vehicles are gone, and we're all just zipping across the earth like this, just our bodies in space going very, very fast.

But once we had arrived and I stepped down from Made's elephant of a car, how very real it all became.

YOU KNOW. IT'S funny how scared I was. That was only a few hours ago, and already I'm looking back at that person—that person who was me—and feel like I should have just relaxed and waited to see what would happen, instead of imagining all sorts of terrible things. I mean, what good does that imagining do, anyway? You won't know what something's like till you're there.

Take my roommate, for instance. The only thing I knew to expect when I got to my lodgings in Penestanan was that

I would have a roommate waiting for me. We spoke on the phone a month or so ago, very briefly, but her voice on the line was light and airy and she said something about *seeing where the spirit takes us on this journey of the self* and that we would be on a *wisdom quest* or *vision quest* or something like that, and so I was pretty sure she was of the New Age. Indra had told me that Jessica was a massage therapist, but on the phone Jessica called herself a bodyworker. I had no idea what a bodyworker was, but I suspected that it was someone who did not wear deodorant.

Made dropped me off in a parking lot, really just a gravel road. To my right, the gravel mixed with dirt until it became a trail leading into woods that looked as cool and damp as the woods at home. To my left, green rice paddies stretched to the horizon.

Jessica, pink-cheeked and lion-headed, stood where the gravel parking lot met the sea of green. About my height, but smaller in build than me, more willowy. She wore a ballerina-pink sarong, a white camisole tank top, and ancient-looking Teva sandals. She's very pretty, like a muse, and her blonde hair is something else—it was held off her heart-shaped face by tiny headbands of her own braids woven around her skull. My first thought was, *I want that.*

As if I could buy her braids.

The best news of the day? Jessica smells amazing. Like vanilla and amber. Not a dirty filthy hippie in sight! Feels like something to write home about. She doesn't shave her legs, though. But you know, I went through my own experiment with hardcore feminism in high school, so I know all about it. I'm with ya, sister. At least Jessica has the balls to exhibit her hairy legs. When I stopped shaving, I wore lots and lots of tights. If I could've worn tights under my bathing suit, I would've. Since I couldn't, I just never swam.

Jessica had come to meet me with a Balinese girl named Su. Su is about sixteen, I think, maybe even younger, and she wears her jet-black hair in a long braid. Her family runs the compound where we're staying. It was sort of funny to me that Jessica, this willowy blonde, was wearing a sarong while Su sported capris that could have come straight from the J. Crew catalogue. But just when I was thinking that perhaps Bali was going to be more westernized than I had imagined it would be, Su bent down to pick up my enormous suitcase and placed it on her head.

I couldn't believe it. I tried to protest (holy colonialist, Batman!) but she wouldn't hear of it. She just clasped either side of the suitcase in her smooth, brown arms, and lifted it onto her head. Talk about shame. Before I left Seattle, my friend Dan gave me a bumper sticker to put on my luggage (along with his advice to tell people I'm Canadian) and there it was, his bumper sticker screaming out at me from right above Su's forehead: MARXISTS GET CRAZY LAID.

Su giggled, clearly amused by the look on my face. "It's not hard," she said.

And that was that.

Next I found myself following Jessica and Su past the pavilion and into the hot green labyrinth of terraced rice paddies that stretched across the earth everywhere I looked. Some fields looked like wheat, with long, thin stalks shooting up around us. I ran my fingers through them as if they were hair. Others were clearly younger fields, just mud blanketed by a thin sheet of water, like acres of mirrors spread out across the earth. I caught our reflection in these mirrors as we leaped from one terrace to the next and navigated narrow pathways of mud and grass. Su could actually jump with my luggage on her head. Amazing.

Everything smelled like heat and duckshit. My eyes were blinded by the green.

After about twenty minutes we arrived here, at Bali Hai Bungalows, my home for the next two months.

And remember what I was saying about how it's crazy to get all worked up in advance about something when you have no idea what you're in for? Here's why. My mud hut? It's actually a *mansion*.

MARXISTS GET CRAZY LAID.

When I looked up the hill to see our house shimmering down at us, partly obscured by palm trees, I thought of that song from *The Sound of Music*, the one that goes, "So somewhere in my youth or childhood, I must have done something good."

And then I thought: When the people revolt, they string up the folks in these houses first.

But then I became distracted by the pool.

Actually, there are three pools. Three pools! One regular pool, one kids' pool, and one that's even smaller…the infants' pool? The pet pool? I imagined the murderous pack of wild dogs lounging about in their own pool, sipping umbrella drinks.

The compound is made up of five big houses, three just off the dirt road, two up another thirty stairs or so from there. We're butted up against the forest, looking out over the rice paddies.

Ours is the corner house, farthest from the road. Tiled veranda, shiny marble floors, teak furniture throughout the house. A vaulted ceiling on the first floor, where there's a futon with a batik print bedspread, a cozy corner by the windows with a table and chairs. To the right, a steep staircase; to the left, a full kitchen with a refrigerator stuffed full of pineapples and papayas. And tucked at the bottom of the staircase? A bathroom that defies all expectations: gleaming gray and blue tile, a vase full of jasmine on the counter next to the sink. A long, deep bath with faucets for both cold and hot water.

Upstairs, which is where I am now, is one big bedroom the size of my apartment in Seattle. In the center is a king-sized bed with mosquito netting cascading from a hoop in the ceiling, like a long and gauzy chandelier.

I JUST WENT downstairs to use the bathroom, and on my way down, I stopped to stare at these incredible, bug-eyed monsters carved around a glassless window—the only light source on the dark steps—and I almost knocked into Su. She started giggling at once.

I told her how beautiful I thought the bungalow was, and she just giggled.

"Yes," she said.

"I didn't expect to have three pools on my yoga retreat!"

Her brow furrowed and she picked at her lower lip. I thought maybe she didn't understand me, so again, I said, "Three pools, it's great."

"Two pools," she said. Her expression grew serious as she gathered her words. "The smallest pool is reserved."

"Reserved," I repeated.

She nodded and pivoted around me to continue up the stairs.

I turned and watched as she took the steps two at a time. She was almost buried in the shadows at the top when I called out for her to wait.

"Who's the smallest pool reserved for?"

She barely turned around as she answered me. "For God," she said.

Midnight

I think I've pinpointed the characteristic that makes Jessica so strange and new to me: she's earnest. Like, really earnest. Most of my friends are funny, ironic, sarcastic types. Theater people, writers, readers. You know, um, smokers. Smokers are always ironic, aren't they? (Although I've been hearing rumors that we're all going to lose our irony soon, now that 9/11's happened. Apparently the age we've been in was an ironic one, but now it's over. Which is a weird thing, considering irony has survived most recorded wars, revolutions, and plagues, but whatever, we're a sensitive nation these days.)

No, Jessica's earnest, and perpetually inspired. It's like she's piped into some incredibly moving radio channel that keeps telling her the Greatest News Ever. When she's especially excited, her voice climbs to a silvery blue pitch and I start to wonder if she's going to break into song. When she told me about the bodywork she does—something called craniosacral massage—she said, "It's just! So! Amazing! That I get to do this incredible! Ah! *Work.*"

After I unpacked my things, I went downstairs just as the sun was setting and found Jessica sitting at the table on the veranda, writing in a spiral-bound journal. I sat down across from her and we stared out over the darkening rice paddies and listened.

There's a gamelan orchestra that practices in a pavilion in the middle of the rice paddies. All women, Jessica said. The sounds they make are incredible, like a delicate silver web hanging in the air one minute and the next, medieval knights in chain mail and armor start slam-dancing. I'd bet you can hear them throughout the village. My first boyfriend after high school—the one who liked to read my journal— used to say that the gamelan was the most transcendent and mystical of all musical forms. He would point out the percussive clanginess of it all as if it were a direct link to the divine. At the time, in his smoky apartment, I listened to it and hated its lack of melody, its unpredictable noise.

But in this environment, this dark green night, it makes perfect sense.

Jessica disappeared into the house for a while, and when she came back out she had a plate of rice cakes and tahini, jam, and avocados. I dug around in my straw bag and pulled out all the hippie snacks I bought at Whole Foods last week: unsalted almonds, soy crackers, hemp seeds.

And then, with the courage of a dozen resistance fighters, I added a few pieces of the German-style beef jerky I had swiped from the pub after my last shift a few nights ago.

"Oh, heavens to Betsy!" Jessica cried.

Naturally, I started to move the contraband back into my bag, figuring Jessica's a vegetarian who can't eat in the presence of my jerky. She was looking at me with wide blue eyes, her lips puckered in disgust.

"There are ants in the tahini!"

She pushed the jar aside and I tried to keep from laughing. I've never heard anybody say "heavens to Betsy" before, especially not over tahini. But mostly I was just so relieved. I could keep my meat. After tonight, I'm pretty sure I won't be allowed to eat animals for two months. Who knows? Maybe I'll even go home a vegetarian?

Um, I can actually hear my brothers laughing at that last thought, from ten thousand miles away. They like to say that they are *meatatarians*. In their preferred diet, the only food other than meat that isn't verboten is butter, or anything that can be dipped or drowned in butter. I suspect Jessica would probably pass out if she had to eat dinner on their terms.

She's sleeping next to me right now. We're sharing a king-sized bed that could sleep an entire family, it's so big. She's lying on her back, with her head propped between two pillows to keep her spine straight.

I don't want to sleep. The darkness here is so heavy and warm, and the mosquito netting is distracting. It reminds me of the forts the sibs and I used to make when we were little. Like I should be wearing Underoos or something. How can I sleep? Being under a canopy is too thrilling. And I'm in such good company; Bali's wide awake, like me.

Crickets. Frogs. Dogs. A rooster—isn't it a bit early for a rooster? Sounds of the women packing up their gamelan instruments. A clang, a gong, chatter. It's all perfect. More perfect than I ever could have imagined.

I wonder what everyone at home is doing. Jonah, is he at work? At home? God knows what time it is there. Or if he's thinking of me, here on an island I hardly knew existed a year ago, with no responsibilities to anyone but myself. I'm absolutely on my own.

February 25
Morning

It's 7 a.m. I'm up at 7 a.m. This is incredible. I wish I could call everybody back home and tell them SEE? I CAN GET UP EARLY.

Especially if I'm insanely jet-lagged, I guess.

We have class in two hours. I'm sitting on our tiled veranda, watching Jessica. I'm eating papaya with lime and drinking ginger tea, even though it's about four thousand degrees out here. I would love some coffee, but Indra told me before I left Seattle to prepare for a "cleansing" two months. Which means no coffee, no sugar, no alcohol, and no meat.

Oh, and no sex. I told Indra that wouldn't be a big deal, since I was leaving the boyfriend at home, and she gave me this funny look and then said, "No sex of any kind. You can just as easily drain your own battery as another's."

Exclamation point!

Jessica is sitting lotus-style on the edge of the veranda, her head tilted back, eyes closed. She's pressing a large Starbucks travel mug against her chest, and every few minutes she lowers her head to the mug and sips from it, then she raises her face back up to the sun, smiling slightly, as if in worship.

I don't blame her. For worshiping this place, I mean. Except that I don't want to close my eyes, I don't even want to blink, I just want to take it all in. It's spectacular. Palm trees, papaya trees, a slice of the turquoise pool sparkling below us. It's like eating breakfast in a glinting emerald sanctuary.

There's a small temple off to the left of the veranda, with a sculpture of a tiny, sexless god peeking out at us, smiling placidly. It almost looks like the god and Jessica are smiling at each other. Like they're both in on the secret.

I did ask Jessica if she thought it would be bad if I allowed myself coffee in the morning. She said yes. Which is an understatement. She basically responded as if I'd suggested it might be okay if I freebased cocaine before class.

"No biggie," I said, but it came out in a sort of ragged whisper. The thought of going without coffee made my throat hurt in the way it does just before I break into uncontrollable sobs. But that was fifteen minutes ago. I'm better now. I think.

OH SHIT. Oh my God. Oh God, gross. I just reached

out to take one of the prickly-looking lychee fruits from the bowl in the middle of the table, thinking that maybe some natural sugar could be my replacement for caffeine, but just as I was figuring out how to remove the skin, a tickling on my forearm drew my attention to a parade of ginger-colored ants marching from the fruit in my hand up to my armpit.

Only now do I notice that the fruit is swimming in a soup of ants.

I can't stop wiping my arms of both real and imaginary bugs. There's a never-ending line of ants climbing up the table leg like pilgrims on their way to the promised land of lychees.

The only good thing about these ants is that they are distracting me from my nerves about class. One hour till we have to be there. Please, God. Let it go well.

Evening

Oh no. Oh God. Oh Jesus. Oh, this is bad. I don't even know how to say it.

No, wait. I do know how to say it. They're a cult. A cult!

But it's not Kool-Aid they're drinking.

Shit, Jessica's coming. I've gotta go. I know what's in that Starbucks mug of hers. Run, run.

Okay. I'm ready to get this down, now. I've escaped the house and am safely ensconced in a little restaurant called Wayan's Warung. Wayan is this great big woman with, like, five babies on her hips at all times and a booming laugh. I wish I could tell her why I'm here alone.

But I don't think it would translate.

Today started off so well. I got to class this morning a little bit nervous, but excited to see Indra. And right away I felt like things were going to be okay. Everything was going to be just fine.

Class was held in that big wooden pavilion where Made dropped me off yesterday. It's called a *wantilan*. It has a pointed roof woven like a wicker basket and a panoramic view of green fields and forest that makes me want to stand in the center of the wood floor and spin like a top. All along one side are the women's gamelan instruments, a million different xylophones and gongs encased in wood painted red and gold. When we jump or fall, you can hear them reverberating for minutes afterwards.

Indra and Lou arrived holding hands, both of them dressed from head to toe in flowing white linen. I realized right away it was the first time I'd seen them together. They smiled at us, and then at each other, and then back at us. I was struck by their commitment to being so yogic—I would probably laugh if I tried to be so serene.

We quickly formed a circle, and Indra and Lou took their places among us, Indra sitting on her heels, Lou cross-legged. Indra looked into each of our faces before welcoming us. When she looked at me with her big brown eyes I couldn't help myself—GOD I am such a nerd—I broke into a huge grin. It was just such a relief to see her. She laughed.

As Indra talked about the two months ahead of us, Lou massaged his entire body. He was constantly working on himself, either his toes or his heels, his calves or his hips. His earlobes, even. I wanted to tell him to calm down and just hire someone to do that for him. Someone like Jessica! But he just kept right on milking his toes, and seemed to be only slightly there with us.

So we went around the circle, checking in.

Lou said, "I'm looking forward to our practice together. It's not going to be easy. It's going to be hard."

He said some other stuff, too, but that's all I really heard.

Indra said, "I'm excited for this great group of yogis and yoginis to get to know each other! And Lou"—she turned to him, her whole face brightening—"what do you say we make these yogis into teachers over the next two months?"

And I felt like jumping up and cheering.

When it was my turn to check in, Indra made my day, saying, "Suzanne is my plant, everyone! In Seattle, she always asks for the things I want to teach. So tell me, Suzanne, are you ready for some core work?"

"Yup, definitely core work," I said.

"And how are you today, Suzanne?" Lou asked, cracking his toes five at a time.

"Oh, fine," I said. "Ready to stretch after the plane ride yesterday." Everyone laughed as if I'd said something very true and funny. And then something awful happened. Without a thought, I announced to the circle, "And also, I'm fearing death."

A moment of silence followed, and I felt the faucets in my pores turn on. Then Indra looked into my eyes and I stopped sweating. "We all are. That's why we're here. Good for you, Suzanne." And then we moved on.

So, right away, I felt that I was in good hands, that it was the right choice to come here and get my head together before I move to New York. It occurred to me that maybe this feeling of safety and understanding is why some people go to therapy. And just when I was about to float up to the rafters with relief and happiness, Indra said she wanted to have a little chat about health precautions for our time in Bali.

"Don't drink the water," she said. We all laughed. I mean—

we all pretty much know this, right? Doesn't everybody know that you don't drink the water in developing countries?

Well. Indra says that when you're in a place for two months, it's almost impossible to avoid drinking the water at some point. For instance, one morning when you're really tired you might forget and run your toothbrush under the faucet. Or you might be singing in the shower and not notice that the water is running right down your face and into your open mouth. Give that water a little time in the petri dish of your stomach, and voilà: you've got the Bali Belly.

The thing about the Bali Belly is that it's really nasty. It's amoebic dysentery, just like Montezuma's Revenge or the Delhi Belly, but Indra says it has a particularly bad caboose on the end of its long, mean train. Apparently, after you spend several days on the toilet, you start leaching toxins out your tongue.

And you know, I hate leaching toxins out my *anything*. I'm completely against it.

So this layer of toxins, it starts out green—like mucus—and then it turns gray, as if that mucus were decomposing in your mouth. And then, when you're dangerously dehydrated, your tongue turns black.

The second she said this, I started thinking about Umberto Eco's *The Name of the Rose*, all of those poisoned priests found with blackened tongues. I pictured my yogamates sprawled across the floor of the wantilan, inky squids exploding from their breathless mouths. And I quickly descended from the happy rafters.

"But no worries!" Indra said. "Nothing to worry about. There's a really easy way to avoid contracting the Bali Belly, and you don't even have to take antibiotics. I've never had to worry about the Bali Belly or a black tongue—because I drink my pee."

Right, I'm thinking. No antibiotics, great. Then: *Wait.*

Now's when the wantilan became a carousel in the middle of the rice fields, spinning and spinning.

"People," Lou said, "I know it might sound strange to you, but urine therapy is a common practice outside the Western world. It's a natural way to fight aging, disease—"

"And it makes for a great facial," Indra added.

Lou was rubbing his neck something fierce. He seemed suddenly very tired of having to explain all of this to us. "Urine is very pure. It has a bad rap as a waste product. But urea," he finished, sighing and speaking at the same time, "is a great toxin-killer."

Indra said that urine has cured people of everything from acne to AIDS. Like, they drink the urine and then they say good-bye. To their AIDS.

I wasn't even thinking about how crazy that is. All I was thinking was, "But is it *worth* it?"

Indra was still talking. I got the feeling she'd delivered this speech a few times. "Tonight, before you go to bed, drink a glass of water. *Purified* water, that is! Then, tomorrow, when you wake up, go into the kitchen and fetch a tall glass. Your glass should be able to hold about eight ounces of liquid."

I know from my career as a cocktail waitress that eight ounces equals about four double shots. My mind sat with that knowledge for a long, grave moment.

"Now, take that glass with you into the bathroom and pee into it," Indra said, "catching the midstream, just as you would at the doctor's office. And then—drink it." She rubbed her hands together as if she was just getting to the good part. "If you do this every day of your stay in Bali, I can guarantee you won't leave with a black tongue."

"Do it for the rest of your life," Lou added, looking at us

one by one, "and you will have greater health, happiness, and, most important—a deeper yoga practice."

Oh, Holy Jesus.

My teachers have told me to drink my pee. To partake of my own piss. That urine is a beverage. I know from years of cleaning up after both babies and grandparents that urine is not a beverage. Urine is *urine*. So, were they joking? They didn't look like they were joking.

Indra and Lou went on to discuss the tasty option of mixing urine with fruit juice, and I felt that familiar seizure in my stomach, that feeling I used to get in church when I knew at any moment I would burst out laughing and piss Mom off. And just as I did as a child at St. Monica's, I started looking around to see if I could get anybody else in trouble.

As I made my way around the circle, my eyes landed on Marcy, a middle-aged woman from San Francisco with a thick white ponytail. She was smiling. An easy target.

But then I noticed something. She wasn't just smiling. She was also—nodding.

And Jason, sitting next to her, nodding.

Jessica, my *roommate*, nodding.

They were all nodding. As if this were something we all already did. As if one day our parents taught us how to pee into the toilet, and the next day how to pee into our sippy cups.

And then it dawned on me: *I am the only one here who doesn't already drink from the midstream. I am the only one here who hasn't tasted my own waste. I am the only one here who isn't out of her fucking mind.*

Looking around at my nodding yogamates and beaming teachers, I knew that I had made a huge mistake coming here. I had left my home, my people, and for what? To join a cult? But I had to be careful. I've seen enough zombie movies to know that your doom lies in your discovery. So even before I made the conscious choice, my neck tensed, my chin lowered—and I nodded. I tried to smile, like *great, so great to be here with other people who drink pee*, and I kept on nodding. I doubt I was convincing anybody, but what else could I do? I'm outnumbered, there's no escape. I'm stranded on an island, among pissdrinkers.

2. Holy Ghosts

To become aware of the possibility of the search is to be onto something. Not to be onto something is to be in despair.

— WALKER PERCY, *The Moviegoer*

I know people who would have left my yoga retreat after that first day. People who, when they find themselves in bad situations, say, *This situation is not for me.* They say, *I will leave this bad situation, because it is not for me.* And then, having acknowledged this in thought, they honor it in deed. They leave. They leave cities, families, relationships. They leave yoga camps when they discover that they are surrounded by pissdrinkers.

I stayed.

It's very difficult to look into the murky past and know, for sure, why we once did the things we did. So all I can say is that I know my staying in Bali—when my brain was screaming at me to get the hell out, to go be a tourist for a few weeks and then catch an early flight home—had something to do with penance. Penance is in my bones. So's a desire to confess, even when it isn't technically necessary. I think it stems from seeds of superstition left over from a childhood belief in an omniscient creator. I imagine this creator, this observer, as a sort of annoying sibling in the sky, forever calling me on my bullshit. When I lie or cheat, I actually feel like that annoying sibling in the sky calls down, "Bullshit, Suzie, BULLSHIT!" and that anyone nearby, if they're at all sensitive to the catcalls of the gods, can hear him. And so I behave accordingly, and try to make amends for what I have done.

This sounds like a rigid sort of self-discipline, doesn't it? As if I'm the sort of person who has a fight with her mother and then, out of regret and devotion, spends a month of atonement picking up trash on the streets, like a criminal who will eventually have served her time.

Forgive me, but no. Time served? No, no, no. As I

understand it, the best penance is the free-floating kind
you vaguely engage with every day until you die, like a
mild flu bug that doesn't keep you from going in to work
but ensures that you won't enjoy yourself while you're
there. The longer you can suffer, the more you please God.
Self-loathing, you see, is nothing more than agreeing with
Him. This type of penance takes no self-discipline, just a
good memory on repeat.

I deserved to be stuck in the land of the pissdrinkers,
you see. I had sinned against the very teachers I was there
to learn from.

I had vowed not to censor myself in my Bali journal, but
even as I wrote that, I knew I wasn't going to tell the
whole truth. There was something I simply couldn't bring
myself to write about, it was so mortifying, so childish and
selfish and, I hoped, out of character. I wrote that Lou
intimidated me, but I wasn't ready to admit why Lou scared
me so much, or why I felt like he looked down on me like
the most judgmental priest from my Catholic girlhood.
I wrote that I suspected Lou thought I was weak—but I
never admitted why.

I had spent months saving every penny for both my move to New York and my trip to Bali. I sold books, clothes, returned Christmas presents. My one luxury was my yoga pass. When I started at Indrou Yoga, I was still taking one final college course for my Comp Lit degree, a class called "Terror, Apocalypse, Revolution," which was perfect, really, for my state of mind. But it was also perfect for my wallet: taking that class meant I was eligible for the discounted student yoga pass. When that class ended, I was no longer a college student, which meant I had to pony up almost twice the amount each month to keep practicing yoga.

According to the Yoga Sutras, we're supposed to be grateful for what we already have and avoid focusing on what we don't have but would really like. (Like the forty-dollar candles at my yoga studio, the ones with the matching-scent organic beeswax body butters that promise to balance my Ayurvedic *doshas*.) This is called *the practice of abundance*, and it seems to me that it would be much easier to practice if you had lots and lots of money.

Enter Karlee, one of my best friends in college, and a woman in possession of profoundly flexible morals. (Here's where that annoying sibling in the sky says, *And you're one to talk?*) Karlee thought that no one who was serious about yoga would care all that much about taking money from artists, which is what we were. "That would be against samtosha," she explained one day, as she blithely stole three Odwallas from the QFC on Broadway. "Or, no. Wait—that would be against, you know, *ahimsa*. Or whatever, you know. The one that's all about not being greedy. The practice of abundance. You know. Also? Everything's an illusion. So nothing really matters."

Karlee believed in the yogic idea of abundance, but with a twist: The yogic idea is about not fixating on what we don't have, but instead appreciating that we already have everything we truly need; it's about focusing on our abundance rather than on our poverty. In Karlee's world, this meant that everything was in abundance, and the world was your community garden: Pluck at will. In other words, everything belongs to everyone, including sun, rain, time, Odwallas, and ninety-minute packages of sun salutations and *pranayama*. In Karlee's world, if a yogi cared about money, she might as well be an aerobics instructor. "A yoga teacher who seriously cares about money is no yogi. Yoga is a gift from the Ancients, and a true yoga teacher is the conduit. If money becomes important, the entire transaction is corrupted and the cycle of karma continues."

Karlee had read a lot more yoga books than I had. I had read none. I didn't even have a subscription to *Yoga Journal* yet.

Which is not to suggest that I was a complete moron. Well, obviously I was, for going along with her plan at all. But I knew what we were doing was sketchy. I knew that we weren't so much proving our yogic righteousness as our corrupt judgment and bad morals. But here's the problem: I needed to save a lot of money. My future depended on it. I needed to save every penny I earned, but what I wanted (yoga) required me to spend a lot of those pennies. There was no way to resolve such a conundrum without changing the terms. So now I could continue to save my money, but I could get what I wanted for a more reasonable price: the price of my soul.

"Suzanne, are we doing yoga tonight?" This was at 5:25. Class began at 6:00.

"Can't."

"Why not?"

"I'm going drinking with my sister and Fran."

"Can't you do that after? It'll be out by seven thirty."

"Nope. I'm broke."

"So?"

"So, Karlee, it's wine or yoga, and the wine's winning."

"Just don't pay."

"Don't pay?"

"Yeah, don't sign in, it's like you were never there."

"Oh. Okay."

And that's how it happened. See, every month Karlee and I bought passes to the yoga studio. The way the system worked was that you signed in at the door, and Indra or Lou would check off your name against their books, which told them who had paid their monthly pass and who hadn't. Karlee's idea was that if you didn't sign in, there was no way to check to see if you were paid up or not. It seemed brilliant, especially since Indra and Lou weren't actually there that month. They were teaching a retreat somewhere, so the teachers that month were all substitutes who didn't know us. As Karlee suggested, they'd never catch on.

I'm more than willing to throw Karlee under the bus here. It was her idea, and she never got caught.

I was the one who got caught.

It was after Indra and Lou came back. When my teachers were in town, I attended Indra's classes four times a week, and I rarely went to Lou's. But with Indra and Lou gone, I didn't pay as much attention to the schedule, and one afternoon I found myself in class, facing not the substitute teacher I anticipated, but the male half of Indrou Yoga.

I had lured my friend Joni to the studio with the promise that ninety minutes of sun salutations would tone her upper arms. It wasn't until we were set up on our mats that I saw who the teacher was. Lou's black-brown eyes burned through my forehead.

At the end of class, Joni hesitated by the sign-in sheet. "Keep moving," I said. "We didn't bring any money, so how can we sign in?"

She looked fretfully to the front of the room, where Lou was levitating three inches off the ground while chatting with a few advanced yogis. He glanced at us, then turned back to his serious students, and I had the uncomfortable sensation that he was reading my mind.

. . .

Well, as it would happen, he was reading my mind. I summoned the courage to go back to the yoga studio the following week. I was craving a class, but I had to be at my grandparents' house for dinner, so I braved another of Lou's afternoon classes, hoping his eyes on me the week before had indicated curiosity rather than condemnation. I had passed most of the last week sleepless with shame, vowing never to cheat my yoga teachers again. What would Indra think if she found out? How could I risk everything I was learning from her just to save a few bucks? And what was especially absurd was that I was saving money to go to Bali to study with her! I was cheating her so that I could pay her! As Lou raised his ropey arms to the ceiling for the first sun salutation, his eyes landed on my face. He lowered his arms.

"What's your name?"

I swallowed. "Suzanne Morrison," I said.

He nodded, taking note. His arms flew up, and we were off.

At the end of class, after an all-too brief period of lying flat on my back in a pool of sweat, Lou said, "Suzanne Morrison, can I see you for a moment?"

It turned out that the substitute teachers were smarter

than Karlee had thought. They did know who we were, and they had kept track of how often we came and failed to pay.

"You're five classes behind in payments," Lou said. His eyes bored into mine. "And you and your friend walked out last week without signing in."

"We did?" I whipped out the checkbook, sweating, blushing, trying not to stammer. "How much do I owe?" And then I wrote a check for twice the amount, the remainder a down payment on future classes. A show of good faith, as it were.

Classic behavior on my part, like the time I gave my dad my piggy bank as a gift on Christmas Eve, because I was worried that Santa Claus had noticed all the pennies I'd swiped off his dresser.

Lou watched me as I wrote the check, his eyes full of disappointment and a sort of kung-fu madness, like he was ready to kick my ass *with his mind* if I didn't write that check fast enough.

I could've killed Karlee. I called her the second I got home. I was tempted not to, since she deserved to go through the same humiliation I went through, but I took pity on her. Or, to be honest, I was afraid that if she got

caught she'd own up to the scam and then my half-baked
explanation that I'd forgotten to pay five times in a row
would be yet another infraction in the judgey eyes of Guru
Lou. So I told her, and the next day she arrived in class
prepared with a story about how she "was just wondering"
if she might not have forgotten to renew her monthly
pass. "I get so lost in my yoga practice each month, I forget
about the earthly details, you know?" Meaningful eye
contact, sheepish shrug, bit of a blush. I could've killed her,
and then myself.

I went to Bali to study yoga with Indra. But I also had
something to prove to Lou. I think I would have liked
for him to believe that I stole from his yoga studio only
because I was *that serious* about yoga. Lame? Well, yeah.
But also typical of someone who has all the guilt and none
of the faith: true penance would have been coming clean
and then scrubbing Lou's toilets for a year. That's what
disciplined spiritual practice gives you, a finite punishment
that fits the crime. Instead, I tortured myself thinking that
every time Lou looked me in the eye he saw my sin, the
one I didn't fess up to even though I might've felt relieved

later—even though I might have enjoyed that nice clean slate my mother taught me to expect after confession.

But the truth is, I needed to stay. Not just to do my penance, but because I was onto something, I could feel it. That moment in our check-in circle when Indra looked me in the eye and said that we all fear death felt like a promise; she could help me, she knew what I was talking about. Living embedded in a cult of pissdrinkers would be worth it if it meant Indra would help me find a way to live without fear. The other option—leaving, giving up, going back to my old life with no promise of liberation—was no option at all. That road led to death. Indra could lead me to life.

I felt nauseous every time I thought about what my yogamates and teachers did first thing every morning, sure. But I was also fascinated. It was a mighty strange way to live, that first week in Bali, one moment struck by how diverse the world was, that it was full of so many crazy motherfuckers, and the next moment clutching my throat in horror to think that there might come a day when we would be expected to drink pee together, like wine at the Last Supper. But I had to stay. I wanted to stay. Those first weeks

I felt like Dante working his way through the bowels of hell, searching for the escalator to purgatory, only half certain of ever finding it. But if I did, it would be only a matter of time before I would work my way free of Lou and my debt to his studio, free of fear and self-loathing, and begin the journey to paradise, in blissful contemplation of the future.

February 26

God, it's so hot here. My whole body is prickling and covered in tiny red bumps, as if colonies of ants have burrowed beneath my skin while I sleep. If I'm in direct sunlight for longer than a few seconds, I start to panic. I come from a land where the sun is kept in a bomb shelter for nine months a year. I am lunar white. Sometimes I run toward shade only to find that *there is no shade*. Just this fire on my skin, under my skin, fire everywhere, boiling sweat and sunscreen dripping into my eyes and mouth and pooling in my sports bra.

Lou quoted Milton today: "The mind is its own place, and in itself can make a heaven of hell and a hell of heaven." He said artists have always understood the power of the mind to warp reality. I swear he looked straight at me when he said, "If they're strong enough of mind to understand that."

And I thought, *I'm in hell.* Perhaps Milton spent time on a yoga retreat?

HERE'S WHAT I keep wondering: Is Indra brave for drinking her pee, or is she crazy?

Why would someone so disciplined and smart and kind do something so disgusting? I see no other signs of craziness. Other than this one big billboard.

She was telling us about the Self today, how we're all a part of the same giant Self, and she said that our ability to have compassion for others is proof that we're all connected to one another. She was so persuasive on the subject that when it came time to meditate, I almost made myself weep, having this gorgeous fantasy about hugging children at the Special Olympics and people telling me how compassionate I am.

If anybody at home knew that I wait around after class, hoping that Indra will come by my mat to talk, they would look me in the eye and say, *I don't know you at all anymore.* And I would say, *Well, shit—me neither.*

So maybe I'm the crazy one.

February 27

We're three days into classes and I've figured out that the only thing to do at yoga camp is yoga. When we eat, it is with mindfulness. When we walk, it is in silent meditation.

Even in downtown Ubud, where the streets are lined with taxi drivers who call out "Transport? Transport?" to every tourist who passes, even there, my yogamates walk serenely, with Mona Lisa smiles on their lips. We speak of little other than our processes and our progress and our spiritual, psychological, and physical wellness and how the Balinese people hold the key to all three. Lou said we should try to be like the Balinese. "They have such childlike innocence," he said, which made me cringe. The whole purpose of my college degree was to learn that no one has a childlike innocence, except for maybe Zorba the Greek and a handful of actual children.

Wellness is very big among my yogamates. If Wellness were a person, it would be Michael Jackson circa 1984, and my yogamates would be screaming, crying fans, jumping up and down just to be so near to it. Kind of the way I would act around a cup of coffee and a pack of cigarettes right about now.

Everything must promote Wellness. What we eat, drink, put on our skin. Jessica complained of chapped lips this morning, and when I offered her my Chapstick, she was as horrified as if I'd offered her crude oil straight from the barrel. "Petroleum!" she said, her lip curled in disgust. Clearly, my lips are not Well.

We spend about six to eight hours a day in the wantilan, stretching, lunging, backbending. Being in the middle of the rice fields, there are a lot of bugs and we sweat a great deal. There are also geckos in the rafters, and they occasionally drop soft little pellets of gecko shit down onto our mats. People cry a lot. Not because of the gecko shit, although I might if it falls on me one more time. No, they cry because, as Indra said, we hold repressed emotions and traumas in secret stashes throughout our bodies, and the complex yoga poses are designed to ferret these out, so they can be purged and we can be purified.

After that first class a few days ago I went to the Internet café—it was called Ubud Roi, which made my inner theater geek very happy—and dashed off an e-mail to my folks and Jonah. I really wish I hadn't done that, now. They already think I'm crazy for being here, when I could've just gone ahead to New York with Jonah.

God, am I here just to procrastinate moving to New York?

No. I know why I'm here. And I'm staying.

Anyway. I dashed off a quick SOS e-mail to the fam, which, in its essence, read, HELP ME. I'M STRANDED ON AN ISLAND AMONG PISSDRINKERS. (Why, oh why, must I confess everything to my family? Why can't I just write them e-mails about the temples and the gamelan music and make them resentful of the never-ending sunshine here? Why must I overshare?)

Today I went back to Ubud Roi and had three new messages.

My sister: That's hilarious, do they eat their own shit, too?

My mother: For God's sake Suzanne Marie, why would you sign up to study anything with anybody who was so foolish as to drink her own urine? I've spoken with Dr. Randelkin about this and he says urine is a waste product, sweetie, not a beverage!!!

My dad: Don't even think about it. Love, Pop.

NOTHING FROM JONAH. He doesn't move for another six weeks or so, but I'm sure things are already getting busy for him.

I'm going to practice the *niyama* of contentment. *Samtosha.* What that means is that you practice being content. Everyone here talks about it all the time, it's all samtosha-this and samtosha-that, and that's why yogis smile even when they walk through downtown Ubud and have to say no to three thousand taxi drivers wanting to drive us the three miles home.

February 28

Penance at yoga camp is called karma yoga. You do chores to burn up past sins and please the god in charge of reincarnation. Doing lots of karma yoga means you won't end up spending your next life on the lowest spiritual plane, as a cockroach, say, or a reality TV star. It's a really neat trick for getting people to scrub toilets and lift heavy things. We practice it every morning in the wantilan when we move the women's gamelan instruments to one side of the floor to make room for our mats. The effort is spiritual, if you want it to be. But I'm having a hard time seeing how pushing a four-million-pound xylophone is going to make my soul sing. So far it just makes me sweat.

Occasionally someone will accidentally bump one of the instruments so that it reverberates for a few minutes in a deep, low, metallic thrum. When this happens I always think of that Soundgarden palindrome of my Seattle youth: *Satan, oscillate my metallic sonatas.* If there is a God, I'm sure he's saying, "Seriously, Suzanne? This is how you please me? Seriously?"

BALINESE HINDUISM INCORPORATES many yoga practices, but not the same kind of yoga we do. Theirs is a bhakti yoga, which is a devotional yoga—no exercise, just lots of rituals devoted to pleasing God. It's what we Catholics call a "smells and bells" religion.

Every morning while Jessica does her morning beverage

meditation on the edge of the veranda, I sit at the table with Su and watch her make offerings. She weaves pale green banana leaves into square or circular shallow boxes, each one about the size of my hand. She makes dozens of these little containers, filling them with flowers, wrapped hard candies, incense, and cooked sticky rice. When she's finished, her work tray is stacked two feet high with these little dishes and their contents, like little miniature Easter baskets without handles.

Once you've noticed one offering, you start seeing them everywhere. There was one on the dashboard of Made's car on the drive from the airport when I first arrived. They're on the backs of the toilets at Casa Luna, the bright, open-air restaurant in downtown Ubud where we eat lunch almost every day. There are dozens of offerings littering the steps in the wantilan. It isn't customary to clear them away after the dogs and chickens and ants have eaten everything in them and all that's left is a dried husk and a candy wrapper. So there are piles of these desiccated offerings cluttering every corner of every building, surrounding the base of every scarecrow in every field, and even beneath the icebox in our kitchen.

Su has to do all of the offerings for the entire guest compound: our five guesthouses, the pool and grounds, and then she does the same for the family compound in the back, which is a collection of ramshackle one-story dwellings and a temple devoted to several Balinese incarnations of Hindu gods. She makes and distributes the offerings every day.

My yogamates have pointed to Su as an example of Zen calm and wellness, but she told me that she only gets one day off a year, and that her brothers and her father get most days off a year. She said that she and her mother and aunts and girl cousins do all of the work around the compound. I suppose she was calm when she said this, so who knows? Maybe she's got some sort of Zen magic going on. But I keep wondering what would happen if we got her to do a few rounds of sun salutations? Would there be secret stashes of resentment and animosity hiding in her muscles and tendons?

LOU IS VERY direct and often seems frustrated when I can't hold a pose as long as he wants me to, but Indra says things like, "Offer it up, Suzanne!" or "Make it an offering!"

Reminds me of my mother. When I used to complain about my knees aching from kneeling for forty million hours at Mass, she'd always tell me to offer it up to Jesus. I thought that was the craziest idea I'd ever heard. I mean, why on earth would Jesus want my pain? What would he do with it, put it on a shelf? Add it to my trousseau for when I get to heaven? "Oh, look! Jesus saved my knee pain! That Jesus, he's just so thoughtful..."

I sort of like the way Indra says it, though. She says that everything we do should be an offering, from our karma yoga in the wantilan to our studies to picking up after ourselves. She says that if you're practicing yoga, even washing the dishes is a meaningful, meditative activity. I sort of love that.

Maybe that's how Su sees her offerings? Not as something to resent as bondage, but as a meditation. As a path to clarity, or to her God.

Or maybe she weaves those little dishes thinking, "I hate my brothers, I hate my father, I hate my uncles..."

Later

Tonight we drank tea on the veranda with our next-door neighbors, Jason and Lara. Jason and Lara are here en route to Australia. They're from London, but they've spent the last two years applying for visas to move Down Under permanently. "All we need are two certificates to teach yoga," Jason said, "and we can begin living the kind of life we want."

Jason has a very kind face, with soft features like a kid's, and bright white teeth. He looks like he should be wearing a newsboy's cap, or playing the lead in *Oliver!*

He and Lara must use the same toothpaste; she's got the same movie-star teeth. Lara's hair is thin and dark brown, as shiny as coffee. Her eyes are an arresting grass green, and a little buggy—when she laughs, they water so much she looks like she's crying. Both she and Jason are in their early thirties, and they look like they've been doing yoga for years. They have incredible arms, like they lift each other instead of weights.

"So you're Indra's pet," Lara said, fixing her big eyes on me in a way that made me wonder if she was joking or judging.

"Her pet?"

"Of course," she said, leaning back in her chair and putting one leg up on the table. A flowering vine tattoo crept up her tan leg from her ankle to just below her knee-length white linen pants. "She mentioned you before you arrived— you're the only one from Seattle here, so we've all been dying to meet you and hear what their studio is like."

I pictured their warm, bright studio in the middle of the dark city. "It's an oasis," I said.

All three nodded. "You can just tell," Jason said. "Indra and Lou are something special. I think they're *there*."

I didn't know where *there* was, but Jessica nodded vigorously. "We have so much to learn from them!" she said, beaming around the table.

Lara laughed. "Jessica," she said, "you are the most excitable girl I've ever met."

Jessica smiled. "But Indra is just so inspiring, and Lou—"

"Lou's a sweetheart, isn't he?" Lara said. "He's a love."

They went on about Lou's gentle spirit, how tenderhearted he is, and I sat back, wondering who the hell they were talking about, and could I please have some of whatever they've been smoking?

Nobody's afraid of Lou but me, it seems. How is it possible that I'm the only one who feels like Lou can see my smudged-up soul when he looks in my eyes? You'd think he was a Care Bear, the way they talk of his cuddly personality. I'm shocked.

"It's so sad," Lara was saying. "There aren't any enlightened yoga teachers in London. They're not the least bit enlightened! They really don't get it at all. They're all a lot of climbers who worship their celebrity students. So pretentious."

"Really?" Jessica said.

"Oh yes. All they care about is what you wear and the bag you're carrying and whether or not Madonna and Gwynnie have visited the studio, isn't that right, Jason?"

Jason murmured his agreement, a pained expression on his face. His eyes were focused on his lap.

"Are you okay, Jason?" Jessica asked.

"He's fine," Lara said. Jason nodded. "He's just been a little unwell. Anyway"—she pushed her water bottle over to Jason, who unscrewed the cap and drank—"Indra and Lou, you can tell they're in it for the right reasons. Something about them—you can tell they're living it, not just preaching it, isn't that right, Jason?"

She reached across the table to tap her finger on his

open palm. He had been sitting still with his eyes closed, which he now opened, and then his face broke into a grin.

"Sorry, ladies," he said. "I'm a bit preoccupied with my netherparts at the moment. Nothing new. In Africa I could hardly fart, I was so backed up. These days it's the opposite problem."

I discovered I no longer wanted my tea.

Jason has been all over the world—Cambodia, Laos, and North Africa just in the past year alone—and he collects parasites like some tourists collect postcards. Apparently he's unwell because he's suffering from a particularly bad one right now that he can't seem to shake. Before they left London, he went in for a series of tests and the doctors thought he had stomach cancer. But he had been into town early today to check his e-mail and got the good news that it was just a parasite.

"So, I thought you were all drinking pee in order to avoid parasites!" I said. I couldn't help blurting this out—for all my years of acting classes, I'm a terrible liar, and I couldn't go through this conversation pretending to be like my yoga-mates in this regard. "I hate to say it"—I didn't, really—"but maybe this urine therapy thing is a New Age snake oil."

"Oh no," Jason said. "You've misunderstood me. It's not that urine therapy failed me so much as I failed urine therapy." Jessica and Lara cracked up knowingly. "I take breaks sometimes. You know, when you're traveling it's hard to keep up with any discipline, and some of the places I've been asked to piss in haven't made me feel all that thirsty, if you know what I mean."

"So it was probably during one of your breaks that you caught your parasite!" Jessica said.

I shuddered.

Lara looked at me pityingly. "So you've never even tried it?"

"Nope. Never even heard of it till now."

Jason cut in, "But listen, here's what Indra told me yesterday: she said that if it's cancer, I shouldn't go home. She said I should go on a urine fast instead. She said all I'd have to do is drink nothing but my own urine for eight days, and by the end of that"—he snapped his fingers—"gone. Just like that."

Jessica became very enthusiastic about this. "You should do it anyway, Jason," she said. "You won't believe how amazing you'll feel afterwards!" She beamed at Jason, her eyes bright with the possibility. She made a tumbling gesture with her arms. "Cycle it through," she said.

This passion for cycles is something I'm learning about Jessica. She loves cycles. Everything is about cycles of the moon, cycles of life, cycles of the soul. So even her piss-drinking is cyclical. Or, rather, *re*-cyclical. She doesn't just drink her pee first thing every morning like everybody else at yoga camp. No. She actually recycles it continuously throughout her day. She starts every day standing in the shower to pee into her gigantic Starbucks coffee mug. She takes little nips from that first batch throughout the morning before class. And then, when next she feels the call of nature, she repeats the process. So she is constantly recycling her pee. She doesn't flush a drop.

"I'm so glad it's just a parasite," I said. Lara and Jessica looked at me sadly. I am a disappointment to them. "Sorry, guys," I said, "I guess I'm just sort of chickenshit when it comes to consuming my own bodily fluids. I don't like drinking blood, either."

But it turns out that Indra's treatment for a parasite is almost identical to the treatment for cancer. Only difference is that he can eat fruits and vegetables.

March 2

I'm sitting at the table on the veranda, waiting for Jessica to finish her morning Starbucks *mugeus nauseous* so we can walk to class. Honestly? I'd rather stay home. But I'm practicing contentment. I'm just waiting for it to kick in.

I feel like a lump of flesh in class. Nothing works right. I'm not as strong or as flexible as my yogamates, I have no muscle tone, I shake in every standing posture. I look at Lara and Jason's arms holding their bodies up in handstand and feel so inferior, like some pale, wheezing, consumptive character out of a nineteenth-century novel.

Lou came over to my mat yesterday and you'd think I was shaking on purpose, he was so affronted.

"Watch the knee," he said. "Watch it."

So I looked at it and I watched it and I couldn't see anything wrong.

"Your knee!" Lou said. He grabbed my knee and adjusted it. "It should always be at a ninety-degree angle in this pose. Yours is more like forty-five degrees, and it's turning inward, and it's because you aren't supporting yourself."

I was panting. "I don't have any muscles, Lou."

"Well, you'll never build any like that."

When I rested in Child's pose a few minutes later BECAUSE I WAS DYING OF TIREDNESS, Lou stopped by my mat and said, "Take a few breaths and get back in the pose."

What is this, the army?

THERE IS ONE posture I excel at, however: Corpse pose. It's my favorite. I love any exercise that involves lying on my back pretending to be dead. Lou says I have a particular knack for it. Har-har.

We were lying in Corpse pose today when I noticed a sound collecting in my ears as I drifted in and out of focus. It was a buzzing sound, coming from the rice fields, like someone doing wheelies on a Harley-Davidson. It took me a minute to realize it was a chainsaw.

Lou asked us to lift ourselves out of Corpse so that Indra could lead us in guided meditation. We rose from the dead to meditate, and I couldn't help but look around to see where the sound was coming from.

"Eyes closed, my plant," Indra said, winking. I quickly closed my eyes and tried to look meditative. Indra's meditation began with the usual business about focusing on the breath, and then after a few minutes of heart listening and all the usual stuff, she said something that I believe was just for me. She said, "Sometimes during meditation it's easy to become distracted by noises and movement happening around you."

I almost laughed, because just then the chainsaw roared, and then roared again at a higher pitch as if to say, *Distracted? By this?*

She asked us to imagine that the chainsaw wasn't coming from outside the wantilan, but was actually emanating from deep within our own bodies.

The chainsaw sounded like it was right outside the wantilan. I was thinking of *The Texas Chainsaw Massacre* now, and that sound definitely wasn't coming from within. It was coming from Leatherface. I half listened to Indra as she gently spoke about our inability to control our surroundings—"We can rent the wantilan, but we can't control the Balinese who need to build more bungalows, we can't control the Tiger Economy!"—but that we could control our response to it, if we discipline our minds.

"So, just for a moment, let's imagine that the chainsaw isn't some worker sawing a piece of wood. It's you, sawing away at your...nagging thoughts...your regrets, your fears.

"That incredibly distracting noise is, in fact, your own inner hand, sculpting your energy, cleaning away the rough branches of attachment that are covering your chakras, blocking their light and suffocating your potential for transcendence."

Honestly? I couldn't fathom what she was talking about. So I imagined Leatherface crouching on the floor of my inner landscape (which, inexplicably, resembled a Russian prison cell), sawing away at the version of me who was afraid of the future and ashamed of her past. My fearful doppelgänger.

"And as your chakras are, one by one, released from the wood of attachment and the branches of indecision and dysfunction, you feel lighter..."

Leatherface was chopping off my doppelgänger's arms and legs.

"You feel happier, brighter..."

My doppelgänger's severed limbs flopped about on the floor of my Russian inner cell. Her stumps gushed cranberry-red blood.

"You feel closer to oneness with the indivisible unity of life, the great Self..."

Suddenly another version of me stepped into the cell. Brave, pissed off, and carrying a semiautomatic weapon: my kick-ass triplegänger. She pointed the gun at Leatherface, who snarled through beef-jerky lips dripping with saliva, and revved his chainsaw in her direction.

You want some of this, you sick bastard? My triplegänger asked him, waving her gun. *You want a taste of this?* And just as Leatherface started toward her, chainsaw raised, my triplegänger doused him in a stream of bullets. I watched as Leatherface flew backward in slow motion as the bullets entered his body, then shook and twisted and flopped to the ground, where he convulsed a few times before lying motionless. His chainsaw kept revving, reverberating against the cold cement walls of the gulag cell as if in mourning.

Then I remembered my chakras. I pictured my triplegänger claiming the still-revving chainsaw and hacking away the branches and stuff surrounding each chakra. I know that chakras are energy centers, but I couldn't remember how many I had or where they were in my body, so my triplegänger was forced to saw through what appeared to be a half-dozen multicolored lightbulbs covered in leaves.

I got back to my doppelgänger. She wasn't dead yet. And even though, technically, she was the one who was holding me back, I watched as my triplegänger picked up her limbs and reattached them to my doppelgänger's body with a soldering iron she happened to have strapped to her belt. Then she sent her on her way with a wink and a spank to the derriere.

"Now take a deep breath," Indra said. "Hold it, release. Good. And now, breathe as if you are *alive*."

March 3

So, I've established that I'm really good at Corpse pose. But I'm really bad at walking meditation.

This morning, for instance, Jessica and I took a walk through the village, single file. Jessica was showing me how she does her walking meditation so I could do my own. The idea is to move through space without becoming distracted or desirous. To focus on the horizon, living in each footstep. You step only for this one step, not to reach any goal.

White people all over the village are practicing their

walking meditation. It's sort of like Dawn of the Yogic Dead around here. Except that, if we were zombies, we'd be looking for human flesh to eat. But since we're not, we're just looking to—um. Shoot, I guess we're just looking to meditate while we walk? I don't know, I'm new here. And like I said, I'm really bad at this.

At first, walking through the rice paddies, I thought, *No problem. I'll just keep my eyes focused ahead, and let this green sea flow along in my peripheral vision.*

But soon we headed back into the village, and I began to wonder how anybody would ever want to transcend such a place. The day was clear and bright. Hot, but not hellishly so. Creamy white frangipani blossoms literally filled the air; they drifted on soft breezes and landed in the path in front of us as if they'd been strewn there by invisible flower girls. The air was full of their sweet perfume. I instantly started to think about how I wanted my entire apartment to smell like that. And I wondered if it came in oil form, and if so, if I could buy some to take home for all my girlfriends.

Or soaps! People love soaps!

A few paces ahead, Jessica lifted and dropped her shoulders and let out a long, melodious sigh. I refocused my gaze and went back to living in my footsteps. That is, until we passed Balinese women dressed in sarongs of yellow and white, their lacy tops stretched over camisoles or bras and tied at the waist with thick silk sashes. On their heads they balanced large square offering boxes made from palm fronds, their lids stacked high with fruit and flowers. The scent of cooked chicken wafted from the boxes, and it occurred to me that all I really wanted in life was some chicken. Oh, chicken! Oh, delicious meat!

We slowed at the bottom of a hill and looked down into

a deep ravine. Its dimples and paths were clogged with garbage, some of it on fire. The frangipani and chicken were smothered by the pungent reek of burning garbage and decomposing leaves. I could hear a river down there somewhere, but I couldn't make it out through all the trash. The path inclined in front of us, deep grooves on either side where mopeds churn up the dirt countless times a day.

Everywhere I looked, life was being lived differently than at home. I couldn't help but feel excited by so much possibility. I drank it in, I wanted to become one with it, I wanted to own every second of it, every piece of it.

The wet sheen of the banana leaves, the sweetish smell of jungle rot, the reek of animal dung, the blossoms on the road, the women who passed me, smelling of jasmine oil and incense and a god's supper.

Who in her right mind would want to transcend any of this?

Later

I've been imagining Jonah and myself on one of those mopeds, scooting around town, having parties for our friends at the mini-mansion. I thought that maybe I'd rather stay here and bring Jonah out than go to New York. Because there are three things New York doesn't have:

> One: frangipani blossoms
> Two: gamelan music every night
> Three: women who carry roast chickens on
> their heads.

Oh, and rent here is five dollars a day. I don't think we'll find anything like that in New York.

I e-mailed Jonah something to this effect, and he responded right away, laughing it off. But part of me is serious. Jonah says I need to let him get through one move at a time.

March 4

Jalaneti: the art of cleaning snot out of your nose. Having clean nostrils is a big thing around here, so I started my very own jalaneti practice this morning. Honestly, I barely survived.

Jason and Lara are very sweet, like older siblings to Jessica and me, and they offered to teach me. They set me up in their bathroom, which is practically identical to ours, where they had already filled a tiny white plastic teapot with salt water. They said a funny little blessing over the pot ("let Suzanne's nose know what is known by our noses, Namaste") and then watched, calm and expectant, like godparents at my baptism, as I took the neti pot from Lara's hands and acted like I knew what I was doing.

But I'm such a klutz. I couldn't help but laugh at Jason, who started chanting, "Clean that nose, clean that nose," just as I slid the spout in one nostril and tilted my head to the side. And apparently I laugh through my nose, because the suction from my laughter acted like a vacuum on the tiny teapot, the contents of which I snorted up like an aardvark. The salt water went straight up to my third eye, where I was treated to a flash memory of being dunked in the pool by my older brother. I started sputtering and laughing and crying all at once. Lara pressed a towel to my nose. "Breathe," she said, giggling. Jason was laughing so hard he had to sit on the edge of the bathtub.

"Tha—that—" He took a deep breath and wiped his eyes, still laughing. "That's what happens to everybody the first time they do it." He sighed and then started giggling again. "But I've never seen anyone spray so much water out their nose as you just did."

I'm thinking that maybe my nose is fine the way it is.

Now I'm sitting here with a spongy nag in my sinuses. My head is waterlogged. And I'm thinking, this is why we must transcend our physical bodies. Because a body is always going to piss you off.

Later

I'm lying on the bed between classes, slathered in tingly arnica gel and Tiger Balm. Every muscle in my body resents me today. When I sit down I hum with pain, like my grandfather. I wish Jonah were here, and that he'd rub my shoulders. Though I suppose I'm being unrealistic. Not about my desire for Jonah to be here, but about him being willing to rub my shoulders. I'm kind of an affection whore—it drives Jonah crazy. But what can I do? I was raised in a family of affection whores. In my family you can't leave a party without hugging everybody at least three times. And that's even if we're going to see each other again the next day.

Anyway, it's only been a week and I'm already even more affection-starved than normal.

I am doing everything I can to be a good yogi. I'm reading my sacred texts. Well—I'm reading *The Autobiography of a Yogi*, at least, because it's got lots of great Hindu saints in it who float through the air and can breathe underground. I would like to be able to do both of these things. I love Yogananda, the author. He's funny and chubby and loves to eat sweets. I wish he were here. I think he'd understand why my walking meditation is going so poorly. Also, he looks pretty snuggly.

I'm practicing contentment, which means that any time I think a bad thought I try to counter it with a good thought. For instance, today I thought, *I would like to punch Louise*. And then I thought, *I love Louise*.

Ah, Louise.

There are only six of us who will be here for the full retreat. This month we've got visitors stopping in for a week here, a week there. And so arrived Louise. She does Burning Man. She said it right away, like the statement was a secret decoder ring or something. She's in her early forties but in that arrested Burner, I-still-think-I'm-twenty way. She sports a wiry red pixie cut and wears a lot of purple and semiprecious stones.

Louise is a type-A yogini and—if you ask me—a bit show-offy about how hard she's working. She complains endlessly about how hard everything is. Take yesterday, for instance. We were having lunch at Casa Luna, and the woman wouldn't shut up. She's an American who has lived in Australia and has a British husband. So she has an accent that makes no sense whatsoever.

I was saying how I found guided meditation to be very relaxing, and she looked at me with wide blue eyes and said, "Relaxing, are you mad?" in her Madonna accent. And then she sat back in her chair and wiped her mouth with her napkin. "Right!" she said. "So, let's be honest, meditation is hard!"

An endless monologue ensued about how difficult it was for her to concentrate for such a long time. "It's too *hard* for me!" An eternity of her complaining about her brain interfering with her serenity. "It's just that I was really precocious as a child, you know? I was quite keen on learning, so my mind has always been overly active." She smiled with what looked like faux modesty at Jessica, who smiled back, because Jessica is an inherently kind and patient person. "In my family the joke was always that I was 'intellectually hyperactive.'"

I started laughing, the way you do in a straitjacket. When she looked at me I played it off as if she were just terribly amusing, a real comedian.

"But meditation is so *hard*. It's the first thing in my life I'm not good at, and it's really starting to get to me."

"I think you need to relax," I said. I passed her a dish called *kangkung*. "Have some more green leaves."

"But you know what's even harder than meditation?" she said, leaning in and lowering her voice. She sounded really perturbed, like she was going to admit something she'd never admitted before. It had to be something good—I was hoping she would say something like, "I keep dreaming of Lou spanking me," or "I secretly want to smoke behind the wantilan between classes."

But no. What's harder than meditation?

"Chanting."

I love Louise. I love Louise. I love Louise.

Later

Here's the thing about yoga: people are farting all the time.

I am not a squeamish person, not at all. I've changed diapers on young and old since I was in junior high. But that doesn't mean I enjoy hanging out and farting with a bunch of people I don't know. Generally speaking, I think farting is something to be enjoyed on your own time, in the privacy of your own home, especially if you've been on a diet of greens, rice, and soy for a week or more.

But the problem is—farts are funny. So I simply can't

keep it together when my placid-faced yogamates start honking at each other like Ganesha the elephant god.

You'd think Jason, being the only guy, would be the worst offender, but no. He's the one who makes the funniest noises, little toots, like a princess. And when he does it, they don't smell and his giggling about it makes everybody laugh. We have a very healthy relationship with Jason's GI tract.

It's the girls who wage silent warfare, surprise attacks that could destroy whole villages if employed properly. They never acknowledge what they've done. It's like they've all been holding in these farts for their entire lives, just waiting till my mat is next to theirs so they can unload a few decades' worth of steam. But of the girls, no one compares to Louise.

My good sweet God, I can't handle it. Today she didn't even make a sound, it was completely unfair, no warning at all. And suddenly I was drowning in a vat of rotten eggs and fried bananas. A sweet, sulfurous smell, as if her body had fermented the food in her stomach for years before deciding now, finally, to digest it.

The force of her fart literally knocked me over. I didn't even realize what had happened till I was on my hands and knees. Without thinking about it, I got into Child's pose, as if I were tired and needed a rest. But what I was really doing was plugging my nose with my fingers so I could breathe through my mouth.

I was trying to be content about it. I was trying to tell myself that in yoga people are more liberated, that they see farting as a sort of letting go of the past, that we're all one Self, after all, so when one of us farts, all of us fart, and that I should just, you know, enjoy the wind on my face.

But suddenly it hit me that I was trying to *understand*

Louise's fart. I was trying to *relate* to a *fart*. That's when my diaphragm started to quiver, and then the giggle just sort of popped out of me in a rush of air. It was trouble laughter, the kind that you might not be able to stop and that always happens at the wrong time. It just rushed right out through my nose. But, oh my God, it's so much worse, because my nose was plugged by my fingers so it came out in more of a snort, which, you know, sounds a lot like a fart. So suddenly my nose and lips were emitting all of these horrible fart sounds, snorty fart sounds which only made me laugh louder, because now I was sure that nothing worse could ever happen. Because now my yogamates, immersed as they were in their Camel poses, must have thought that my wet, snorty sounds corresponded to Louise's smells.

When I finally caught my breath and looked up from child's pose, Lou was glaring at me. He came by my mat after class and said, "Suzanne. You are only the person you are RIGHT NOW."

That could be the most depressing thing I've ever heard.

Later—almost dawn

This is the third time I've had this dream:

> I am in a white padded cell, on all fours, and I'm wearing white leather chaps and nothing else. I have clothespins sucking on my nipples like they are alive, like they are baby clothespin-sucklings. And I'm just hanging out like this when Lou enters the room, looking even taller than he is. I am aware of every muscle in his body, and he keeps saying, *These are yoga muscles. Yoga muscles are better than other muscles because they are made out of GOD.*

And then he gets behind me and I slap my ass
and say, *Just do it, Lou. Do it. I've been bad. I've
been so bad.*

Holy hell.

March 5

Louise left today, and everybody cried to see her go. I didn't,
but I did give her a warm hug that I actually meant. What is
it about yoga that makes us all so stupidly emotional?

Evening

I'm feeling a little depressed today. Lou was being *muy* pan-
theistic in class this morning. Well, I guess he's always pan-
theistic in the sense that he sees the universe as God and
God as the universe—all that *We are all One Self* business—
but today he was treating all religions as yoga. We were
chanting when he switched from the Sanskrit *Om Namah
Shivaya* to *Kyrie Eleison, Christe Eleison, Kyrie Eleison.* My
mouth opened but the words wouldn't come out.

It pains me to admit this, but Louise was right: chanting
is hard.

I grew up in that Church, and I did not confirm in that
Church, and I don't want to be reminded of that Church.

Ugh. If I'm only the person I am right now, then I am a
person who does not fit in at yoga camp.

It feels like it's been months since I was home. I still
don't quite *get* my yogamates, nice as they are, and it's been
impossible to get any time with Indra. That's really it. She's
kind and attentive in class, but if I approach her after class,
she gets this distant look in her eyes, as if she has to protect
herself from her students. During practice it's clear that she

favors me. Or, at least, I hope it is. I really want to be her favorite. That is unabashedly unyogic of me, but I want to be the one student she looks back on and thinks, *She is the reason I teach. She has made it all worthwhile.* Indra spends more time helping me than the others, and I don't think it's just because I'm the least experienced. Well—I hope not.

If all I'm here to do is be abused by Lou, chant Christian prayers, and endure the myriad bodily functions my yoga-mates insist on sharing with one another, then I'm a bigger fool than anyone could have guessed.

Jonah is winding down his life in Seattle, meeting with our friends and my siblings for final drinks, final dinners. And I'm not there. I feel so disconnected from him, and I keep thinking about all the negative things. I'm not think-ing about how sweet he is, how he cooks for me or brings me Swedish Fish because he thinks it's funny that they give me such an incredible sugar high. No, I'm thinking about the fact that we watch too much television together, that I wish we would travel together, that I don't know what it'll be like living with him.

My sister is alone in our apartment. We might never live in the same city again. We spend every night together. I can't imagine how I'm going to live without her, and yet I'm wasting two of my last months before moving to New York here, among strangers.

I keep picturing Seattle the last night I was there, driving through downtown, the streetlamps festooned with plastic, talismanic American flags. I had just come from my grand-parents' house, where I sat with Grandpa and watched *All Creatures Great and Small* on PBS before going down the hall to say good-bye to Gram.

She was in bed at four o'clock in the afternoon. I sat

down next to her on the raspberry-colored bedspread and told her I was there to say good-bye. Just then, the new home nurse came in, the one who took over the days I used to stay with Gram, and Gram said, "Mary, I'd like you to meet my granddaughter Suzie. She lives in New York with her boyfriend Jonah."

I said, "No, Gram, I'm just going to Bali for a couple of months. I haven't moved yet."

She smiled, flashing her dimple at Mary, cocking her head in that flirtatious way she has. "Suzie's come all the way from New York just to visit me." She patted my hand.

I smiled at Mary as she left the room—we'd already met a half-dozen times at least—and listened as Gram prattled on about a dream she'd had, which she clearly thought was real. I tried not to think about what she might be like in two months' time. She changes dramatically on an almost weekly basis. I started to get antsy, trying to skirt the guilt stabbing at my stomach and throat. Her room, as always, smelled strongly of dusty rose potpourri and faintly of urine, and even though I've spent hours in there with her over the years and am quite used to it, I suddenly felt a strong need to leave.

I kissed Gram good-bye and put my head on her chest while she chatted away about how her dog, Blitzen, had been in the room earlier, and how my father and his frater-nity brothers had gotten the dachsund drunk on German beer last night, so his little legs kept giving out. I murmured to let her know I was listening, and gradually she slowed down, her words drifting off. I sat up to look at her. She was dozing, her mouth slightly open, exposing her small yellow-ing teeth. I rubbed the space between her eyebrows with my thumb, the way my father did when Gram was upset, and then I slid off the bed. I spent a few minutes tidying her room, putting her nightgown in the hamper, straightening the stack of notebooks on her bedside table. I tried not to think that this could be the last time, that I was trading time with my grandmother for an Indonesian adventure. As I walked through the doorway I heard the sheets rustling and then her voice, childlike and full of joy, exclaimed to the empty room, "I am so lucky."

It was like being hit in the stomach with a baseball bat.

Where's the positive thought to counter this one? How do you look at a deteriorating woman and practice contentment? I mean, if you're not a sociopath?

I haven't looked at a newspaper since I've been here. Supposedly that's what it takes to get enlightened, to live without fear: withdraw from the world, retreat from the people and things you're attached to.

But all I can think is, if the world were to end tomorrow, this is not where I would want to be. I wouldn't want to be enlightened. I would want to be in Seattle, with my family and friends, toasting the apocalypse.

March 7

The last thing I expected at yoga camp was Christianity. For the past three days, Lou has been bringing that Catholic prayer, that prayer of my every Sunday for eighteen years, into the wantilan. This:

Kyrie Eleison, Christe Eleison, Kyrie Eleison—which means "Lord have mercy, Christ have mercy, Lord have mercy."

Did I accidentally go to Bible camp?

I've always had this little problem with my childhood faith: I can't seem to believe in the Catholic God. I'd love to, but I just can't, even if I find myself calling upon Him and occasionally praying to Him, and name-dropping Him and His pals, Jesus and Mary, as if they were celebrities I once had cocktails with.

I go to church for family functions, and I always take part. I take Communion, I say the prayers. I still like the rituals.

So I'm a bit surprised at my reaction to this little prayer. The second the words came out of Lou's mouth, I felt like snickering. I literally felt my face and posture turn sour and teenaged, exactly the way I used to sit in the church pews when I was in high school.

To be fair, I had a lot of reasons to snicker in church. Our pastor was a real bastard. Every week he looked down on us from the pulpit and told the women in the pews that we were impure, dirty, that we brought about man's fall. I actually learned the word "bristle" because of him. "That priest makes me bristle," my mom said on the drive home after Mass one Sunday when I was ten. That day our priest had begun his sermon by declaiming, "Sin was originated by a woman."

This was the same priest who laughed when I told him, at eight, that I wanted to be an altar boy. He laughed! So it was my brothers who were allowed to participate in those rituals, who rang the bells and wore the white robes and got to sit on the stage—or the altar, I should say—throughout mass.

Kyrie Eleison. Lord have mercy. On women's souls, for we are temptresses. Too dirty to stand on the altar, so close to the Host.

As a kid, I was disappointed, and maybe a little convinced that I *was* bad. I had a terrible fear of hell, which seemed inevitable given all the bad thoughts I indulged in.

But as a teenager, I was outraged. I was being condemned, in the twentieth century, by a *myth*? Eve eats an apple in a story, and you want me, sitting here in my blue jeans and Nirvana T-shirt, to feel bad about it? *Fuck off, old man.* That's why I didn't confirm in the faith.

Turns out there were many Eves offering their apples to our pastor, and many of them were married. One was a teen-aged girl. So our pastor is serving the Church no more.

God be praised.

ANYWAY, IT JUST doesn't make sense, mixing a Christian prayer with yoga. Is this yet another 9/11 thing? It seems as if, in the six months since the attacks, everybody around me has been talking about God a lot more than I ever would have thought possible. God, and revenge.

But as I understand it, yoga is about getting away from the ego and seeing that we are all one. I was raised to believe that God watches your every move, taking note of every single little thought, desire, every imaginary sin, as if you were the center of His universe. Doesn't that reinforce your ego, your sense of being separate from others?

I thought that what we were doing here was the exact opposite, not seeing ourselves as separate and special and spied upon twenty-four hours a day by a Taskmaster God, but rather as part of some big energetic force that isn't judging us all the time and making us worry we'll go to hell if we don't atone, atone, atone! I mean, Christ. I've been doing penance (or at least some of it) my entire freaking life, and this Christian God probably doesn't even exist! It's just my inner knuckle-dragger that is too primitive to get that through her beetle-browed skull.

I already feel guilty around Lou, as if he can see straight through my façade to the weakness at my core, just like the priests at home made me feel when I was a kid. As if it is a man's job to judge me, to tell me if I'm good or bad, holy or impure. Listening to those words fall from Lou's mouth, I want to burn this church down.

Later

Jessica says that I overthink things. She says, "Let go, and let God!"

Funny—my cousin Gabe said the same thing in his first sermon as an ordained priest. Let go, and let God.

Jessica said I overthink things because I'm a Scorpio, which made me split in two: one part of me wanted to say, *Well, maybe Aquarians don't think hard enough—if you did, you'd know all that astrology stuff is hogwash!* While the other part of me wanted to sit her down and make her tell me everything else she knows about Scorpios.

That, I believe, is the very definition of dueling egomaniacal urges.

March 8

Indra stopped by my mat after class this morning to "check in," and I was so ecstatic—this was the first time she's done that—that I blurted out, "What is up with the kyries?"

Then I went off for about twenty minutes, I think. Like, bring me my soapbox, children, and let me debunk your God. I should have been in a college dorm room with a can of PBR and a joint.

Indra sat there on my pink mat, listening. She nodded slowly, not to agree, exactly. More like she wanted me to keep talking. So I told her about sin being originated by a woman, I told her about how that prayer doesn't work with yogic philosophy, and then I told her I thought we had all decided that God didn't exist.

"We?"

"Yeah, you know…"

"What, educated people? Liberal people?"

"Um, no. Modern people, I guess."

"You were raised Catholic?"

I laughed. "Isn't it obvious?"

"I was, too," she said, "and there was a time when I thought religion was all about guilt and power and politics."

"Absolutely," I said, "and you were right."

"But my whole purpose in being on this planet is to love God. Yoga is about learning to love God. We are God, all of us, and when we ask God for mercy, we are asking ourselves to be merciful. Don't you think we could all stand to be more merciful with one another?"

And what was I supposed to say to that, *No?*

When I was little I thought I could sense God following me around, observing my performance as a human being, watching me pull my sister's hair or pretend that Barbie was having sex with Ken. And Skipper. And My Little Pony. These days, if I sense that audience—and I do, more often than I care to admit—I remind myself that it's just that my narcissism is so powerful it has actually splintered off and begun to live outside of me.

Indra asked if I'd studied my *niyamas*. The *yamas* and the *niyamas* are sort of like the yogic Ten Commandments. You abstain from the yamas—sex, lying, stealing. And you observe the niyamas—you practice contentment, that sort of thing.

Indra said there were three niyamas she wanted me to

focus on. "You could think of them as a trinity, since you're familiar with the term." I groaned and made the sign of the cross, which made her laugh.

So she told me that the first was *tapas*, which means to heat or cleanse. It's what we're doing in practice, heating up our bodies through the postures in order to purify them. The idea of tapas, she said, is to learn how to suffer gracefully. To sit with pain until we can transcend it. An idea I love, in theory. It sounds incredibly badass, very Linda Hamilton doing chin-ups in *Terminator 2*. In practice, however, it makes me want to lie down on the floor and become a lima bean.

The second was *svadhyaya*, or self-study. This I can accomplish by reading my sacred texts, and witnessing my emotions instead of identifying with them. And keeping this journal. She told me to read the Yoga Sutras, the Upanishads, the Koran, and yes, the Bible.

"Christ."

"Exactly. Christ was an avatar. He came here to teach us about loving God and each other."

"Maybe, but I don't think he wrote that prayer!"

"Well, fine, let's continue. The final niyama I want you to think about is *isvarapranidhana*."

She looked at me, and her eyes were warm and expectant. I wanted to make her happy, but all I could say was "Ishwarra whatana?"

"Love of God," she said. "Surrendering yourself to God."

I nodded, like, sure, Indra, I'll do that right now.

The weather shifted, suddenly. A gust of wet wind moved across the floor. Indra pulled her hair into a ponytail without missing a beat.

"You're afraid of death," she said. "You said so our first

day in Circle. You see death everywhere you look, so you're afraid to act. If you can love God, surrender to God, you can live in the moment, free of anxiety. Without God? You look ahead and see traps and pitfalls, you look behind and you see loss and death."

Rain started beating down on the roof of the wantilan. Indra told me to think about Lot's wife.

"You know the story—God destroys the cities of Sodom and Gomorrah and spares Lot and his family, provided they leave the city immediately and without looking back? He is asking them to have faith. Until you have faith in God, you will always be turning back, like Lot's wife, looking back out of fear of death and change. And we know what happened to her, right?"

"Pillar of salt."

"Right. Loving God allows you to simply move forward without trying to relive the past or divine the future. At your age you need to be moving forward, don't you think?"

"Okay," I said. I swiveled away from Indra to stretch my legs in front of me. "But…ah!" I shook my head. Could I really practice loving God? *God?* I felt like I could hear Richard Dawkins and all my old professors snickering from thousands of miles away.

Indra lifted herself off the ground and crouched in front of me. "Answer me this," she said. "Do you like chanting in Sanskrit?"

"Yes! Why can't we just stick to Sanskrit?"

"Well, you realize we're essentially saying the same things. We're asking God for mercy. It seems to me that, since you can chant in Sanskrit but not in Greek, your problem isn't with God. It's with language."

And that was that. She stood up and left the wantilan,

and I joined my yogamates in their color wheel of mats for a between-class meditation session. I watched Indra walk down the steps, into the rain, her eyes fixed forward.

All this coming from a woman who drinks pee, I thought.

Later

When I was about four years old, Grandpa and I went for a walk in the woods behind my house. It was Easter morning, and I was wearing my ballet clothes—powder-blue leotard, skirt and tights, pink ballet slippers, and a tomato-red T-shirt over the whole thing. I'm told I wore this outfit most of my fourth year.

I carried an Easter basket full of jelly beans and Cadbury Creme Eggs, which were, and are, my favorite Easter candy. But I couldn't make sense of how a rabbit could have gone to the grocery store and bought a bunch of Cadbury eggs without someone noticing him. Which would mean that he might have stolen them in order not to be seen, something that I knew from a traumatic paper-doll experience was a sin.

Naturally, such a possibility troubled me, and Grandpa must have picked up on it. Grandpa's always been intuitive like that. But I didn't know how to articulate such a complex ethical issue, so when he asked what was wrong, I told him I was wondering if the Easter Bunny was real.

"No," he replied. "He's not. Neither is the tooth fairy."

I nodded.

"But Santa Claus," he said. "He's real."

I had total faith in Grandpa's knowledge of the universe, so I believed in Santa Claus for years longer than I might have otherwise. I keep thinking about that, about what a relief it was that he gave me Santa Claus. I was at the age, I suppose, when all the older kids knew the truth about our holiday gods, and it was a relief to have the big-kid knowledge that some of our gods are imaginary, more customary than anything else, but that one is real. My grandfather confirmed that I was right to have doubts while still giving me permission to believe.

I thought of it the moment I sat for meditation with my yogamates, after Indra had left the wantilan. And I keep thinking of it because in the strangest way, I feel relieved.

Not *convinced*. But relieved.

March 9

I love the church of my youth, I love the church of my youth, I love the church of my youth.

I'm practicing loving it. Samtosha!

You know, it occurred to me today that even if I hated our priest and his rhetoric, there were a few things I loved about Catholicism growing up. The bhakti elements. Like the Balinese stuff, the offerings, the incense, the rituals.

I keep thinking about Gabe's ordination. It was at St. James Cathedral, in Seattle, before it was remodeled, when the altar was in the nave of the church, not in the center as it is now. We rarely went to the cathedral when I was a kid, but when we did I imagined that there were secret chambers just beyond the altar and the tabernacle, rooms where secrets were kept—secret objects and secret books, maybe even secret people like Opus Dei. Those imaginary rooms were where the sacred mysteries of the world were kept, and the Gregorian singers' bell tones hung in glass webs like a force field between us.

The ordination Mass was long and repetitive, a real knee-breaker. Every priest in the archdiocese was there to welcome Gabe into the brotherhood, and there were several occasions in the Mass for the priests—hundreds of them, thousands of them!—to approach my cousin in the sanctuary and bless him. Toward the end of the Mass, Gabe was made to lie facedown in front of the altar, the priests surrounding him, so many that they spilled down the altar steps and into the aisles. Gabe's arms stretched in front of him like Superman flying to heaven.

The priests gathered around, all of them in white robes like so many stern and aged altar boys. They encircled him, each with one arm stretched out, their palms facing the prostrated body of my cousin, and they muttered prayers we in the congregation couldn't hear. And, oh, the smells and bells were wafting and ringing, and I breathed excitement and jealousy. I wondered what would change if there were women on the altar with them. What if I were up there? In spite of myself, I wanted to be in my cousin's place, who now would have access to all those secret rooms and secret books. I wanted to be indoctrinated into a mystery.

The Catholic faith is predicated on mystery: the mystery of the Trinity, the mystery of the Immaculate Conception. Miracles abound. I've always liked that; if I were to practice, I wouldn't want my religion to be too practical, lest I start to believe we really know what we're talking about. Because honestly? I just can't believe that anyone really knows who God is, if God really does exist.

Gabe quoted Saint Augustine to me once: *Si comprehendis, non est Deus.* If you understand it, it's not God. That day I imagined myself in my cousin's place, being knighted in order to guard over those secrets of life that can't possibly be understood, but only expressed through ritualized mysteries. I didn't want to take on any of the duties of a modern priest—from soup kitchens to church renovations to preaching a knowledge of the afterlife and the character of God. No—I wanted to be a knight.

But of course, I can't expect the Church to conform to my idea of what its rituals should express, can I? And even if I could, they don't want me. Mystery and reverence belong to the men. And I never saw anything sexy about cutting all my hair off and becoming a nun.

March 10

This morning Indra and Lou told us that they were canceling our afternoon class due to an issue at home. Neither one slept much last night, because just as they drifted into sleep, a ghostly whirring sound came from the kitchen. They got up to see what it was, and discovered that their blender, without any human assistance whatsoever, had somehow managed to plug itself in and start blending.

Why does a blender plug itself in and blend in the middle of the night?

Simple. *Because it is possessed.*

Indra and Lou have a poltergeist in their blender!

Apparently this is quite a common occurrence on Bali. According to my teachers, legions of spirits wander the island every night, just looking for their chance to break into your house, animate your kitchen appliances, and fuck your shit up.

Indra said that she tried to talk the spirit out of the blender, but it didn't work. She shrugged and gave Lou a wry smile. "It's a pesky spirit, this one, but we have to be kind and remember that half the reason a spirit possesses a blender is just to get a little attention."

Lou was massaging his quadriceps. "Listen, people," he said. He paused, breathing in sharply through his nose, collecting his thoughts. "Sometimes when you give the spirit the notice it craves, it will move on and leave you alone."

Indra nudged his shoulder with hers. "We're pretty used to this sort of thing," she said. "Spirits just seem to follow us around."

Jason looked at Indra with wide eyes, like a little boy. "What do you say to a blender to give it the attention it craves?"

Indra laughed, looking down at her legs as she adjusted them in lotus. "It might sound a little funny, but I said, 'Spirit, I recognize you, you can leave the blender now. Release the blender, spirit, we acknowledge you.' That sort of thing."

Baerbel was sitting on her heels next to me. She's a sixty-five-year-old grandmother from Berlin, and the only person in the wantilan besides me who thinks everything about yoga is funny. She tittered. "Well," she said, "if you believe in spirits you will see them. If you don't, you won't!"

And I thought, *Maybe that's how I feel about God.*

Anyway, Indra and Lou have invited some of us over to their house for a ritual purification of the blender. Which would be hilarious to me if I weren't ecstatic at the prospect of seeing Indra in her natural habitat. I'm a little embarrassed about how happy I am to be one of the chosen four. Jonah wouldn't recognize me. I can't stop grinning. Maybe I'm just another pesky spirit who needs to find an appliance to possess in order to get some attention. The first thing I'm going to say when I meet this blender? *I understand you.*

Sundown

Made is picking us up to drive us to Indra and Lou's in just a few minutes. Jessica, Lara, Jason, and I have spent the last four hours getting ready. Jessica lit a dozen aromatherapy candles she brought from her massage studio at home, and as the sun went down we turned off the lamps and let the candle-light bounce off the shiny tile floor. Indra and Lou told us to wear sarongs. Su brought over a half-dozen for us to choose from, but we girls couldn't resist dressing Jason first. He's prancing around the house in his gold sarong, looking splen-did and cheeky in a skirt. He's wearing a sash of the same gold, a blousy white shirt, and a thick, gold, bandanna-like headband wrapped around his forehead. He's performing a t'ai chi dance in the candlelight, his shadow looming large against the back wall like a human shadow puppet.

When both girls were out of the bathroom, I stared at myself in the mirror with a candle at my back, so that my brown hair, which is frizzing like all get-out, appeared almost as red as my rust-colored sarong. I looked like I was on fire. In the candlelight my eyes looked deep and round and dark and I could see the shadows of my eyelashes against my upper lids and forehead. I looked like a woman going to an exorcism.

Sigh. My first exorcism. So far, it's everything I ever dreamed it would be.

The house reeks of sandalwood, amber, and lavender. Lara has joined Jason in his t'ai chi and now they're doing a sort of mock kung fu. Jessica is laughing hysterically and rolling her eyes around in her head like the *satsang* danc-ers we saw the other night. But now the women's gamelan music has begun, and my yogamates are filing through the shadows and out the door with great solemnity.

See you on the other side.

Later

If I could have designed a house in the trees when I was ten years old, it would have suffered from a poverty of imagination in comparison to Indra and Lou's home. They live in a secluded corner of the village, in a house they built at the bottom of a long road ending in a cul-de-sac of bungalows just along the edge of the forest. We could still hear the gamelan when we got out of the car, but now it was punctuated with the screams of monkeys coming from just beyond the house.

Their bungalow is nothing like ours. If our place is a mini-mansion, theirs is a cross between a seraglio and a tree house. Only the kitchen and the bedrooms have ceilings. Instead, tall trees grow right through the center of the house, and their glossy, yellow-green leaves provide a natural canopy. You can see patches of darkening sky through the branches.

Gauzy purple and burgundy curtains hang in the doorways along the central corridor. Candles in rice-paper lanterns lighted our way down this main thoroughfare of the house, which is in the open air as well. Made led us through the house and out to the living room, which is more like a large deck that juts into the forest like a dock into a dark green sea.

The purification ritual was conducted by Noadhi, a small, seventy-year-old man Lou referred to as a *balian*. Balians are healers and scholars of Balinese Hinduism, and they are the most important people on this island with all its pesky spirits. You might say Noadhi is a cross between a priest and an exterminator.

Noadhi was working at a makeshift altar in the middle of the balcony. He was laying out fruits and flowers, cigarettes and cakes, all chosen to entice the spirit out of the blender. Four unlit red candles waited on the edge of the altar, and a long glass bottle filled with an oily-looking orange liquid stood just to the right of the blender. My mouth went dry when I considered what might be in that bottle, and what was to be done with it, if anything. I hoped it was some sort of oily orange holy water—add ice and blend, and you've got a specter-free kitchen appliance. Just don't make me drink it.

Lou was hanging out near the altar, dressed in white with a matching piece of fabric wrapped around his forehead. Jason, Lara, and Jessica made a beeline to join him. I hung back until a voice drifted over from a shadowy corner of the balcony. It was Indra, calling me to join her.

Sitting with Indra in a tree house in the middle of a vast green darkness, drinking spicy tea from a jade tea service among crimson and deep blue pillows: that is what I came here for.

Indra's different outside of the wantilan. More relaxed. More glamorous, maybe. She reminded me of an actress entertaining at home. Her dark blonde hair was free and ran straight down her back like a sheet of water. She wore a silver and purple silk sarong and a white flower tucked behind her ear. When Lara and Jessica burst into laughter at something Jason said, Indra sat up and spoke in a stage whisper. "Yogis," she said, "*hush*. We use our spa voices here."

I felt a little embarrassed by her choice of words, but my yogamates were duly humbled and took seats facing the altar. Indra turned to me and asked how things were going.

I don't know how Indra does this, but it's her greatest power. All she has to do is ask me one simple question and it's like my head splits open and the contents of my brain spill into her lap. All Indra asked was, "How are you, Suzanne?" and I found myself telling her about Jonah and our plans to live together in New York, I told her about my grandparents and my sister and how sad and guilty I feel moving away from them. I told her that I wanted to change and I feared changing. I told her what I have done and what I have failed to do.

And then something slipped out that I didn't even know I was thinking. I said, "I don't even know if I *want* to live with Jonah in New York."

The balcony was so quiet; I heard no voice but my own. I glanced at the altar to make sure no one was listening; thankfully my yogamates were meditating with Lou.

After a moment Indra said, "We've got a lot in common, Suzanne."

"Yeah?"

She nodded and went silent. Lou and my yogamates began chanting. The sound wrapped around to our end of the balcony. I felt like a character in the *Mahabharata*, receiving counsel from some otherworldly sage. Or from a god who had once been mortal.

Indra sipped her tea with both hands wrapped around her green cup. "That's one of the problems with doing anything for a long time. Staying home, for instance. The longer you stay, the more you believe your identity is wrapped up in the people and things around you. You become trapped. It seems as if you fear change because you can't let go of this illusion of yourself as being what? The good granddaughter? The girlfriend who can't choose between her boyfriend and her family? Seems as if your fear of change is really just the same fear of death you mentioned in our first class."

"So how do you fix all of that? How do you leave your family? When you love them, I mean."

"Practice dying."

I laughed, but she was serious. She said to embrace each change as if it were a small death. That I should just dive in and let my world fall apart and rebuild itself. That if I can embrace change, I can embrace death, and that is the secret to liberation.

"But, Indra," I said. "That sounds *hard*."

Indra smiled and glanced at the altar, at my yogamates chanting with Lou. She was silent for a long time; I was beginning to think she wasn't going to talk anymore when she started to speak very softly, very gently, as if the words were sharp and she had to ease them out in order to not be cut.

She told me she was married once. "A long time ago. And I loved my husband. But I could never shake the feeling that I needed to leave. When I imagined a future with him, all I felt was dread. I think I knew that if I stayed, I wouldn't be brave enough to change in the ways I needed to change. You know how people who love you hate it when you change?"

I nodded.

"So, one day—it was actually after my first meditation class—I did it. I left. Got in the car, drove cross-country. Left the house. Left the husband. Left the dog. It was the hardest thing I've ever done. But then! Then I could *grow*. I could find God. Until I met Lou, I lived like a monk. Just me and yoga."

I didn't know what to say. Well, if I am completely honest with myself, I think I felt both inspired and judgmental. Inspired because I think there's a secret part of me that would like to drop my entire life off a cliff and watch it break into a million pieces. But judgmental, too: I knew what my family would say. Gram would say, *Marriage isn't a bed of roses, it takes work*. My mother would say she was selfish, that she had broken a vow. Isn't that what Indra just said? That her own needs were more important than her marriage? Her desire to find herself was more important than her promises? But before I could find the words to articulate all of that, Indra stood up. I looked over at the altar to see Noadhi lighting the first of the red candles. The ceremony was about to begin.

The moon was three-quarters full, illuminating the altar and making Noadhi's white costume glow. Noadhi asked us to stand in a semicircle facing the altar, and then he walked among us with a bowl of holy water in one hand and a lotus flower in the other, the bloom captured between his third and fourth fingers, facing his palm. He dipped the lotus flower in the holy water and then sprayed each of us in turn, just as priests do in Mass. Next he splashed water into our cupped palms and told us to drink. And we did. We slurped it up like it was spring water at the end of a long hike.

The water was just trickling down my throat when I thought, *Holy shit. Is this water purified?*

I really, really hope that Noadhi used an actual filter to purify the holy water, and not just prayers. But after a half-dozen palmfuls of water, I relaxed a little, and then I found myself hoping that the water wasn't just pure, but purifying; that it would clean me out, make me new.

Noadhi pressed white rice kernels to our foreheads and temples. Then he turned toward the altar and lifted his arms above his head and closed his eyes. He stood like this for a long time. I was about to nudge Jason to see what we should be doing when I realized that everybody around me had their arms up and their eyes closed, and they all appeared to be praying fervently for the blender. Which begged the question, *What sort of prayer does a person make for a possessed kitchen appliance?*

I lifted my arms and closed my eyes, blinking away a few errant rice kernels. *Out, spirit!* I commanded. In my head.

And then I almost lost it. It took some serious deep breathing to keep myself from cracking up.

Purity, Tranquillity, Calmness, Bliss. I pray to Jessica's aroma-therapy candles, including the one called "Tibetan Rejuvenation," please calm and purify and rejuvenate this poor blender, which is so dear to my teachers.

I opened my eyes. Twelve arms were still up in the air.

Hail Mary, I prayed, *fix the blender. Let it blend only when expressly asked to do so.*

Pretty soon I let my mind wander away from the blender and back to my conversation with Indra. I imagined a younger version of her driving cross-country, alone. Throwing herself into her car. Her long hair whipping in the wind. Surrendering herself to whatever life brought her. Her heart so open she could even find God.

Hail Mary, full of grace, the blender is with thee. Blessed is it amongst kitchen appliances, and blessed is the fruit that it shouldst be blending.

Oh, help. My arms were so heavy. There were rice kernels in the corners of my eyes, tickling my eyelids. I was starting to panic. *Heal, blender, heal! Go toward the light, Carolann!*

I opened my eyes and decided that I didn't like rituals that made me feel like my arms were going to break off at the shoulder. Come on, y'all, I wanted to say, we're praying for a *blender.*

And then I smelled something marvelous. Something familiar and comforting. Noadhi was sitting on his haunches next to the altar, smoking a cigarette and watching us. He smiled at me. "So, that's the end," he said.

We sat as Noadhi passed out the blessed fruit and flowers from the altar, his cigarette dangling from his mouth. He told us it's good luck to eat the offerings from a purification ritual. We formed a small circle in front of the altar, Indra and Lou looking casual and relaxed, as if we were just a group of friends gathered for a party. We were chatting quietly and eating apples and rice when Lou cleared his throat.

First he wanted to offer Jason the bottle of oily orange liquid that was still sitting on the altar, next to the blender. It was some sort of Balinese concoction for ridding the body of parasites. I was so relieved by this news, I actually wrapped my arm around Jason and side-hugged him. "Can't wait to watch you drink that," I said.

He put on a thick Cockney accent. "I'll pour it down me froat like a pint," he said, tipping the bottle back and pretending to chug it.

Lou laughed at that, which I found shocking. "It might not taste as good as a pint," he said, "but it should make you feel better." He rubbed his knees. "We also have a small announcement," he said, looking around at each of us before settling his gaze on Indra. "Indra and I have decided to get married. We'll be celebrating with a Balinese wedding at the end of our retreat." He rubbed his neck, and for a moment a sweet, modest smile softened his features. "Noadhi will be performing the ceremony."

My yogamates and I burst into applause, and Noadhi watched us, laughing and shaking his head. We clapped and whistled, Noadhi laughed, and Indra leaned into Lou, fitting herself right under his arm. Her sarong spread into his lap where her leg rested on his. Lou looked down at her, and his eyes on her were kind and soft, completely unlike the Lou I was afraid of in class. For an instant, my eyes became wet and I didn't know why. Something was piercing me just below my sternum.

I've been thinking about it all night, and I know what it is, now. They were transformed by their affection for each other. Singly, they were two teachers. But at their home, telling us of their future together, they were something else. They were a world unto themselves. That is something I have never experienced before. Something I want. Maybe Jonah and I can create that kind of love when we start living together. But what if we can't? God, when I think about what Indra had to do to get where she is now—the years of solitude, leaving a man she loved to follow a path with no guarantee that it would lead her to wisdom and a new, deeper love? Terrifying. And, well—inspiring.

Before we left, I excused myself to use the bathroom, and crept past the bedroom and the kitchen, dying to look more closely but not wanting to be a snoop. The bathroom is as much of a curiosity as the rest of the house. The floor around the toilet and shower is a loose bed of smooth river stones. There's no ceiling over the toilet, so I peed while looking at the stars. Then, washing my hands, I couldn't resist the urge to look around. I lingered over Indra's toiletry bags, and without touching anything I could make out mascara, eyeliner, lip gloss, and lipsticks. She has as many organic and "all natural" beauty products as Jessica. Tucked in the corner of the countertop, between an olive-green bag that was as rough as burlap and the oval-shaped mirror, was a tiny yellow travel candle. I picked it up and smelled it; it smelled like Indra, clean like lemon, and warm with something like clove. I turned it over to see its name. "Renaissance Woman," it read.

3. The Body Electric

O I say these are not the parts and poems of the body
  only, but of the soul
O I say now these are the soul!
— WALT WHITMAN,
"I Sing the Body Electric"

Have you ever stood near a drum circle and secretly wanted to join in? To just throw aside propriety and irony and get all sweaty and Noble Savage-y?

Yeah. Me neither. Drum circles look strenuous. And smelly. But drum circles are probably the only ritual I haven't wanted to try. I love rituals, even toasts at weddings. I love them for the way they bookmark time, for the way they enable us to say, out loud, that this moment means something. That we must remember this. These

words and choreographed gestures pull us back from
oblivion to insist that this life matters, all of it.

I suppose I've spent much of my life trying to find the
perfect ritual. When I was a kid, I relished the elaborate
rituals my elementary school best friend and I made up to
worship Mary, virgin queen of the baby dolls. In middle
school, as I began to think that I couldn't be both a feminist
and a Catholic, I joined a Presbyterian choir, hoping
maybe the Protestants—my father's people—would have
something for me. That didn't last long, simply because
there weren't enough rituals to keep me excited. Everything
with the Presbyterians was so practical, so pragmatic, as
if Jesus himself were just a dude and a buddy and not a
man-God who could walk on water. The closest thing to
a ritual I could get consisted of sitting around with a cool
youth leader, talking about what a cool guy Jesus was until
I turned into a cool bowl of mush, inspiring my mother to
say, "For the love of God, Suzie, will you stop saying 'Jesus
was totally cool'? You sound like a Valley Girl!" After the
Presbyterian girls got all the good parts in the Christmas
concert, I gave up on my Protestant experiment.

I grew up in a Jewish community, and in seventh grade

I spent more time in temple than I've spent in church
in all the years since. Sometimes, in the privacy of my
mother's bathroom, I would pretend it was my bat mitzvah,
reciting parts of my friends' Torah portions. I loved the
thought of being Jewish. My Jewish friends had it all:
beautiful rituals in an exotic language, ancient history,
family in New York, and some of them, the ones from the
reform temple, could look forward to having sex before
marriage without fear of going to hell.

In high school I cast longing looks at the chalices and
blades my Wiccan friends kept on their altars, and went to
the Fremont Solstice Parade hoping that something beautiful
would happen. All I got were naked bicyclists. Which was
exciting for a girl from the suburbs, but not exactly *spiritual*.

But whenever anybody brought up God, or the
existence of God, I would shake my head. That was the
right answer, as far as I could tell. Didn't mean I couldn't
play at worship. I have a friend who calls himself a Jewish-
Buddhist, or a JewBu—he attends a synagogue where
they meditate and chant *Shalommmmmmmm*—and when
I asked how he reconciles the God of the Old Testament
with the absence of a supreme god in Buddhism, he said,

"Maybe I don't believe in God. Maybe I only believe in
culture."

Maybe he's on to something.

After the night we exorcised my teachers' blender, I
wanted my entire life to be a ritual. I felt like a novitiate;
the Mother Superior, Indra, had given me my orders: be
brave, be strong, read your sacred texts, and practice death.
That was what I was going to do. I set about reading my
books. I meditated between classes, each day training my
mind on a different sutra, the way we used to contemplate
mysteries while reciting the rosary when I was a kid.

Sometimes my meditation centered on the image of
Indra and Lou. On the magnetism between them, that
perfect balance of truth and love I saw in them. One day,
quite by surprise, I found this in Swami Satchidananda's
translation of the Yoga Sutras:

"The entire world is your projection. Your values may
change within a fraction of a second. Today you may not even
want to see the one who was your sweet honey yesterday."

The moment I read these words I wished I could forget
them. They acted on me like an incantation, calling up
something I had been trying, for months, to put down.

. . .

Jonah liked tarot cards. It was one of the things I loved about him. When I first discovered Jonah's interest in tarot, I found it very appealing—I imagined us raising our children with weekly tarot readings instead of church, and maybe we would attend the occasional Ren Faire. It made me want to wear moonstones and watch people joust.

I was only slightly disappointed when Jonah told me that his interest in tarot had less to do with *magick* and more to do with Jungian psychology. He liked working with archetypes. He would choose a number of cards, lay them out on the floor in front of him, and then sit and tell himself a story connecting the archetypes that would illuminate the darker corners of his subconscious.

We were in his apartment late one night, drinking cheap red wine, when I decided it was time. We had been together for over two years, and I was finally ready to ask Jonah to read my tarot cards.

We set up a spot on the floor and lowered the lights. I put on the soundtrack from *The Last Temptation of Christ*, which was perfectly moody, I thought, just right for the occasion. But Jonah asked me to turn it off, saying it was too cliché. I suggested Dead Can Dance, then, or perhaps Enigma; something with Gregorian chants or stylized wailing in it. No dice.

"Let's not embarrass ourselves," he said. "That music makes me feel like I'm at a Ren Faire."

"Right," I said, "Ren Faire, yeah. That would be lame." I was disappointed. If you're going to perform a ritual, why not go whole hog? It's all playacting anyway. But my desire to be transported was overwhelmed by my desire to be cool. So I settled in for my reading, happy that Jonah at least allowed the candles to stay lit. The light flickered on the shiny cards as he turned them over: Death. The Magician. The Tower. The Lovers. I looked at the cards for a minute, maybe longer. And then I felt so strange; flushed and cold at the same time. I didn't want to know what the cards were telling me.

Jonah must have noticed, because he said, "Do you see something? Do you see a story?"

I said no. "No, no," I said. "I was just spacing out."

But that was a lie. I couldn't tell him what I saw—I didn't even want to tell myself what I saw. Because what I saw was: You. Are going. To leave. This man.

But I love him, I pleaded. *He's my best friend.*

But the cards didn't change.

Six months later, I didn't leave him. I went to Bali.

That night, when Indra told me why her marriage ended, I knew exactly what she was talking about. I didn't want to acknowledge it, because I thought that my urge to leave Jonah was pure selfishness. How could I throw away a perfectly good relationship just because I wanted to find myself? Why sacrifice Jonah to the whim of some tremulous inner voice that told me to change, but that couldn't possibly tell me how or why or even what I was supposed to become?

If Jonah and I were terrible at working through problems, it was only because we were too busy having fun together. Discussing our future wasn't nearly as fun as watching horror movies and seeing how many Bundt cakes we could eat in a week. No one wanted to be the killjoy. So, one minute I thought that it was better to be with Jonah, to enjoy the good things about our relationship and squelch that pesky inner voice that told me I needed to change. The next minute I could see myself on the Aurora Bridge, the suicide hotspot in Seattle, my life with Jonah like a bundle in my hands to be dropped into the cold, dark water below.

But sometimes I thought that maybe all I needed was a change of location. Maybe moving to New York and living with Jonah was the change I needed. Maybe I could prove the cards wrong. I mean, really, when your subconscious pops up with unpleasant surprises, it's best to ignore it or it'll have you doing all sorts of crazy things. Better, perhaps, to treat it like an alarm clock and hit snooze until it stops on its own.

March 12

Beneath every banyan tree in the village there's such an abundance of offerings that every other tree seethes with envy. Papaya trees get nothing, and yet they provide me with my breakfast every morning. The manly, coconut-laden palm trees, same. Maybe they'll get one or two every few days, but nothing like the banyan. The banyan has as many offerings as some temples.

Today, Jessica and I spent an hour beneath an enormous

banyan on the walk between home and the wantilan. We talked about love. We spend a lot of time talking about love.

It's cool and shadowy in a banyan. I say *in* a banyan because it's almost like walking into a room. These trees are enormous. If a ficus plant took a bite out of one of the cakes in *Alice in Wonderland* that turns you into a giant, it would become a banyan. But what really makes the banyan special is its trunk. It consists of hundreds of roots bulging aboveground that taper upward into as many skinny trunks, like a forest's worth of saplings huddled together for comfort. These branchlike trunks climb toward the sky in a disordered cluster that unfurls at the top in an explosion of limbs and foliage.

If people and trees are both blessed with personalities, then this ecstatic tree is Jessica's soul mate. While we were under its cover, Jessica started to weep. Jessica is always weeping, it's one of her *processes*, I think, but this was the most euphoric form of weeping I've ever seen, her head tilted upward and her eyes joyful as tears streamed from them. She shook her head from side to side and said, "Oh, Suzanne! It's just so beautiful!"

Su told me that the banyan is sacred because each trunk is both separate and part of the whole tree. Each trunk is an offering to the banyan tree and the banyan tree itself. That's why it gets all the good offerings—because the banyan tree symbolizes the nature of existence.

Lou's still chanting the kyries, and I've joined in, but when I say *Kyrie Eleison*, I think *banyan eleison*. Banyan have mercy. I'm turning into a pagan. Indra told me to think of God this way; she calls God the Great Zucchini. I told her that it was a shame that even her vegetable God had to be phallic.

March 13

Today I stumbled upon Jessica weeping again, but this time she was sitting on the veranda in her loose cotton pants and white tank top, listening to her yellow Walkman. I was squinting in the sun—I had been lying down upstairs, resting after a hearty lunch of green leaves and fermented soybeans, so it took me a minute to adjust to the brightness. I crouched down next to Jessica and put my hand on her shoulder. I know this is her process, but I'm always afraid when I see her crying that it's something serious.

Which is funny, really—because it's always something serious. Jessica is processing her childhood and her relationship with her parents. When she discovers something particularly disturbing, she cries with joy, as if she has uncovered some ugly but invaluable prehistoric fossil. She told me she has dreams in which she makes love to her mother using her *sister's* detached penis, which she calls a *lingam*, and when she told me about this dream she described it as "a reminder of my own repression, the necessary repression we all must suffer if we're going to live within society. But, ah! This necessary repression takes us so far away from our Ancient Selves! Our animal selves! I don't want to make love to my mother with my sister's lingam," she said. "I want to love my mother *with my sister*." She cried and spoke as if she were reciting something memorized. "I want us all to love each other."

"I know what you mean," I said.

But on the veranda today I was nervous to see her crying again, so I put my hand on her shoulder and she opened her eyes. "Oh, wow," she said, speaking a little too loudly with the Walkman on. "My teacher is talking about the lingam and the yoni and it really makes me think of Indra and Lou." She sighed. "Ah! He's so good!"

"What kind of teacher is he?" I asked.

"Gender clarity." She wiped her chin, catching a few tears that clung there and then studied her hand as if her tears were tea leaves. She was still looking at her hand as she spoke. "Did you see Indra and Lou in the rice fields yesterday?"

I told her I hadn't, and she whipped her headphones off. "Ah," she wailed, "they're just so beautiful!"

"Yeah, I know," I said. "But what were they doing?"

Jessica said that when she went for her walking meditation yesterday, she broke out of her reverie when she noticed that Indra and Lou were about ten feet away from her, walking single file through the rice paddies. They weren't speaking to each other, just walking, their posture exquisite and their faces serene.

I've seen them walk like this. Jessica's not wrong—it's arresting. They could be dancers, both of them.

"They weren't speaking or anything, but then—" she laughed up at the sun, shaking her head until her dangling coral earrings were shivering.

"What happened, Jess?"

She wiped her eyes, sighing, still laughing a little. "Oh, gosh," she said. "Well, there was a two-foot jump between where one path ended and another began, and Lou turned around to Indra and—still! Not saying a word!—he took her hand and helped her across to the other path!"

She smiled and laughed and cried all at once.

She didn't have to explain to me why this moved her to tears. I'm still thinking about the way Indra and Lou looked together the night we exorcised their blender.

She pushed her hair off her forehead. "It was just so beautiful," she said. "They really love each other. As man and woman." She sighed and looked out at the green. "As lingam and yoni," she said softly, "in their truest nature."

You know what's crazy? This girl is for real. She means every word of it. Those *lingams* and *yonis* are coming straight from her heart. Which sounds sort of icky. But what's crazier still, if you translate what she's saying into cringe-proof English, I kind of know what she means.

Later

Jessica's diary is a spiral-bound notebook covered in construction paper cutouts of flowers and vines and Sanskrit symbols. Faceless male and female forms dance hand in hand around its border like pygmy paper dolls. In the center of this spiritual garden her prize roses bloom:

> Loving-kindness
> Mindfulness
> Serenity
> Bliss
> Bounty

Beneath this list she's taped a small white tag from a tea bag that reads, *When you worry, you're praying for what you don't want.*

Evening

I was doing a backbend over the open side of the wantilan this afternoon, looking up into trees and blue sky, and it occurred to me that this is exactly where I'm supposed to be. There was a light breeze, and it made me notice that I've actually grown accustomed to the heat. I don't feel like I'm in a sauna anymore. I've figured out where to put my mat so that the geckos don't shit all over it in practice. Things are looking up.

Jessica and I are sitting on the veranda right now, both of us writing in our journals. The sun is setting and I can hear the women getting their instruments out in the wantilan.

Now they're beginning to play. Why don't we all have symphonies playing for us as the sun goes down? It's hard to imagine how I could ever feel troubled in this environment. It's perfect. It's especially good for daydreaming, which is something I've been doing a lot of lately. I've decided Jonah and I need to completely remodel our life together. If we're going to live together, I want it to be a new start. I'm picturing us in an apartment in New York that's like a citified tree house. Plants and natural fibers everywhere—pussywillow branches, river stones. I want us to sit on the floor. I don't want a single chair in the house! I am going to be the anti-chair brigade! Chairs tighten your hips. I want dozens of meditation pillows and open hips.

Now, I'm not saying I'm going to insist we start referring to our privates as lingam and yoni or anything. But I must persuade Jonah to try yoga. I want him to start meditating. I feel like we'll be better together if we meditate more. We'll be less resentful of each other. I'll be less resentful of his independence, and he'll be less resentful of my inability to say no to my enormous family and all the demands they place on us. Even at three thousand miles away, there will be demands, mark my words. But we'll roll with the punches, breathing deeply and wearing loose, comfortable clothing. We'll have sex by candlelight and wrap ourselves in silk sarongs afterwards. (NOTE TO SELF: Buy sarongs.)

March 14

So, today I wrote a long e-mail to Jonah. I told him I wanted us to be better, to grow together. I told him that if we were going to live together, we needed to be equals and that I needed to learn to put him before my family.

The hardest thing for me to admit is that I have a tendency to act as if I love my family more than I love him. This past year, Jonah went away for the holidays and came home on New Year's Day. He and I hadn't seen each other in two weeks. He called me the morning he got in, and his voice was so excited, he couldn't wait to see me and he wanted to have the whole day together, cooking and talking.

I wanted to see him, too...

But my sister and I had already rented four movies and bought our body weight in German Gummi Bears. So I told Jonah we'd get together the next day. He was so angry he hung up on me. It makes me want to cry just thinking about it—how could I be such an asshole?

Sometimes I think I love Jonah the way a child loves. I accept his love as a given, and I don't think about giving much back. I'm sure Jonah would rather have one of those thoughtful girlfriends who makes homemade cards for his birthday and surprises him with cupcakes when he's had a hard day.

I will become that girlfriend. I will learn to live in the moment, not always thinking about how cool it would be if we did this or that, but actually doing those things. I will surprise him with cupcakes. I just have to learn how to make them.

Flour. I bet they have flour in them.

There's a picture of us on my nightstand. I'm sitting on

Jonah's lap and kissing him on the cheek while he looks at the camera. When I look at it, I can feel his clean-shaven face on mine. It makes me miss him terribly. I look at it every night before bed in the hopes that I'll dream about him.

March 15

Love. Jessica and I are all about it. We are in love with love. We stayed up late last night talking about our relationships. Or rather, my relationship and Jessica's desire for one. Jessica's path seems to be about finding a spiritual connection with another human being more than anything else; I think she considers a love union the only spiritual happiness she'll ever need.

I told her I wasn't so sure about that. But now I think I said that because I'm afraid that what I have isn't a spiritual union. What I have is fun, and it's deep and dear and familiar. But spiritual? Huh. I don't know. But does a relationship need to be spiritual to be good? I don't think so. Quoth the Beatles: *All you need is love.*

That said, our conversation started after I went into Ubud to check e-mail. Jonah had written me, but he didn't respond to what I had said about how I want us to be better. How I need us to be better. He said nothing about it. Just that he missed me and loved me and that getting ready for New York was extremely stressful.

I'm trying to be understanding about it. Maybe he's not in the right space to talk about heavy stuff when he's trying to move. But neither one of us is ever in the right space to talk about this stuff.

So I told Jessica about Jonah, and then—perhaps because Jessica isn't from my world, and so I feel like I can tell her things—I told her the story I've never written about, because it's too—something. Too potent, too much of a fantasy? I think I'm scared of it. I don't know. I told her about the Sailor, and the novel he gave me that I keep cracking open but can't bring myself to read. Maybe talking with Jessica has emboldened me, but for the first time in three years, I want to write it all down.

The Sailor is too old for me, but I love the idea of him. I've clocked many hours daydreaming about the few times we've met. He's eighteen years older than me, and when we're together, we talk books. That's all. In groups, he stays quiet until the conversation turns interesting. But when he gets talking, he can talk books like nobody I've ever known. His eyes are very blue and there seems to be no end to his mind.

If it weren't for my office job, we probably never would have met. As I told Jessica, about a month before Jonah and I started dating, I ended up at the fortieth-birthday party of my co-worker's brother, the Sailor. This would have been three years ago, right after my twenty-second birthday.

I had heard about the Sailor for years. When the phones were slow at work, my bosses were lenient enough to let me read at my desk. The Sailor's sister stopped by to chat occasionally, and when she noticed what I was reading, she'd often start laughing. "You and my brother are reading the same book, *again*," she'd say. "I need to put you two in the same room together."

During my freshman year of college his sister gave me an issue of *Harper's* to read, and it had his name on the mailing sticker. I remember I spent a lot of time looking at it. Maybe it was the thought that there was a man out there reading the same books I was, thinking about the same characters, the same ideas, that excited my romantic sensibilities, but I was already primed when I met him. In person he was bigger and more grizzled than I had imagined. He looked like a man who went to sea. He had a beard and a broad chest. I had never kissed a man with a beard.

All it took was a glass of Scotch and a conversation about Russian poetry to change that. The next day he went back to sea, I went back to school, and by the time he came ashore again, I was in love with a sweet, funny guy my own age. Jonah.

I told Jessica this story only because there are times when I feel like I have to talk about the Sailor. I wonder, now, if it's because Jessica is such a romantic that it inspires me to dive into emotions I haven't indulged since my first months with Jonah. Like passion. The Sailor is so passionate he almost scares me. What I have with Jonah is sweet, settled, real. There aren't a lot of illusions between us anymore, and it's the illusions, the mystery, that make a love romantic.

I couldn't help but show Jessica the book he gave me, and his Bon Voyage note, which is completely innocent and yet thrums like an amulet.

I'm both attracted to and repelled by this novel. Its cover looks like the Balinese night; green and dark blue, jungly, mysterious. I feel like I know what the Sailor was trying to tell me in giving me this book. As I told Jess, it's not just any book.

After the Sailor came back from sea, he called me and wanted to take me out, but I said no. I was in such a deep swoon over Jonah that I wanted to spend every minute with him, and when I couldn't be with him, I listened to the mix tape he made me over and over again, replaying the moment we met, our first kiss, our first nights together, on an endless loop.

I told the Sailor as much, and then he asked if he could at least take me to lunch to give me a Christmas present. He said he'd been thinking about my green eyes, and that they made him think I'd like some Spanish literature.

I still said no, although I liked the thought. The rest of the day I couldn't stop guessing what book he might have meant. Was it a Spanish writer, or a Spanish-language writer? Modern? Classic? *Don Quixote?*

I never asked him.

The next time we saw each other, it was at a dinner party a year later. He showed up late, and we found our way outside so I could smoke. We did nothing but talk about books for a few hours, but the conversation was almost too good for it not to be cheating. We were both reading Anna Akhmatova at the time, and her poem "Lot's Wife" brought tears to both our eyes, especially the line I keep thinking of since my conversation with Indra: "But in my heart I never will deny her / Who suffered death because she chose to turn."

Finally I said I had to go. He pulled me into him as we said good-bye, and told me he was waiting for me. His blue eyes were intense and sad. And this is what was strange—he said that, about how he was waiting for me, and there was a part of me that wanted to tell him I was waiting for him, too. Which is just crazy.

I didn't say I was waiting for him, of course. I just sort of giggled and reminded him that I had a boyfriend, and then squirmed away. Very suave. Since then he's been nothing but friendly, and I try not to mention what I'm reading when I see him.

But there have been times when I've been walking somewhere, or up late at night, and I find myself silently chanting, *I would love some Spanish literature. I would love some Spanish literature.*

I saw him briefly just before I left for Bali, when his sister and some friends from the office came by the pub while I was working my shift. He told me about a book on Indonesia by V. S. Naipaul that he loved, and I said I'd like to read it. He promised to send it in to work with his sister.

The next day I went into the office, and from ten feet away I could see that his sister had left not one, but two books on my desk. I knew that the second book would be the one from three years ago, the one he had wanted to give me, that I had refused. The book is by a Colombian writer, Álvaro Mutis. It's called *Maqroll*. It's languishing in my suitcase in the armoire. I can feel it in there, thrumming.

Later

I'm just up from a dream that I was in a museum, or an armory, someplace grand and old. And the Sailor was there, and he picked me up in his arms and walked toward a sweeping marble staircase. And I was happy. I looked over his shoulder and saw Jonah weeping. And this is the worst part—Jonah was crying, and I felt nothing.

I snuggled into the Sailor's arms just as Indra had nestled into Lou's side, and let him carry me away.

March 16

Talking about the Sailor makes me think about the Sailor, which makes me dream about the Sailor, which makes me want to talk about the Sailor even more. But the thing I must remember about him is that he's just a fantasy. I don't even really know him all that well. I just like the idea of romance. But dreaming of Jonah crying while the Sailor carries me away? That's not romantic, it's heartbreaking. I don't want to start thinking there could actually be something real with the Sailor.

Romance cannot be trusted. What's real is me and

Jonah. Our future together, our community of family and friends, our plans.

Can you imagine what our people would say if I told them I was leaving Jonah—funny, kind, age-appropriate Jonah— for a grizzled, taciturn sailor eighteen years older than me? Holy hell, they'd have me committed. Absurd. Impossible. And you know what? This is probably typical. I am a little restless—and, if I'm honest with myself, a little scared.

In just a few months, Jonah and I will move in together in New York, and I'm going to have to let go of the idea of other options, other possibilities. It'll just be a matter of time till we get married, and so these are my last months of independence. Better to get these dreams and fantasies out of my system now. And how perfect to do that in Bali, where I can't act on them or fool myself into thinking they're anything bigger than that, dreams and fantasies. Illusions.

I wonder what Indra would say if I told her about the Sailor? I feel like she already wants me to think about leaving Jonah and being on my own for a while. Even today in class she said something about how you can't be with another person fully until you are fully with yourself.

I'm with myself now. I'm doing everything Indra told me to do: tapas, svadhyaya, even isvarapranidhana. As Lucinda Williams says, *I wanna get right with God.* Even if God is just the energy that animates us all.

I'm trying God on.

And, God, if you're there, *please* let me dream of Jonah and no one else.

Later

Looking back through this journal, I found some language that makes it look as if I idolize Indra. Saying she's like a god who once was mortal, that sort of thing. It makes me feel sort of icky. Or creepy, like I'm the sycophantic young assistant in *All About Eve*. I mean, sure—I admire Indra. I love it that she calls me her plant. I want to learn from her.

But Jessica, now she can be downright worshipful of Indra. She and Lara and Jason talk about how Indra's probably enlightened, and Lou, too. Which makes me feel funny. It feels a little too much like a fan club. Makes me look for things in Indra that bug me, just to prove that I still have some objectivity.

Here's one: The night we exorcised her blender, Indra hugged each of us good-bye, and when she did, she said, "Goodnight, Sister Suzanne. Goodnight, Sister Jessica."

I hugged her back, and, not knowing what else to do, I sort of mumbled, "Night Sisterndra."

I've never been anybody's groupie, I've never had any mentors, I've never liked authority figures. So I don't intend to start worshiping Indra. I just want to be around her a lot.

Jessica and I hung back after class this afternoon because Jessica wanted to get Indra's advice. It seems that—well... So, Jessica's pH balance is off in her netherparts and she was wondering if Indra knows of any good home remedies. I believe Jessica's words were "My yoni is imbalanced."

I don't make the news, I just report it.

Jessica asked if we could speak to Indra in private, and honestly? Indra looked a little put out. Maybe she wanted to go to dinner. When Indra is distant like this, the feeling I get reminds me of being a kid, when my mother was distracted. I would get so nervous and upset, as if she would never look at me again or love me again. Like I was out in the cold, all alone and without a sweater.

Indra agreed to walk us home, and she slipped on a pair

of sleek red sneakers, the heels smashed down so they were more like mules. As we walked, Jessica told her about her imbalance, and Indra looked straight ahead. When Jessica finished detailing her symptoms, Indra said that the first thing Jess needed to do was to get into the habit of peeing immediately after sexual intercourse.

Jessica turned bright red. "Oh, no, no, *nonononono*, I'm not having sex," she said. "I'm basically a virgin."

And I've gotta say, my head about spun around when she said that. Jessica's a virgin? I can't help but wonder if she was lying. I mean, she knows we're supposed to be celibate, so maybe she wants Indra to think she was already being celibate before coming here? Like she's some kind of perfect yogini who goes around being celibate and drinking pee all the time? And I'm thinking: *Apple shiner.* And suddenly I wished I had a yoni issue to talk to Indra about, too.

Wait. No. I didn't just write that. Sweet Jesus, how embarrassing.

Anyway, Indra told Jessica to douche with lime juice in water. So, after Indra dropped us off, we cut up a few limes and squeezed them into a plastic water bottle. Jessica added a few drops of tea-tree oil for good measure and then lay down on her back in the tub with her feet up the wall, and went for it.

This is so typical of yoga camp, I just have to record it. I don't know if I'll want to read about Jessica's douching experience later, but this is what my life is like here. Bodily functions are absolutely fair game for discussion over dinner, in mixed company, with perfect strangers you meet at the Internet café. Jason and I had an intense conversation about intestinal flora with a yogi at another computer just yesterday. In class we do partner exercises in which you end up as drenched in your partner's sweat as in your own. Jessica's usually my partner, so it wasn't a big deal at all for her to douche in front of me. Our bodies are just the same stubborn material as our minds, both of which we're here to discipline.

That said, my tenure in the douche-room was a short one. After the first go, Jessica's entire body contorted with pain, and I cringed in sympathy. I imagine it stung something awful. Pretty soon she figured pranayama breathing would help—sort of like yogic Lamaze—and I left her alone to huff and puff and do her yoni thing.

Standing outside the bathroom door, I could hear the crunch of the plastic water bottle as she squeezed it, and then the most awful sound coming from her throat. Awful, like the involuntary sounds a dying animal makes. That, or an air-raid siren: *MmmmhhhhaaaaaAAAAAA*. Like there was a war raging in her privates.

When she emerged from the bathroom she was more subdued than usual, as if she really had just fought a war and now needed to sleep for a few weeks. Her cheeks were bright red and her eyes sort of glassy. She practically collapsed on the futon, and I came up here to the bedroom to record the latest episode of *Your Friends' Privates*.

Later

I had to follow up with Jessica about the whole "practically a virgin" thing. I am terrible at minding my own business, but I don't think it bothers Jessica. She's probably the most open and honest person I've ever met.

I brought it up over dinner at Casa Luna tonight. Green leaves, tofu. A side of resentment as I watched the waiter deliver a pork chop to the table next to ours. Jessica had made a full recovery from her lime-juice experience and was happily drinking peppermint tea and cutting into a brick of lemongrass tofu.

"So, you're not really a virgin, right?" I said.

She smiled, forking a big bite of tofu. "Well, I haven't had sex in five years," she said. "And then I reclaimed my virginity after I decided no more sex until I found a man who could be a man to my woman."

"Oh," I said. "Sure. That makes sense."

Jessica told me that the way most of us girls lost our virginity was wrong. She said that in the Ancient Days women lost their virginity at the hands of another woman. "So it wasn't a traumatic experience!" she said.

"Sounds very *Red Tent*," I said. I've read that book, I know all about the ritual deflowering of Old Testament times. They did it with some sort of ritual deflowering stick. The ritual dildo. Sounds a lot more traumatic to me than my own deflowering, but who am I to judge?

So what does Jessica tell me? She's been *revirginized*.

"Like—surgically?" The thought of getting sewn back up made me choke on a green leaf.

There are about four thousand waitstaff at Casa Luna, all beautiful and wearing dark blue or pink batik sarongs, white shirts, and a flower behind one ear. They were hovering nearby, so I leaned in to get the details from Jessica. But she continued to speak at full volume, telling me about the healer she visited in Boulder who helped her reclaim her virginity.

"This woman was just so amazing! She does all this energy work, and breath work, and massage, and when you're spiritually, um—"

"Intact?"

"Yes! When you're spiritually intact, she takes away your new virginity the way it ought to have been done the first time."

I considered this for a moment. "You mean she—"

Jessica literally cackled. "Yes!"

"With a ritual, um—device?"

"Yes!"

"Wow," was all I could say. "Jess, you are really hardcore."

JESSICA HAS TAKEN about a million workshops to help her find love. After dinner we walked all over town just as the sun was setting, and Jessica told me about her favorite classes and teachers. At first it was hard to listen, and not just because some of the things she's learned, like that "the feminine bends to the masculine," make me bristle with indignation. No, it's just that it's so damn pretty here. Sometimes I'm so struck by the beauty here, it actually physically hurts. My eyes start to ache from the strain of trying to take it all in.

We walked up to the village of Campuhan just as the sky was darkening into streaks of violet, black, and gold, and Jess told me about an exercise in which you learn how to be womanly by mirroring a truly feminine woman, usually the workshop leader. In Campuhan, the ground became sticky with some sort of bloody pulp from the fruit that fell from the low-hanging trees above, and Jessica taught me how to wobble my head like an Ancient Goddess. We wandered around, heads wobbling, until the stars came out, and then we started home, falling into silence.

The stairs from Campuhan to Penestanan are the most brutal part of our daily walks to and from town. There are ninety-six stairs in total. Jason and I counted them last week. We had a bet. I lost. I thought there were at least two hundred. Walking up the stairs is absolute torture, but they are a sight. They are framed on either side by thick green vegetation, from which squirm all kinds of creatures—reptiles, cats, the occasional chicken. A canopy of trees is balanced over our heads, whiplike vines hanging listlessly from their branches. Craggy stones, laid down by the Ancients, make up the wide stairway.

A quarter of the way up we were tired and Jessica started sighing, which usually suggests she wants to talk about something, so we stopped and sat in the middle of the dark stairs. The stone beneath me was hard and lumpy with moss and God knows what else, and the only light source came from a million miles away, or halfway up the stairs, where an ancient-looking lamppost was swarmed with bugs and geckos. In the distance I could hear the faint dissonant tones of the women's gamelan.

"I know I should be patient," she said, sitting lightly, her torso stretching up from her seat, "but it's so hard. I want a man who can say yes." Her moonstone necklace caught the light and blazed blue for an instant, then folded back into the darkness.

"A man who can say yes," I said.

"I took this workshop once, gender expression?"

"Okay," I said. I took a deep breath and exhaled. "And that is different from gender clarity, I assume?"

She nodded vigorously. "Oh, it's amazing! Basically they help you learn how to express your sexuality and gender to yourself and the opposite sex. So, we were doing this exercise. You stand face to face and take turns." She stood and pulled me up so that we faced each other, green vines hanging between us. "I was paired with a man I thought was so attractive, oh, Suzanne! He was so big and tall!" Her hands rested on my shoulders.

I laughed. "Go on."

"So, I would say the word *yes* to him, having yoked all of my feminine sexual energy and directing it toward him with the one word, right?"

"Okay," I said in a deep voice. I grabbed Jessica's arms. "Did you feel that? I just said *okay* while yoking all my feminine sexual energy—did you catch it?"

"I'm serious, Suzanne. This is very real!"

"Sorry," I said, straightening up again. I put my hands on her shoulders, repentant. "I'm sorry, please continue."

"So I would say *yes*, and then, depending on whether or not he could feel my feminine energy, he would say *yes* or *no*.

"So, when it was his turn, he looked into my eyes and said, *yes!* and he had the most feminine voice I'd ever heard. It was the last thing I expected from him, because he was this large African man, so, so masculine-looking!

"So I said *no*, and he said *yes!* again, still in that high-pitched girly voice! I couldn't believe it."

"So I said *no* again, and then!" She breathed in quickly, her hand on her heart. "And then!"

"What did he do?"

"Then, he said"—she lowered her voice to sound deep and throaty, giving herself a double chin in the process—"YES!"

She clapped her hands, squeezed her eyes shut, and jumped up and down. "And oh, Suzanne. Then he sounded like a man!"

"So did you, m'dear," I said. I turned back to the stairs, leaving one arm around her shoulders. We started walking again, slowly, three feet to a step, four feet to the next, until we reached the top of the stairs.

This is our favorite part of our nightly walk. From the top of the stairs you can see the rice fields and the whole green expanse of the village. Small and large bungalows pop out of the green, lit up like lanterns. The forest holds the village in on all sides, but here only a few trees obscure the view of the sky. So many stars. My God, there must be more stars visible here than anywhere I've ever been. Or maybe I'm just looking more closely. Maybe all this turning inward is making it easier to look out at the world and really see.

We stopped without planning to, and I watched Jessica's face turn rapturous. She looked like I felt. The gamelan floated across the village, expanding the sense that we had ascended into another world. I looked at my new friend and felt charmed. We linked arms and resumed our journey, necks stretched back, shoulders down, eyes on the skies.

March 17

Noadhi, the balian, told me to be careful walking alone at night. This was at Indra and Lou's. I raised my eyebrows at him. Rapists? Muggers? Nope. *Leyaks.* Evil wizards. Well—he didn't exactly call them evil wizards, I just like the way that sounds. No, he said that leyaks are men and women who practice black magic. They appear as monsters, sometimes, or giant birds. He said that if you see a leyak, you could be dead in a week and nobody would know why or how you died. A leyak kills you by spiritual, not physical means.

The most interesting thing Noadhi said was that leyaks aren't evil, just gifted in the dark arts and so they must practice them. It's their dharma, I guess. You can tell that a leyak is nearby because your vision darkens, and you might smell a sweet, earthy scent in the air. I thought about telling him that I smell something like that every morning in the wantilan when my yogamates do their first abdominal twists of the day, but I kept my mouth shut.

I call this *practicing maturity*.

March 18

Noadhi came over today to give Jason a massage, and while he was waiting for Jason he stopped by our veranda and we sat on the steps, chatting. I noticed right away that his eyes were shadowy and a little bloodshot, so I asked him if he was tired.

"Yes," he said. "Very tired. I've been up since early morning."

He said that his father was very sick with spirits. A year ago he took his father to the ocean to heal him by appeasing the bad spirits, who like to be near the sea, but he said the effect was wearing off. I asked him what his father was doing, exactly, to make Noadhi think he had spirits, and Noadhi basically described a man with dementia or Alzheimer's, as I understand it. He raves and sees things that aren't there; he's himself one minute and a child the next. Gram has dementia and is always having these incredible hallucinations about African priestesses performing healing rituals on her, or hundreds of police officers showing up in her room after she thought she'd accidentally dialed 911. She often thinks her mother is in the room with her, or her grandmother, both of whom are long dead. She tells me about wonderful parties she attends with all her dead relatives, or, on bad days, parties where her dead relatives and friends ignore her.

I told Noadhi my Gram has the same thing, but that in the States we call it dementia. He was very interested in that, and I told him about Alzheimer's, too. He asked what we do for Gram, and I told him that we mostly let her believe that what she sees is real, unless it's upsetting, and then we try to calm her down. But if she's at a great party, we let her enjoy it. There isn't really much else to do. He nodded. He said his father was violent and that the only thing that helped was getting him to the sea for purification. He rubbed his bald head and gave me a wry smile. He looked very beautiful and sad. "Life," he said.

March 19

Mornings are a riot of roosters, dogs, birds, all yelling at once. It's like the WTO out there.

We're learning all sorts of meditation techniques and breathing exercises, chief among them *bastrika*, or bellows breath. I am addicted to it. Here's what you do: You sit in lotus and put your hand on your diaphragm. (You only have to do the hand on the diaphragm until you know how to do it.) Take a full, deep breath in, and then exhale all the air out. Inhale halfway, then exhale forcefully through the nose over and over again. After a minute or two of this you inhale again, exhale fully and then hold the air out, lifting the diaphragm and clenching your privates like you're trying to keep from going to the bathroom. This is called engaging the *bandas*.

The bandas are a big thing around here. We're always turning them on. The *mulabanda*, especially, which is basically a muscle that's located between your rectum and sex organs. When I first heard about it all I had to do was translate: he meant *the gooch, the chode*. What some of my friends call *the taint*, because it *taint* your balls and it *taint* your ass.

Guess what Lou calls the mulabanda? The anal lock. Woof!

Guess what else? I'm engaging it *right now*.

Later

Lou says that there are steps that precede meditation. First you withdraw from your senses by closing your eyes. Next you concentrate on a single image or mantra. Once you can concentrate, you can begin to meditate.

But even when you're meditating, there are levels as well. You don't go directly into a deep meditation. You sort of find deeper levels as you go.

It feels like sinking, sometimes. I focus and then I feel like I slip down a rabbit hole. I always come back up almost immediately, because it feels a little like I'm going into a lucid dream.

Or maybe I'm just hungry and about to pass out. I'm turning into a vegetable, I've eaten so many. I'm a green leaf. I'm a papaya.

March 20

I can't stop looking at Marcy's hands. Marcy's from the Bay Area, and she's probably my mother's age. Definitely a baby boomer rich former hippie type—lots of gold bracelets and a big ol' diamond ring, and the kind of language that people acquire after years and years of New Age therapy. She told me the other day, while running her fingers through her thick white hair, that she didn't want to be "ageist," but that I would understand the importance of engaging the mulabanda in every pose after I'd had some kids. "My sexual health is vital to my sense of self, especially at my age, when it's easy to give in to fear-patterning about death and aging. Engaging the mulabanda in practice frees me up to not have to do my Kegels every day. I really don't want to be ageist, but you couldn't possibly understand the importance of a tight womanplace at your age."

And you know, she's right. Frankly I don't think about a thing called *womanplace* ever, if I can help it. *Womanplace* is even more embarrassing to say than *yoni*.

Marcy's nice, though, even if she is a little annoying with all that ageist talk. But her hands just make me want to weep. Today at lunch I couldn't stop looking at them, resting one on top of the other just at the lip of the white tablecloth. She was chatting with Lara, and she was laughing, but her hands looked forlorn. Around her rings her fingers are dry and raw, as if she washes her hands too often. The backs of her hands are just beginning to show sunspots, or liver spots, whatever those big brownish spots are called, and the skin is starting to cave at the knuckles and around her tendons and veins.

Marcy's hands are the last hands one wears before one is the owner of old hands.

She's my mother's age.

The thought of my parents being old makes me want to die before them, so I won't have to see it.

When I think of being my mother's age, I feel so tired. What if nothing changes? What if I'm fifty-five and still feel like I haven't started to live yet?

I'm afraid of losing everything. Of life being over before I can get a grip on it. I can't die before I understand why I'm here, what it means; before I have at least one moment of living my life in a way that is both authentic and connected.

March 21

I've been practicing this mantra Baerbel told me about. We were sitting on her veranda a few days ago—she lives down by the pool, closer to the road—and she was rolling around on a giant blue exercise ball, her table overflowing with books. She's been talking me through the Upanishads and the *Bhagavad Gita*, her reading glasses propped on her nose, her short gray hair messy as if some friendly person had just tousled it.

Baerbel reminds me of a female Jesuit; warm, learned, with a wicked sense of humor. I was feeling kind of down, thinking about Gram and Noadhi's dad. She told me that the Buddhists try to accept death in everyone and everything. So they say, *I am of the nature to die. All of my loved ones are of the nature to die.*

It reminds me of Indra's instructions to practice death.

So I went through the rounds: *I am of the nature to die, my parents are of the nature to die, my siblings are of the nature to die. Jonah is of the nature to die.*

And if I can be honest? My God, I will have to burn this book before I leave Bali. When I thought about Jonah dying, I felt sort of relieved. Which is so horrible it makes me want to kill myself. But it's not a wish, of course. My God, no. No, it's a question: What would I do if I were unattached?

For a second, I was going to write: *I would read the Sailor's book.* But when I think of actually doing that, I get kind of scared. I don't trust myself to read it, somehow, though I realize that might be a bit absurd. It's only a book.

Oh, but there's no such thing. When a person gives you a book to read, he's asking you to look into his soul. And I think it would be a bad idea for me to see any more of the Sailor's soul than I already have. And I wonder now—is it because I'm afraid that it won't match up with my fantasy of him? Or because I'm afraid it will?

But even as I write that, I notice something: nothing.

You know, I think I may have burned myself out on this story. I've used it up. I haven't been thinking about the Sailor all that much lately, but today I'm antsy and a bit bored and I think I'm trying to give myself a charge from a dead battery. It's so much more fun to think about romance than it is to think about death. I told Jessica this, just now, and she said, "God gave you the Sailor to remind you to give that romance to Jonah! He's giving you a lesson in the cycles of love. It's time for you and Jonah to have a renewal!"

That made me feel great until I started thinking about that chant again. *Jonah is of the nature to die.* If I were still in the clutches of the Sailor story, my relief would make sense. But now I keep thinking, *What if we were to get married and then he died when I was in my forties or so?* Then I could still do something different with my life before I die! I would be free. God, what an awful thought to have about someone you love. Sounds like the start of a Hitchcock film.

I am of the nature to die.

God. Buddhism is *depressing.*

March 22

Baerbel told me that she lives in Berlin, and her husband lives in the countryside an hour outside of Berlin. She spends the week on her own in the city, and then takes the train to the country to be a wife every weekend. I am so impressed by this schedule I can't stop thinking about it.

She must have noticed that I was impressed, because she said, "And so what? I have been a wife since I was young. He has been a husband since he was young. What a boring way to go out of life, being what you've always been. So I get five days a week to be myself now."

Later

If Jonah would go for it, I would totally do what Baerbel and her husband do. Just weekends. Five days a week to do whatever I want!

I wonder if she can do *whatever* she wants.

March 23

It's after 1 a.m. and I have just come home from a bar. My clothes smell of cigarettes. How strange that that is strange!

Tonight we went to a club called the Jazz Café, a crowded, overpriced jazz club in a dingy part of Ubud I hadn't been to before tonight. It's a bit off the beaten track. There are fewer tourist spots along the street, no transport guys or tchotchke shops. Fewer smiling faces. The street was lit with sputtering street lamps. Broken palm fronds and piles of garbage burned in the middle of the street.

Before we went in, Jason and I paused in front of a tiny pedestal altar at the corner of the gate. It looked like an altar and a nest; stringy patches of thatch burst from its center, where a pile of offerings was laid on a stone ledge. Next to it, a demon guardian carved into the stone wall stuck its tongue out at us. A dog howled, and then another, and then as many as eight mottled and flea-bitten mutts ran toward us from across the street, turning just before they reached us and running away again.

I smelled a sweet, earthy smell as we walked into the club. I raised my eyebrows at Jason. "Leyaks?" I said.

He sniffed the air dramatically. "Beer, I think."

The Jazz Café appears to attract every tourist under fifty in the area. It looks like most Balinese structures, open, airy, lit mostly by lanterns and candles on the walls and tables.

Jason reserved us a *bale*, a raised platform with a canopy, where we sat at low tables littered with plastic water bottles, candles, and stone vases full of jasmine and frangipani blossoms. We sat on square silk pillows of green and gold and drank virgin cocktails out of pastel-colored martini glasses.

From our perch on the bale the entire club sprawled out in front of us. Behind us a dark courtyard full of plants and dotted with small rice-paper lanterns squirmed with couples. Their cigarette tips glowed like animals' eyes. I looked up, leaning back until I could see beyond the canopy to where the full moon lit up the sky. Then I sat forward again, to check out the action at the bar, the restless activity on the dance floor, and the band—a cover band playing near-perfect imitations of Louis Armstrong and Frank Sinatra.

It was so strange—I felt shy around my yogamates, being away from the wantilan and in what normally would be familiar territory. But this club seemed to bring out a new shyness in all of us, not just me. We were an island of sobriety in a sea of drunkenness. My yogamates and I sipped our fruit drinks quietly, tapped our fingers against the tables, and eyed the crowd as if we weren't sure how to reintegrate into normal society. I've only been away from home a month, and yet I feel changed in some fundamental way. I don't know how to be myself in a bar anymore. I wanted to make eye contact with everyone who passed me by. Maybe it's all the deep breathing I've been doing, or the meditating, but I felt too open to be there. There's a certain wildness to this state of being that feels very protected in the wantilan, but out in the world it seems almost dangerous, like I'm seeing too much.

We all had our tricks. Jason hid behind a magazine—one of those spiritual tourism rags in which everyone interviewed takes long pauses before speaking with great wisdom.

He'd brought it with him in his cloth satchel, and now he sat quietly, occasionally lifting his eyes to survey the band before returning to his reading. Jessica and Lara were sitting on my other side, speaking quietly about the differences between Satchidananda's and Desikachar's interpretations of the Sutras. I faked comfort by taking pictures. I needed a filter for my eyes. It was so much easier to stare at people through a lens.

Jessica was the one who finally stood up and made everybody dance. She loves to dance; she's part of some ecstatic dancing group at home called Five Rhythms, where you dance at five different rhythms until you hit some sort of ecstatic, meditative state. But it's funny—watching her on the dance floor, she wasn't the ethereal hippie dancer I assumed she'd be. What she does is more hip-hop than Hemp Fest. Her moves are fast and precise and actually pretty badass.

Soon all of my yogamates were on the dance floor, but I held back for a while, saying someone needed to guard our stuff.

I loved being alone. I have so few moments to really be alone here, unless we're meditating, I guess. But I've noticed something. I've learned how to find my solitude while walking with Jessica to and from town. I've found it in class. By the twentieth Sun Salutation I usually forget that there are people around me. And Jessica is so easy to live with. I can do things—writing, stretching, meditating, thinking— exactly as I would do them at home, by myself, and only occasionally notice that Jessica is just a foot or two away. I mean, I'm not about to start douching in front of her or anything—I'm not there yet—but I am getting comfortable in this life.

Actually, being around yogis is not all that different from

being around actors. Before rehearsals, actors do things normal people would find very strange—we pant like dogs, we assume bizarre stretches, we chant tongue twisters. Another actor will never think you're weird if you're lying on your back in the middle of a room, buzzing your lips like a bee.

I'm starting to get that about my yogamates. They're not as different as I thought they were.

Jessica gestured to me from the dance floor to come join them, but I pretended not to notice. Instead I lifted the camera to hide my face. I took a few pictures of my spinning, gyrating yogamates—or the fuzzy shapes I believed to be my yogamates. Then, because I'm stuck on this one mantra, I thought, My *yogamates are of the nature to die. I am of the nature to die.* And then I pointed my camera around the room.

The place had filled up since we arrived. I watched the club through the lens of my camera. One moment the frame was filled by long-haired Balinese hipsters, then by scoping European men flanked by chic, weathered-looking Asian women. The men reclined on pillows in wrinkled linen pants and shirts, smoking, sweating, sunburned. In the camera's view they looked so colonial, so European, lounging as if they owned the place.

I pointed the camera at the tables along the dance floor. There, cocky, short-haired white guys flirted with Indonesian women. Beachy-blonde middle-aged white women with extravagant breasts sat at tables overflowing with drinks and ashtrays, with young, baby-faced Balinese boys at their sides. The bar was packed with shiny-shirted, tight-trousered beautiful people who licked their lips at each other as they flipped open and shut their cell phones. Eyes flitted about the room, following the waitresses as they wove through swaths of drunken dancers, their spines long, trays of cocktails balanced on their heads, a few graceful fingertips holding them in place. I pictured these women returning home to their family compounds and waking up in the morning to prepare the same offerings Su makes each day for the temples and the grounds. The idea of these women appeasing the spirits of the island by day didn't seem a far stretch from their work by night as they handed out shots of liquor and boxes of cigarettes to the Europeans, Australians, and Americans in the club.

As the scene became more animated, it was difficult to capture anything with the camera, so I stared, the camera lifted only halfway to my eye. The music was louder than before. I looked at all the people.

Something shifted in me, then. I looked at all the people, with my own eyes, unfiltered. I had a thought that this might be all there is. And I loved it. I loved the waitresses' gliding movements, I loved the men looking at the women and the women looking at the men. I loved the writhing bodies on the dance floor.

I am of the nature to die?

No. I am of the nature to live!

I leaned back and looked just beyond the fluttering edge of the canopy to see the sky. The moon was perfectly round and perfectly white. A crowd jostled the bale and I thought about joining my yogamates on the dance floor. I leaned back farther, blinking at the moon, and I thought that I would like to stretch the moon open like a hole in dark fabric, pull the sky over my head, and see for myself what lay beyond.

March 24

I don't know how to describe what happened today.

Jessica and I are on the veranda. It's sunset. The gamelan

music is playing. I'm going to try to re-create my day in these pages, although part of me wants to just let it go, to stay in this present moment with the sunset and the music and Su down below, making an evening offering to the temple— something I've never seen her do before.

But I want to remember this.

Today we had already been through several rounds of bastrika when Lou asked us to inhale, then exhale all the air out. Then he told us to engage the mulabanda. So I did, and in that moment the wantilan, my yogamates, and the surrounding fields fell away and I found myself driving a car toward a light that was white, like the moon. But I wasn't driving *toward* it so much as *in* it. The car was a convertible, and I was in a cylinder of white light, as if I were inside a vein of white lightning. Two androgynous people I recognized as family were in the backseat of the car, and they both wore Dorothy Hamill haircuts. They laughed at each other in the backseat, and their laughter was silver and tinkling, falling from their mouths to the floor in glistening drops of mercury.

The light brightened, and I felt, then heard, the thrum of murmuring voices, and I thought that I had fallen asleep during Corpse pose and had had a wonderful dream—the kind of dream you don't want to wake up from. I wanted to go back to dreaming, but I knew I wasn't supposed to be asleep, I was supposed to be sitting up to meditate.

One voice was trapped in a spiral, loud, then soft, then louder and louder. *It's okay*, the voice said. *I've been here before*. I felt as if this voice were hitting me in the face, it was so loud. Finally, the voice took shape in my mind and I recognized the face that went with it.

It was Indra. Her face was a few inches from my own. I was lying in her lap. Indra's hand was over my hand, which was pressed against my heart. Every time she spoke, a wave of air splashed against my face. I looked around without moving my head, and could make out my yogamates, in pairs, massaging one another's feet. Lara was crying. So was Jessica.

I must've said something, because Indra told me not to speak yet. She handed me a blue plastic cup and told me to drink.

I lifted my head just enough to take a sip from the cup, but it was hard to swallow because I couldn't stop smiling. *Look at them*, I thought. *My beautiful friends, rubbing each other's feet.* I smiled at Lara, hoping she understood me. She cried harder.

I started to laugh and then I knew why some laughter is compared to a bubbling brook; I wanted to drink my laughter, it was so clean and clear. *How amazing!* I thought. *How perfect and amazing we all are!*

Lou was in front of me suddenly, and his hand was on my leg. I smiled at him, too. He looked relaxed but inquisitive. He murmured, "How do you feel?" and I just smiled. *I love you*, I thought.

His face brightened like I'd never seen it. Like he really could read my mind. He put his hand on Indra's, which was still on mine, and with his other hand he brushed a few hairs out of my eyes. "Suzanne," he said, "I believe you may have had a kundalini rising."

I felt Indra's arms tense. "Let her drink her water, Lou."

"How do you feel?" he said.

There were no words. "Good," I said. I couldn't stop smiling at him. I'd never noticed how luminous his eyes were. "What's a kundalini rising?"

"Suzanne," Indra said, "what's the last thing you remember?"

I thought about it for a moment, and then told them about the dream.

"But what was the last thing you remember before the dream, the last thing you can recall from class?"

"Bastrika."

"Do you remember which moment during bastrika?"

"Lou said to engage the mulabanda, and I did."

Lou put his hands together in namaste, and nodded. "It was probably a kundalini rising, Suzanne."

"What is that, though?" I asked.

Lou pressed my hands between his while he spoke. He said something about how when there's a blockage of energy at the base of your spine, it can be released through pranayama or meditation, and then it causes a surge of prana to move upward through the sushumna channel... and then I spaced out thinking about what a great word *sushumna* was. He said that it causes spontaneous asanas, mudras, and kriyas.

"It looks like a seizure," he said. "But it's not. It's a spiritual breakthrough."

I felt like I was floating in Indra's arms, like all the tension in my body had been released. I wanted to stay there forever. But I was also confused. "So—*what* happened?"

Indra gently squeezed my shoulders. "Like you were saying, it happened right after Lou asked you to engage the mulabanda. You were sitting up, erect, and then you fell over to the right, at which point you exhibited signs of heightened neurological activity. Your limbs shook, your eyes rolled back, and you gave your brothers and sisters a bit of a fright."

"Wow," I said, and it occurred to me that *wow* was a perfect word. Like *mom*, only upside down. I squirmed happily against my teacher. "I love you," I said. Indra stiffened slightly, but then she squeezed my shoulders again. Lou clapped his hands together like a little boy and laughed. I don't think I've ever heard him laugh before. I smiled at him and he smiled at me. We were a couple of happy campers.

Class ended early. Jessica and I were very quiet as we walked home along the river, and stayed that way down by the pool with Jason and Lara. And now we're sitting on the veranda, each with her own journal, and I keep taking breaks from writing to watch Su distribute her offerings to the temple in front of our house.

The altar looks like a large throne. Like a throne for a god. Su chose one banana leaf dish with its rice and flowers and candy and left the rest stacked on her tray on the bottom step of our veranda. She's placed the dish on the altar and lit the incense, and now, holding a lotus flower between her fingers, she dips the flower into a dish of water and sprinkles it on the altar with a graceful curve of her wrist. She closes her eyes as she makes this gesture, then brings her free hand between her breasts in prayer, bowing her head. It's a lovely, simple dance, one I've seen her perform every morning since we've been here, but today I find it mesmerizing. She's transformed by the ritual. This shy, giggling girl looks older. More grounded. Reverent, as she attends to the invisible.

There's something familiar about this offering dance Su performs each day. And something familiar, and pleasant, about the peculiar yearning I feel watching her.

What would it be like to believe in the invisible? To believe in it wholeheartedly?

She lifts her arms. She brings them back together in prayer. She bows her head. She's strange, her dance is strange, and yet so familiar. Her offering doesn't look like a chore now, the way it did when I first got here. It looks like something I once wanted to do, before I was told that I couldn't because I was a girl.

Jessica sits across from me under the light, which flickers with the wings of a half-dozen moths. She's writing in her spiral-bound journal, looking up at me occasionally with half-focused eyes, smiling at me as a mother might smile at her child after her first day of kindergarten. Su is gone now, and the sky is dark. There's the green forest around us, the blue shimmer below that is the pool by day. The ants of morning are replaced by the moths of evening, and the roosters are upstaged, for the moment, by the croaking of geckos.

The world is transformed, unrecognizable. Here I am. Me, not quite myself.

4. Awakening, Reawakening

The world is deep,
And deeper than the day could read.
Deep is its woe—
Joy—deeper still than grief can be:
Woe saith: Hence! Go!
But joys all want eternity—
Want deep profound eternity!
    — FRIEDRICH NIETZSCHE,
     Thus Spake Zarathustra

God, how I'd love to end my story here! If I could, I would join the ranks of the redeemed, my spiritual journey immortalized at its apex. But that would be a fiction. My kundalini breakthrough was not the end of my spiritual journey, though it seemed that way for a while. No, it was the beginning of a journey that would only get harder, the spiritual switchbacks more frequent, the veil of illusion as thick and obfuscating as Seattle's darkest, most threatening cloud cover.

This was what I had been looking for in religion: *seizures*. I had waited all my life to be seized by a spiritual practice, and now, it seemed, I had been, quite literally. But what caused the seizing? The whole notion of a kundalini experience implies that there is some spiritual order to our world and our bodies, doesn't it? To believe in my kundalini experience, I might have to believe in the designer of such an experience. Was this change purely physical? Me, experimenting on my mind and body to cultivate a more expansive consciousness? Or was I tapping into something eternal? I didn't know. I still don't know.

In the summer of 2009 I met a woman who I believe is a spiritual therapist. I didn't know that when we sat down together—I thought she was just a regular therapist. We met over drinks after a show in Memphis, and soon got to talking about Bali and yoga, and when the subject of my kundalini experience came up, I played it down. I told her I wasn't sure about it, that I wasn't sure I believed in any of this stuff at all. I really wanted her to believe I still had my wits about me. So I said it was possible I hyperventilated, that it might have been a neurological reaction to hyperventilation. Or, I said, smiling to let her know I was kidding, it could have been a seizure brought on by a brain tumor that's gone dormant in the seven years since. I chuckled at my little joke, and then found myself troubled, wondering if it *was* a brain tumor: Am I dying?

Sometimes I'm embarrassed by my kundalini event. My kundalini awakening. My *awakening of kundalini shakti*, I mean, my God, is there anything more embarrassing than saying, "I've awakened my kundalini shakti"? It sounds like next I'm going to invite you to join me in a wheatgrass enema.

The trouble is that no matter how much I employ my brain in analyzing the experience, I can't convince myself that it wasn't a spiritual breakthrough. Meditation became easier afterwards, and for a while I felt like I was on the road to real spiritual progress.

"You know what your problem is?" the therapist said. "You're afraid of being duped."

She didn't have to tell me twice; I knew exactly what she was talking about. It's something I think about, being duped. I don't want to be duped. But sometimes I wonder how much it matters if you *do* get duped. If I were to spend my entire life believing in a system of faith, one with an omniscient creator and an afterlife, only to die and there be no heaven, no God, no reunion with my grandparents, would it matter?

No. I would be dead. I wouldn't know the difference.

In the meantime I'd have all the benefits that come along with faith—peace of mind, an ability to live in the moment without always fearing death. A system of values to keep me honest and disciplined. If a placebo works to cure the symptoms of disease, who cares if it's just a sugar pill?

Well—I do. That's the problem.

It would be great if I could just blame my fear of being duped on my parents. Everything's easier when I can just blame them! I come from a mixed marriage, you see. I was raised Catholic, but my father is Episcopalian. When my father asked my mother to marry him, she said she would—but only if he'd agree to raise a Catholic family. He said he would, but with his own condition: he wanted his children to attend public schools.

Thus my parents began a familial experiment designed to form open-minded but faithful adults, a hazardous experiment considering the profound influences of both the Catholic Church and the public schools. We grew up surrounded by people of many faiths, attending Mass on Sunday and public school on Monday, and at the end of the day, three of my parents' four children were confirmed in the faith.

My father wanted us to think for ourselves. Every day of my childhood, he'd come home from his law firm and transform our dinner table into a miniature debate club. My father trained my siblings and me never to accept an assertion at face value; received opinion was the enemy of our round table. If we couldn't back up an argument with proof, he threw it out. I listened to my father spin his arguments and wanted to be just like him—in part so that I could more effectively vanquish his cool-headed economic arguments with my bleeding-heart social ones. But I didn't want to be emotional, or to claim opinions I received from other people as my own. I wanted to think for myself.

My mother is dreamier, more spiritual. She's a musician, and when I was young she worked hard to be a good

Catholic mother, vigilantly protecting her daughters' virginities and reminding us that divorce and abortion would never be options. But now that her kids are all older, she's slowly letting her true self out of the closet, revealing an unorthodox Catholic who follows the rules she believes in and disregards the rest. She always did her best to represent the scary Catholic God, but even as a kid, I knew her faith was really an artist's faith; she finds her God in beauty, especially in nature. Every summer my family spent a week at my grandparents' place on the coast, and at sunset my mother would take my siblings and me on long walks by the ocean. We would gather shells and rocks and watch the tide come in. And every night, just as the sunset spilled over the sea, she would take our hands and look toward the waves and sky and breathlessly proclaim, "This is the proof that there is a God."

My siblings and I say our mother's line over beers, now, or in reference to the movie *Showgirls*. It's one of our favorite lines: *This is the proof that there is a God.* But when I was a kid I would look at the purple and red sky, the wet gold of the setting sun spreading along the horizon, and ask myself, *Is it?* And I would search my gut, my intuition, my senses, looking for some proof: Do I feel God when I look at this sunset? Do I sense His presence?

A few years ago I went to see Amma, the Indian hugging saint. I didn't know much about Amma, except that she was a guru who dealt in unconditional love. Her thing was hugs. She'd give a hug to anyone who lined up to receive one. But what differentiated Amma's hugs from the type junior-high kids give one another is that her hug was *spiritual*. The simplest expression of the connection between mind and body.

Chubby and smiling, she looked like a female Yogananda, like a cuddly guru who liked her sweets. She received her audience from a throne in the Pavilion at Seattle Center, surrounded by her moony disciples, most of them white and glassy-eyed, wearing yellow and ivory robes.

I had heard that a hug from Amma could awaken the spirit. That it had healing properties. That her hugs changed lives. I was in the market for all of those things.

There was live music, and chanting from the disciples gathered around her. The chanting reminded me of my

time in the wantilan in Bali, as if this cold convention
hall had been warmed by the collective hum of Sanskrit
appeals. I felt hopeful that maybe I'd be able to recapture
something lost.

At one end of the pavilion, a movie played on a screen
above the stage as Amma gave her hugs. It was a movie
of Amma giving people hugs: Amma hugging earthquake
victims, Amma hugging tsunami victims, Amma hugging
cleft-palate victims, Amma hugging Bill Clinton. The
other end was packed with tables and bins of stuff to buy,
like a citywide rummage sale. I was there with an old
friend, Keisha, and while waiting for our turn to join the
darshan line, Keisha and I poked around the bins of coffee
mugs, pens, key chains, and magnets with Amma's face
on them. I bought a magnet for four dollars. Keisha was
entranced with the stacks of photographs of Amma. She
picked one up and caressed it with her fingers.

"Stop that!" one of the robed devotees said, a white
woman with gray hippie braids and milky eyes. "If you get
fingerprints on the photos, we can't sell them."

Keisha looked at the woman as if she were crazy, and
I started to get nervous. When Keisha is angry, I always

end up feeling like it's my fault. She turned away from the disciple and said, in full voice, "Amma, save me from your followers!"

Keisha left shortly after that, but first she looked over at Amma and back at me and said, "You know, it must be easy to love everyone unconditionally when they treat you like a divine mother." I laughed, and Keisha shrugged. "I mean, not that I'm jealous or anything."

We said good-bye, and I was left to experience Amma on my own. I was fine with that—I wanted to find out if I bought it, if I could put my faith in a so-called saint. I wanted to see Amma for myself.

There were people in line who were counting on miracles. Parents with children in wheelchairs. Women with their chemo scarves on. These were people who needed all the faith they could get. As I moved up the line, I saw Amma hug an infant with tubes in his nose, and tried to steel myself against the image; who can be objective when Amma is hugging a sick child? And not just one hug, like she gave to everyone else in line. The baby might have been her own, the way she snuggled him to her chest, rocking him back and forth. I wanted Amma to be powerful, seeing that. I wanted her to be a miracle worker.

I didn't have quite the same response to the seemingly healthy people, like me, in line. The shiny-happy-Seattlites who acted like they'd been struck by lightning after hugging her. They stood around with huge smiles on their faces and tears in their eyes. Really, the demonstrative post-hug bliss-fest was a bit much, I thought. But there must be something terribly wrong with me that I wanted to punch them all in the mouth when all they were doing was enjoying some unconditional yogi love.

The darshan line began at the back of the room, and once you were in it you took a seat and then scooted up a row every few minutes. When you arrived in the inner sanctum, where about seventy or so followers sat meditating and beaming at one another on their soft cushions, you had to hand over your ticket, your purse, anything that might get in the way of your hug. Creeping up toward Amma on my knees, I felt ridiculous, looking up at her as if to say, *Yes, Master?*

She grabbed me and pulled me to her breast, chanting

something in my ear that sounded like "Glug glug glug glug." She smelled terrific, like clean laundry and sandalwood. I could smell her on me the entire walk home.

You can buy Amma's perfume at a lot of health food stores. It's called Amma's Rose.

Walking at rush hour along Mercer Street, I didn't feel changed. It wasn't like what happened in Bali. But maybe that was my fault. I didn't let go and give in to Amma's hug. I was too busy thinking, *Is this real? Do I feel something? Is Amma the proof that there is a God?*

I couldn't come up with a yes. Amma was like the ocean, like the sunset; I didn't feel that she was all that aware of me.

I've read that there are saints who see special potential in one devotee and enlighten them with the touch of a finger. That's pretty much what I was looking for.

That, or another Indra.

What happened in Bali was different. My kundalini experience—it happened *to* me. There was no time for me to question it or look for proof—it was its own proof that there was something to this yoga business. I had laughed at the idea of a mindbody; that mind and body were actually one entity. But now this physical-spiritual experience made it all clear: the division of mind and body was a false one. And if this division was false, then what about the division between me and the rest of the world?

So, was my kundalini experience the proof that there is a God?

Not exactly. But it seemed to suggest that there was something to the science of yoga. That my mind went deeper than I knew. Meditating after my kundalini experience was like spelunking into crevasses in my mind I discovered fresh each day. And the deeper I went, the more I felt some kind of presence in the world that could only be described as god-ish. Not the God I was raised with, but something—well, something loving and beyond the everyday world. Something god-ish.

Lou told me to pay close attention to how my body felt later that day—that if I had a headache or sore muscles, to tell him, because it could mean that the seizure was something more neurological than spiritual. I had no such problems. Instead, I felt like I finally understood everything, and that it was so simple: everything in the world needed love. I was going to save the world with love. If I'd known about Amma at the time, I would've told my yogamates and the entire village of Penestanan to line up for hugs.

Lou did deliver one warning. He told me that I must try not to hold on to my kundalini experience. I must let it go. He said that if I tried to repeat it, I would only backtrack. He said to start fresh every day, to approach my next meditation as if I had never had a kundalini experience, as if it were, in fact, my first attempt at meditation. To be disciplined about not letting my ego wrap itself in a new cloak of spirituality.

I thought it was the silliest way of thinking I'd ever heard. Let go of my kundalini experience? Go back to how I felt before it shook me free? Why on earth would I give up this euphoria, this fearlessness, in order to revert to a version of myself I couldn't wait to relegate to the past?

It occurred to me that maybe I should follow my gut, which told me I had had enough of feeling uncertain and afraid, and now that I had this clarity, this power, I wasn't going to give it up without a fight. Plus, so long as everyone looked at me as if I were a real-life *sage*, why on earth would I disabuse them of the notion?

March 26

When my great-grandmother Nomma passed away, I was four or five and hadn't yet known a person who'd died. My mother told me she was in heaven, which I pictured as a beautiful room with high ceilings and red velvet curtains on all the windows, where someone, anyone, would answer every question you've ever had.

Life, death, why this elaborate and heartbreaking game? I knew life was a game, because I was told there would be winners and losers at the end of it. And I knew it was heartbreaking, because I saw Gram crying, and she told me her heart was broken. Nomma was her mother. If Gram's mom could die—if any mom could die—then what on earth was the point? I thought that Nomma was in that beautiful room, learning the answer now, and that when it was my turn to go there, it would be Nomma who would pull me onto her lap and stroke my thin baby curls as she passed her perfect knowledge on to me.

That room came to me a lot when I was little, in dreams, in reveries. I remember feeling that it was where I had come from, and where I would return someday.

Red curtains? High ceilings? A memory of the womb, perhaps?

I felt it as a peaceful, dreamy place.

That's sort of what meditation feels like, now. Like I dip down into some familiar, dreamy place where I am nothing but a soul waiting to be born.

March 27

Indra and Lou are beautiful and supportive and loving.

Today, Indra kept telling me to slow down and breathe. She says I'm doing deep emotional and physical processing right now and so I shouldn't push it, but just focus on my breathing.

I don't want to. I am kicking ass, spiritually speaking. Everything I do is effortless now, from meditation to arm balances. I don't want to just focus on my breath. I want to stretch and soar.

Later

Lou and I are connected on a spiritual level that no one else could possibly understand. He is psychic.

And so am I.

I sent him a message in class today. We were meditating, and I decided to test him out.

Over the past few weeks Lou has mentioned that my head was turning to the right a little during guided meditation. I used to do that in piano lessons, too—I think I hear better with my left ear. That's my theory, anyway.

We were meditating, unguided. And I said to Lou, in my brain, *Lou, tell me if I'm tilting my head to the right*.

And I swear to God, Lou responded immediately, out loud. He said, "Suzanne, your head isn't tilting. Your posture looks good."

I want to do this forever. I'm never going home.

March 28

Since we arrived, I've had a million questions for my yoga-mates: What exactly is *chatturanga dandasana*? What are the Yoga Sutras really about? Why, in Horse pose, do I have to breathe through my vagina?

But now! Every night we gather around the table on our veranda just as the last drops of liquid sun dribble down our shiny tiled steps, and my yogamates ask me question after question after question about my kundalini experience. When I speak, they lean in and listen.

I keep thinking of sixth grade. That's what this is like, sixth grade, except that this time? This time I'm the first girl to get her period, and everybody else wants to know how soon they'll get to join the club.

God, I really love my yogamates. I feel like I understand them now, truly and deeply.

March 29

Today I found myself bonding with plants. I meditated on these big, green, leafy things stretching toward the heavens and thought, *Yeah. I know what you mean.*

I am detached, and I am engaged.

Lou told me that there is a difference between detachment and disengagement. It took me a while to understand what he meant by that. I think I always thought of yoga and Eastern philosophy as having to do with detachment, that you just sit on a mountaintop not giving a good goddamn about anyone or anything, just zoning out. Lou says that is disengagement, not detachment, and that it's not the goal of yoga at all.

The idea is to be detached from the fruits of our labors, which means that we do things simply for the act of doing them. Today, for instance, I wanted to tip up into headstand, but couldn't get there gracefully. Normally I would waste loads of energy worrying that my yogamates were watching and judging, or feeling superior to me because they can get into headstand and I can't, and so I would muscle my way into it or give up entirely and rest back in Child's pose. But today I realized that the goal of headstand wasn't the point—headstand was the outcome I needed to be detached from. The act of trying to get up gracefully was enough, so I just worked on that.

It's why we try to speak only the truth: because we use language to manipulate one another, to get a particular response. So if we speak the truth, we can't use our words to elicit a particular outcome. For example, telling a waitress, "No, it's really no problem, I mean, you *could* bring me some salt for this underseasoned dish, but it's really no big deal if you don't, I mean, I don't *have* to taste my food" is the opposite of yogic.

It would be a lot more yogic simply to say, "I need some fucking salt." Truth! Oh my, if I brought that kind of yoga practice back to Seattle I would get lynched by the Nice Police. Good thing I'm headed to New York.

Being detached means recognizing our emotions as what they are: clouds, sunbursts, weather. They pass. So rather than feed on my anger or sadness, rolling about in it like a pig in its own filth, I see that it is weather, and know that in time it will pass.

This clarity I've had since my kundalini breakthrough isn't an emotional state. I don't see it as weather so much as a whole new sky. Today, Jessica wondered out loud if maybe it was emotional, if all the attention I was getting from my teachers and yogamates was giving me a sort of well-being high. That would've bugged me if I didn't have this clarity. Which proves my point: it's not emotional.

I wish Jessica would bring it up again, so I could point this out to her.

March 30

Javanese workers have descended upon Ubud and the surrounding villages to harvest the tall stalks of rice. They wear those pointy straw hats that look like the shells my siblings and I used to call Chinese hats. Sitting in the wantilan before class, watching the workers with their strong arms slice through the dry, yellow stalks in the middle of the lime-green rice terraces is unbelievably beautiful. It occurred to me today as I watched them that I would ordinarily feel guilty if I caught myself thinking that the work these men and women do is beautiful: like, here I am, sitting in a yoga pavilion, romanticizing their sweat. But now I'm just taking it in, and it's beautiful to watch.

I accept the world as it is.

ALTHOUGH.

I would like to see more of Indra. I was sort of thinking that now that I've had this breakthrough, we would spend more time together outside of class. That I could come over and hang out with her on the balcony drinking tea, talking about the path, braiding each other's hair. Or something.

March 31

My yogamates keep talking about how difficult meditation is. Not like Louise did. It's not annoying. But Jason and Lara were visiting and they both said they were having such a hard time with it, and they were looking for some advice.

"You lucky duck," Lara said, and I think her green eyes were extra green. *From jealousy.* "You've had what we've all taken thousands of dollars of workshops to experience."

"Tell us about the dream again?" Jason said, and I did, and I just felt so sorry for them. It's like they're in this loop of self-sabotage, telling themselves it's hard and then wondering why it's hard. But it's not hard at all! If you just let go, it's really easy.

But I wonder if I know it's easy because I'm just really *gifted* at meditation.

Later

Class ended rather strangely today. Jason does a pitch-perfect impersonation of Lou, in which he sits in lotus, rubbing himself like a massage therapist on speed and calling us "people" in a faraway voice, his eyes going vaguely cross-eyed as if he were transcending to another planet. We made him do it for Lou at the end of class, and I stood to the side, next to Indra, watching. Everybody was laughing, especially Lou, who looked more tickled than I could ever have imagined him to look. It's hard to believe I was ever afraid of this sweet, gentle man.

I kept stealing sidelong glances at Indra. I could feel her next to me, her posture rigid with tension. She was smiling, but tightly, as if she was just waiting it out. As if she was experiencing something unpleasant and inappropriate. I got the sense she didn't know what to do with herself. I don't think I've ever seen her like that. Ill at ease: it's not how I think of her.

I wonder if she felt that we were being disrespectful? Or did she wish we had a similar tribute to her?

Then again, she's always been somewhat distant after class. Maybe she was just hungry and wanted to get to lunch. Baerbel noticed it as well, though. "Well," she said as we sat down to our own lunch of greens and rice at Casa Luna, "Indra did not like that one bit."

April 1

Easter Sunday.

I'm lying in bed, trying to accept that yes, I'm in a little pain, but it will pass. I'm detached from my pain, and engaged only in this writing.

That said, there is the cutest little baby gecko running around on the windowsill. It's smaller than my pinkie finger!

Anyway, today: Easter. The Resurrection. We didn't go to church. I don't even know if there are churches on this island. We didn't go to any temples, either. I mean—why would we? No, we went to a spa. It was called the Sacred Spa. Which is sort of holy, right? (Sometimes it strikes me as funny, this New Age business. In the eighties, I'd bet the spa would've been called "You're Rich, They're Not! Spa." But these days anything that costs a bit of scratch has got to be spiritual or we don't approve.)

Which is cool. I mean, in a way, my spa experience *did* feel spiritual. But maybe that's just where I am right now— there's no difference, anymore, between my mind and my body, so being touched and coddled is amazing. I feel like Zorba the Greek, opening my arms to the world.

Jessica cried a little while we got pedicures. The woman who was taking care of her insisted on shaving off about twenty layers of skin and calluses from Jessica's heels. She probably lost a shoe size. I'd bet she was the highlight of her pedicurist's day.

"I got those calluses walking the earth," Jessica said, watching the shavings collect beneath her feet like so many slices of Parmesan. "That was my whole life built into my feet." She looked at me helplessly.

"Your heels have been reborn," I replied. "Consider it an offering in honor of the Resurrection. Beginning of a new cycle."

That cheered her up a bit.

Now that I think of it, my time at the Sacred Spa was a bit of a spiritual journey. I walked through fire in order to reach salvation. I scaled the cliffs of fear and suffering and found myself closer to God.

For you see, today I had my first bikini wax.

What's crazy is that I've spent so much time in meditation and yoga practice that I've learned to relax instantly. So even though I howled with pain each time Reni, my aesthetician, ripped a swath of hair off my inner thighs, I fell asleep after each one. I dozed as she smoothed the hot wax on my leg, and gently pressed the cloth to the wax, and then I came awake with a shriek the instant she tugged it off.

I wailed as if she were skinning me alive. But then I fell back asleep until she pressed on a newly bald spot, which made me howl again. Reni winced, but I could tell from the way her mouth twitched that she thought I was completely bizarre.

"Sick, sick!" she said, hiding a laugh with a cough. I opened my eyes and yelped as she tore another patch of hair off. "Sensitive, sensitive!" It looked almost painful, her screwing up her face to keep from laughing at me, so I started to crack up, and once I started, she busted up, too—just as she went to pull at a strip of hair. Her grip slipped a little and instead of ripping the hair out, she just gave it a ragged tug.

I moaned like a dying cat. And then I dozed.

After she was done abusing me, Reni walked me over to the shower, holding on to my arm as I would guide my grandmother. Next to the shower was a large claw-foot tub, the bottom of which was lined with fresh flowers and spices. She ran the water in the tub while she soaped me up in the shower. Now I really felt like a little kid. She even washed me between my legs—which naturally made me start laughing again. I turned my head to the side so Reni wouldn't notice, but she gave me a quizzical look anyway and sort of shrugged, like, *What, you don't want to be clean?*

She guided me over to the bath. The warm water had lifted the flowers up to the top, so I pierced a layer of gardenias and frangipani as I got in. Reni gave me a yellow clay mug of hot water with chunks of ginger and loads of honey in it, and then left me alone. I sank into the water, a gardenia grazing my chin. I watched a little pang of guilt, or maybe fear, drift across my inner sky, and depart. It was the same guilty fear I've been feeling for ages, but now I just looked at it, acknowledged it, and let it move on by.

It struck me that this was the most extraordinary thing I'd ever learned how to do.

I lay back in the tub and looked up at the sky through the glassless window above my head. I kicked my leg through the floating blanket of flowers and rested it on the side of the bath, sinking deeper into the hot water, laughing a little bit at my gynecological shower experience and marveling at this curious, unfamiliar feeling of liberation from myself. I sipped my tea and looked at my body. The flowers were canary yellow, magenta, pink and creamy white, and they cast revolving shadows on my belly—smudges and blobs like Rorschach blots.

The tea was perfectly spicy, and I imagined it cleaning my insides. When all that was left in the mug were chunks of ginger and cinnamon sticks, I dumped these remnants into the bathwater and leaned over the side of the tub to place the cup on the tile floor. I loved the sound it made, that muted clink of clay on the stone tiles.

Thank you for that sound, I thought.

I reached my wet arm over the side of the bath, tiny flowers and bits of yellow and red spices sticking to my skin, and picked the cup up again. I lifted it to my nose, smelling the last traces of ginger. Then I put it back on the ground to hear the clink again. Like dress shoes on flagstones. I lifted it up, I put it back down.

Oh, thank you for that sound! I thought, directing it toward the window. I splashed my hands through the flowers at my sides. *Thank you for this bath. Thank you for the waxing I've just had and the rash that will surely follow.* I thought of my yogamates and my friends at home, my sister, my brothers, my parents and grandparents; my entire family. *Thank you.* I thought of Indra and Lou and Jonah, lifting my arms above my head, flowers falling into my hair, overwhelmed. *Thank you, thank you, thank you.* I lowered myself back into the water until my mouth and nose were submerged and I could hear my heart pounding in my ears. The flowers floating on the surface of the water were at my eye level. From this angle they looked like a bright, colorful jungle. I stared at them like this for a long time until I felt the first few pinpricks of pain in my inner thighs, which swiftly became a crimson irritation that now has me lamenting the existence of wax.

Until I remember, now, that it's just pain. And see? Just like that, it's gone.

Hmm. Well. Almost.

April 2

There was a spider the size of my hand on my bath towel this morning. I didn't have my contacts in yet, so I didn't see the spider until my face was about an inch from its hairy green back. At just that moment, Jessica, who was brushing her teeth next to me, let out an incredible wail of fear, but I didn't even jump. I just moved my face away.

I'm fine with the bugs now. I didn't used to be. But now I look at the bites all over my arms and legs and find myself admiring their differences. Some are as big as quarters and as pink as my lips, others are like a rash of whiteheads. The one on my knee looks like Saturn, a small round bite with a red ring around it. What interesting work you do, I say to the bugs.

I figure, I eat from the rice fields, the bugs eat from the me-fields. We're all working together!

Jessica wouldn't come back in the house until I had tapped the spider off the towel and into the bushes along the side of the veranda. Poor thing. She's really got a ways to go yet.

Later

Something strange and new happened today. I was in Warrior Two pose, feeling very powerful and open, when a teensy-tiny little fart escaped me. A little soubrette of a fart, a light, sweet soprano sigh.

You know what I discovered? Farting in public is fun! In fact, it was liberating! It was like an extension of my mindbody state. An audible meditation. Like chanting, but, um—with my ass.

Ohhhhhh, okay, I'm lying. It was mortifying. I wanted to die. I still want to die. But I'm trying to work with it. I'm trying to be detached from the fart. Farts and emotions are like weather. They pass.

But, oh. Cringe.

Later

It's raining.

I've been meditating on the bed, trying not to think

about certain things. Trying not to relive certain moments when I could've been more repressed. I don't know. I don't want to be repressed.

Oh, goddamn it to hell. Repression is something I *like* in a GI tract.

I want to die. And I can't stop laughing. I'm in strait-jacket territory.

Still Later

I've been a little hysterical. Laughing and moaning and hiding under the covers. Jessica can hardly believe I'm this upset over a little fart. She brought me a tray with some ginger tea on it and a little yogurt. She said yogurt is good for the GI tract, and then she made a farting noise with her lips, like a kid. She sat down beside me on the bed and did it again. "Excuse me!" she cried, and then she made more fart noises until she was giggling uncontrollably and spilled the ginger tea all over herself.

I like her so much.

April 3

I've read all my books! The *Gita*, the Upanishads, the Sutras. I am a sacred text–consuming machine.

Now I'm going crazy without anything to read, so Baer-bel took pity on me and lent me some of her books. She has the unabridged Upanishads, while I only have the paltry abridged versions. She also gave me some books on ancient Ayurveda, which is the medical science connected to yoga. And looky what I found, a recipe for the curing of insanity, demons, and epilepsy:

"Cow's urine is cooked in about three kilograms of ghee, together with about 200 grams each of asafetida, dark salt, and a mixture of black pepper, long pepper, and dried ginger."

If I had to choose between drinking my own pee or the pee of a cow, there would be no question about what I would choose. No question at all. I would choose to kill myself.

> Dream:
> Jonah shows up here in Bali and his face falls when
> I don't recognize him at first. We sit down on the
> veranda steps, open on three sides to gales of wind
> and rain that whip through the trees and spray our
> faces. I get up and stand in the yard, in the rain,
> and Jonah says, "You'll be too muddy to transcend.
> Your little feet will get stuck in the earth and you
> won't be able to go anywhere."

April 4

Jessica has had a breakthrough in her groin openers (she realized in Horse pose that breathing into her vagina wasn't as powerful an image for her as breathing *out of* her vagina), and to celebrate, she wants to go shopping. She's dressing for our outing right now, braiding her blonde hair in sections and wearing rose quartz drop earrings. She's instructed me to wear my light pink linen sundress. She's the boss, I told her. It's her day.

That said, I wonder if shopping is something we ought to be doing. I'm meditating about five million hours a day, and when I'm not meditating I'm in the wantilan exhausting every muscle in my body so that I can meditate. Do we really want to risk our mental clarity by filling our hearts with worldly desires?

But no. I am not going to be disengaged, just detached. Gandhi engaged with the world and so will I!

Jessica sees shopping very differently than I do. She told me this morning that the movement of fashion is a vein of feminine gold in the gray, masculine rock of society. Her gender-clarity teacher told her that femininity reveals itself in adornment. I told her that I felt like fashion was just another industry wanting to take our money. And besides, doesn't it seem a bit crazy, the amount of effort and money it takes to keep up with the changing trends?

"That's the whole point!" she cried. She was standing in long black linen pants and a long-sleeved linen shirt, with a batik-print green scarf wrapped loosely around her neck. She said that it's the ephemeral nature of fashion that makes it a feminine power. "Women are the true agents of change in this world—what changes the world more than bringing new life into it?" I was struck by how elegant she looked, with her delicate rib cage, small breasts, tiny little shoulders.

I suddenly felt like a sausage in my pink sundress, white and fat and mottled, like a bratwurst, and the feeling made me want to shop for a whole new me. Jessica seemed to understand what I was feeling—she lifted her arms above her head, the thin sleeves of her shirt peeling back to reveal her two ruddy elbows: "Today is our day for transformation!"

Jessica says that when we shop, we worship the goddess Kali, goddess of destruction and transformation. She says that when you have a major breakthrough in your life, it's like you become a whole new version of yourself. In order to embrace this new version of yourself, you must destroy the person you used to be—and everything she ever wore.

Evening

What a day, what a day! We're at Casa Luna, adorned and blissed out from a day of spiritual shopping.

I would relive this day a hundred times if I could. I want to own this day, keep it in a pretty little sandalwood box, wrapped in silk, so I can pull it out and look at it whenever I want.

I'm in love. It's a problem. But God, it feels good. I am ENGAGING WITH THE WORLD!

I'm detached, though, too, of course.

We started in Campuhan, where those small red fruits had fallen from the low-hanging trees during this morning's storm and had already been trampled by God knows how many feet. Their sticky pulp made our flip-flops cling to the ground. Campuhan is the last village before Ubud, and it's lined with tchotchke shops. We stepped into one and emerged a few minutes later with batik scarves in turquoise and purple.

And you know what? Suddenly I was right back in a state of spiritual bliss. It was like my kundalini breakthrough had just happened this morning. I'd forgotten that you can get virtually the same high from handing over cash for clothes. Jessica's right about the transformational possibilities of shopping. In a jewelry store, I imagined myself in New York wearing all this fabulous silver jewelry and chopsticks in my hair, decorating my urban treehouse with masks of Shiva and Shakti. When people visit my house they will say, *She is a world traveler. She is worldly. She has exceptional taste in phallic sandalwood sculptures. She doesn't just go on vacations: she goes on* sacred *vacations.*

I did buy a carving of a man sitting in Forward Bend with an enormous erect penis and his hands covering his eyes, as if he's saying, "I just can't believe it's so big."

Conversation piece!

Walking into Ubud, the sun was in our eyes even as

rainwater from the storm rushed down the flood drains. We passed pavilion after pavilion of men in shorts and T-shirts building creatures out of chicken wire and papier-mâché for an upcoming festival.

Jessica's voice climbed higher and higher up her vocal range as she pointed out all the colors in my new moonstone ring. I complimented her on her choice of silver arm cuff. We were best friends.

Until Jessica found her shoes. Then I had to escape for a minute. See, Jessica's idea of haggling is to name her price very low and then never budge. So when she found the shoes—beaded thong sandals, white and sparkling and the shoes she says she'll be married in someday—she offered five thousand rupiah, about five dollars, and the saleswoman countered with twenty thousand, and then moved down to eighteen, then sixteen, and Jessica stayed at five thousand. I tried to stay out of the way, lurking next to a hanging mobile of scarves, but pretty soon I realized it was going to be a long time before Jessica had herself a new pair of shoes. So, just as Jessica reluctantly upped her bid to six thousand, I stepped out onto a busy Monkey Forest Road to see where we should go next.

I walked past a skinny, shirtless man crouched on the corner selling skewers of chicken and beef that smelled delicious and forbidden, poked my head into a couple of shops, and then stopped in front of a glass-fronted store that couldn't seem more out of place in the land of batik scarves and sandalwood sculptures. PRADA.

The store was clean, bright, minimalist. Three sides were lined with thin black shelves upon which purses, backpacks, and wallets waited for admirers like sculptures in a museum. Carousels of lightweight T-shirts spun around the floor.

A small collection of shoes was displayed near the entrance, one pair to a shelf. Pointy-toed leather pumps, three-inch stilettos. Lovely, all of them, but shoes are not my vice, so I quickly lost interest. The same wall bore the weight of a few dozen wallets, satchels, and fanny packs in the black nylon design that is ubiquitous in certain suburbs of Seattle where the women are tan and blond and the men drive Jaguars. I've never understood the appeal of those bags. Especially when I found out they cost as much as half my rent.

I made my way toward the door to return to Jessica's shoe crisis, but something held me back. This something wouldn't let me leave.

I have this vice. Well—I have several vices, or I did before I came to Bali and got all transcendent and kundalinified. But this one is my most girly of vices. Handbags. I adore them. So it was the power of the handbag—the prana of the Prada, you might say, if you were prone to saying such things— that made me turn around and walk to the back of the store where variations on my addiction lined up like an exceedingly attractive Greek chorus, chanting to me in unison.

One voice distinguished itself from the others, low and husky. My breath fell short. My face warmed. I was in thrall to Eros.

Pistachio green leather. Its strap is like a belt buckle, so that it can be adjusted to fit snugly under my arm, or hang loosely if I want it to. Slightly rectangular, slightly cylindrical, I reached for it; I pulled my hand back. We flirted with each other until I couldn't help myself; I had to hug it to my side, my perfect purse, my one true love. I stroked the leather, I smelled it, I wanted to wear its perfume. I looked at myself in the mirror in a variety of positions. From the side, the bag tucked deliciously under my bare arm, the leather rubbing gently against my skin. From behind, its backside round and perfect.

On my knee, genuflecting, its length perpendicular to my thigh, I unzipped it slowly, tantalizingly, and then slid my fingers inside as if to retrieve a compact.

From the street, I heard the screech of tires and someone yelling. I shook my head, caught my breath, and remembered that I was in a Prada store, a place I had never been, for one simple reason: I am not rich.

I put the bag back on its little altar. But first, just to make myself feel better, I looked at the price tag.

The handbag that would complete me as I've never been completed before could be mine for one hundred fifty thousand dollars.

Relief. Of course I couldn't afford it. I turned away, I said good-bye.

But wait! One hundred fifty thousand dollars? No! One hundred fifty thousand *rupiah*. Which is more like one hundred fifty dollars.

I have that many dollars.

But then something struck me as wrong, as terribly wrong about this whole scenario. I looked around. I was at Prada, in Bali. Is this for real? I know most fake bags are made in Asia—could this be the *fake* Prada store? I eyed the saleswomen in their chic black outfits. I envisioned them leaving the store through the door behind the register and walking into a windowless room of long tables at which nimble-fingered toddlers made hundreds of handbags a day in exchange for a spoonful of formula and a diaper change.

But one hundred fifty dollars? That's too much to be a fake.

But it's also too little to be real. Could these be last season's purses? International prices? But if I spent one hundred fifty dollars on a Prada handbag that turns out to be a fake, what would that make me?

That would make me a chump.

I'm not ready for this leap of faith, I thought. I was standing with my arm outstretched, the purse dangling like a drop earring from my hand, when Jessica appeared in my peripheral vision. I didn't know what to say to her, especially when I noted that she didn't have a shopping bag in hand and therefore must have put the shoes back for costing one or two dollars more than she was willing to spend.

We tilted our heads at the purse as if it were a painting. "Beautiful, huh?" I said.

Jessica sighed at the purse and then gave me a look that told me everything I wanted to know: she could see that we were meant for each other. That we had a connection. That I had found my soul mate.

We walked out slowly. I turned back twice, but made it out to the street without my leather companion. Back in the sun and air, I remembered who I was, and who I wasn't, what I needed and what I didn't, and I told myself I had made the right decision. I am in Bali for other reasons. I'm on a path, and that path doesn't go through Milan.

As we walked toward the restaurant, Jessica said, "You know, women experience their purses as an extension of their uterus."

"Mmm," I said. "Do they?"

NOW WE'RE SITTING at Casa Luna, drinking tea and thinking about getting some dinner. And I've got to say there are some scary places your brain can go when you want something. I've been thinking about the idea of dharma. Sweatshop dharma. If we're supposed to accept the world as it is, then maybe it isn't a bad thing to own a purse with potentially sinister origins? Jessica says that this is a bit of a stretch, BUT! She did say that it was true, as far as she could tell, that sweatshops are just a part of life, and that the people working in sweatshops are living with their own karma and dharma and all the same things we live with. Dharma doesn't stop at the sweatshop door.

As Marcy sometimes says, *Everything works out perfectly*. In India, she says, the people are singing in the slums. She says that in this world there's *just enough* happiness, and *just enough* suffering.

When she said that, I looked at the giant diamond studs in her ears and thought, *And I guess there's* just enough *bullshit, too*.

Hmm. Well, shoot. I don't want to be a Marcy, so I'd better put this business out of my mind. We need food.

I want nothing, I need nothing, I am free of all desire.

Oh, but I *wants* it. My precious.

April 5

Ohhh, we're in trouble. Big trouble. I wasn't going to write about this, but Jessica and I did something very naughty last night, at the end of our day of shopping.

There we were, at Casa Luna, singing songs to each other about our day's purchases. As always, we were surrounded by the spiritual tourists that crowd Ubud and fill up every table at what we think of as *our* restaurant. They were smoking cigarettes and drinking martinis and eating all of the foods we've long since renounced: Artery-clogging steak. Shrimp in sickly sweet sauces. Pork that's been marinated in Balinese rice wine. By now we'd eaten our green leaves and rice, and I was feeling pretty good about my ability to be detached from my handbag. Soon I found myself feeling sorry for these poor tourists—I know their trials and tribulations well. After all, I was once one of them. Fourteen days ago, I, too, longed for the worldly pleasures these tourists enjoyed, like food that tastes good, for instance. For cigarettes and cocktails.

But then I noticed the table next to us. A brunette and a blonde, just like us, only these women were wearing gorgeous designer vacation wear. Flowing silk sarongs with matching halter tops that showed off their spectacular and line-free tans. They sparkled all over with jewelry: diamond studs in their noses, diamond rings on their right hands. They looked like they spent every morning in yoga and every afternoon at the spa. In comparison, our purchases looked cheap and handmade. I wished I had bought the purse.

I want nothing, I need nothing, I am free of all desire.

I was about to say this to Jessica when she froze, staring at something in her menu. "Oh no," she said. She looked at me with crazy eyes. "Oh Suzanne!"

"What?"

"Oh, it's bad, bad, bad!"

"What?"

She lowered her voice to a giddy whisper. "It's a milkshake. A coconut. Vanilla. Milkshake!" And then she started giggling again, shaking her head. "Oh no, no, *no*."

I looked at her, not smiling, not joining in her giggle fit. "We have to have that," I said.

"No!" she cried, "we can't!"

"Can't we?" Suddenly I wanted this milkshake more

than I've ever wanted anything in my life, including enlightenment.

Jessica's laughter was starting to get a little panicked. "But, Suzanne, it's full of sugar! Sweetness! Attachment! *Milkshakes are bad!*"

Now, as I saw it, this was a health shake. It was probably fresh vanilla mixed with fresh coconut, probably from the trees right outside. Back home they'd sell it at Whole Foods for twelve bucks a pop. I explained my thinking to Jessica, but she looked skeptical. "Come on, Jess. You only live once!"

Oops. Jessica looked at me as if I was the crazy one in the relationship. I tried to backtrack. "I mean, until the next life."

Ten minutes later it arrived.

And it wasn't a milkshake—I could tell from the little corona of heavenly light hovering above it. It was ambrosia. It was a milkshake for the gods. It made me believe in God, in fact, in a loving God that wants us to be happy. I thought of my siblings for a second, and laughed. "Jess," I said, "this is the proof that there is a God."

She nodded happily. "This is about as God as God gets," she said.

Not too thick, not too thin, a subtle blend of coconut and vanilla. It tasted like an ice cream cone. The wafer kind, not a waffle or sugar cone, but the cheap kind my parents bought when we were kids, when ice cream cones were symbolic of the weekend or summer or anytime when we were liberated from the dictatorial anti-sugar regime of the house. I sipped my milkshake, five years old again.

How something that makes me feel loved by God can be bad, I don't know.

Well.

Lest we forget: certain things are forbidden in the yogic lifestyle, including meat, alcohol, caffeine, sugar, and *joie de vivre*.

This morning, before class, we were being good karma yogis, moving the gamelan instruments to the side of the wantilan, and Jessica and I couldn't help telling our yoga-mates about our brief rebellion last night. Our impulses were good, I swear. We weren't trying to corrupt, we were trying to enlighten.

Jessica was explaining that this milkshake was like a coconut-vanilla *orgasm* when Indra and Lou arrived. Our yogamates looked nervous at the sight of our teachers, and their nerves must've made Jessica repent, because as soon as we were seated for check-in, something terrible happened. Jessica confessed.

Lou looked up for a split second and then returned his gaze to his heels, where he was digging around with his thumbs. But Indra stood up a little straighter, her head tilted as her eyes traveled from Jessica to me, and back to Jessica. "A coconut-vanilla milkshake," she said.

A heroin crack cocaine blood of a junkie whoreshake?

We nodded. "Well now, let's see," she said, looking up at the rafters. "What's in a milkshake like that? I'd guess it's chock full of coconut. And vanilla. And sugar?" She low-ered her gaze, simultaneously thrilled and pissed. "And it's fun to drink sugary drinks, isn't it? Doesn't it make you want to drink more of them? Don't you wish you could have one right now?"

We nodded again. And then things went a little weird.

"Now, I'm sure you remember the man just outside the wantilan today, right? A man cleaning a dead chicken?"

I was a little thrown off by Indra's question, honestly. I

had noticed the man with the dead chicken—he was shirt-less and standing up to his thighs in the river that runs be-tween the forest and the rice fields, and he was cleaning the chicken on the bank where we walk every morning to class. There were chicken guts all over the path, so we had to hop over them, Jessica squealing as she jumped. But I couldn't see what the connection was between a little milkshake and a pile of chicken entrails.

"Weren't you repulsed by those chicken guts?" she said, smiling slyly. "Is there anything so disgusting as the bloody insides of a dead, headless chicken?" She seemed to be waiting for a response, which came in due time—from my growling stomach. Roast chicken. Crispy golden skin. Sides of mashed potatoes and green beans with butter and garlic. So I suppose the answer would be *No. Not exactly repulsed.*

"Well," Indra said, ignoring my stomach's editorial reply, "if you want to experience worldly pleasures like milkshakes, then you must experience the revulsion of the chicken guts." She quoted the Upanishads from memory:

> *Like two birds perched in the selfsame tree*
> *Intimate friends, the Ego and the Self,*
> *Dwell in the selfsame body.*
> *The former eats the sweet and sour fruits of the tree of life*
> *While the other looks on in detachment.*

Indra explained that these two birds, the lower bird and the higher bird, represent the world of attachment and sep-aration, and the indivisible Self. The lower bird is the mate-rial world, and everything in it, good and bad. So the lower bird is Gandhi, but he is also Hitler. He is the milkshake, and he is the chicken guts. "The lower bird," she said, shaking her head sadly, "wants nothing more than to embrace the illusions of this world, and so he must suffer along with his joy."

She paused, thinking. "But the higher bird," she said, "is detached from all worldly illusions, all worldly desires, and so he is at peace."

Jessica sighed and lowered her head respectfully. I looked down as well, studying my hands and trying to figure out what the hell Indra was talking about.

I think I get it now. It's different from the Judeo-Christian view of the angel and the devil, one on each shoulder. In the Upanishads, the angel and devil are on the same shoulder, both trying to keep you attached to this world and believing yourself to be separate from everyone else. On the other shoulder is the higher bird, detached from all pleasure and pain, just sort of chilling out. The higher bird has perspective, you might say. You might say that he doesn't sit on a shoulder but higher up, on a shoulder pad. The lower bird is down in the scrum of life, lost and confused.

"The beautiful thing," Indra said, now smiling around the circle, "is that once you can be detached from that milkshake, you can step over or into those chicken guts and not feel a thing. Just as the higher bird would."

With that, Lou asked us to return to our mats to begin the first rounds of sun salutations for the day. And just as I reached my mat, I heard Indra, her voice smiling, say, "And, Suzanne! Just remember one thing: One kundalini breakthrough? Doesn't mean you've won the race."

Later

Jessica is beside herself. She came home and did fifty sit-ups on the veranda as penance for the milkshake. But then she got up and joined me at the table and said, "Suzanne, I know we're not supposed to want the milkshake, but ever since Indra said those things about the higher and lower birds and how we should be detached from the milkshake, I can't stop thinking about it. I just want another one so badly!"

I told her she'd just summed up exactly what it's like to grow up Catholic.

But then I remembered something: Indra is my teacher, and she knows what she's talking about. One kundalini breakthrough isn't enough. I need another one. And the only way to have another one is to stay on the path. So I looked Jessica in the eye, and said, "Now, we could act like most Catholics I know, and go out and drink ten coconut-vanilla milkshakes in rebellion, or we can think of it this way":

(I felt really wise, like a real yoga teacher.)

"The milkshake, Jessica, doesn't exist. It isn't real, so why would we want it? What is real?" I asked her, rhetorically. "What is real is the Self, and that is what we are here to attain. Union with the Self. Freedom from desire. Desire keeps us attached to life, and attachment to life makes us fear death. No more milkshakes, Jess. Back on the path." I nodded at her, putting my hands together in namaste and lifting them to my lips. "Back on the path," I repeated. Then I went inside, thinking, _I'll leave her with that_.

Hmm. I wanted to record this because I was feeling really good about myself, having seen the proverbial light and imparted it to my friend. But now, reading my words over, I wonder if maybe I spoke less like a sage and more like a douchebag.

The thing is, I'm a little embarrassed, but at the same time I really believe what I said to Jessica. It's time to get back on the path, and stay there. We've got less than a month left here, and soon we'll have to start practicing as teachers. In just a few weeks I will be responsible for teaching an entire class on my own. So today I practiced on Jessica. Maybe I sounded a little douchey, but it's also possible that that's just what a real yoga teacher sounds like. Maybe my ears haven't adjusted to it yet. Maybe my ears are plugged by irony and cynicism. And who knows? I may have gotten through to her. I can hear her out there doing more sit-ups, and maybe that's just what she needs to do to have the discipline to conquer her desires.

I'm going down to the pool. My stomach is a little upset from all the excitement today. Or, who knows? Maybe the sugar we drank last night is affecting my system—I haven't had sugar in over a month. Seems like my stomach is rebelling against it a little. I'm going to take it easy till the afternoon class. No need to push it. A little poolside meditation and I should be right as rain.

April 6

What. The. Fuck. What the fuck!

I am so upset. Indra, my God. I don't understand!

I've been doing every pose for them. For Indra and Lou. In *surya namaskar*, I extend, I reach, I'm watching where my knee is in relation to my ankle. I'm focusing on my breath. I wait for them to tell me it looks good and then I make it even better. And yet! Today, while in *paschimottanasana*, WHICH MEANS SEATED FORWARD BEND AND SEE? I EVEN KNOW THE POSE NAMES IN FREAKIN' SANSKRIT, Indra did something so unexpected, so out of character, so cruel, I can hardly write I'm so angry.

We were in our Forward Bends. My Forward Bend, if I dare

say so myself, is pretty good. I ease my way into it until my rib cage rests on my thighs, and then I fold over like a piece of paper. I might not have any upper-body strength to speak of, but on a good day my hamstrings are so flexible I could jump rope with them. That's not ego, that's an objective truth. I'll be the first to admit that I can't do a push-up. When I try to do a push-up I look like a dog with broken hind legs, whimpering and waiting for the needle to put me out of my misery.

But in Forward Bend I lean into it, I ask for ease in my legs, I search for *sattva*. And I have to say: having had a kundalini experience, I know what motherfucking *sattva* means.

It means balance.

Anyway. So I was in my Forward Bend. My irreproachable Forward Bend. The sun was hitting my back, warming me up so I felt even more flexible.

Indra wove slowly through our mats, speaking in her gentlest tone, the one she uses when we're in restorative poses. "Your Forward Bend is such an important pose," she was saying. "It's one of the most introspective poses, and I'd like to thank all of you who haven't studied at our studio in Seattle for recognizing that."

Naturally my ears perked up at that last bit, because I am the only one in the wantilan who has studied with them in Seattle. I leaned deeper into my Forward Bend, now, thinking that Indra was going to use me as her example. That I wasn't included in her statement because my Forward Bend was simply in another league.

"This is such an introspective pose," she continued, "it deserves to be respected. But I am frequently disturbed to find that the Forward Bend becomes a competition for who is the most flexible in class."

I felt Indra standing beside me, blocking the sun.

"Competition," she said, "is not an introspective activity. So I'd like to thank you all for overcoming that urge to compete."

She put her hands on my sacrum, now, guiding me deeper into the stretch. "With that in mind," she said, "Suzanne, would you please watch the rounding in your thoracic spine? Just ease into it, and remember: there's no need to be competitive."

!!!

Um, excuse me?

I'm sorry, but who do I have to compete with here? Last I checked, I was the one who was so deeply meditative I had a fucking seizure!

I have to go back to class in thirty minutes, but I feel like I should just skip it and stay home to meditate on my own, without that negative energy messing up my practice.

I'm just so humiliated. After she called me out, I closed my eyes and tried to look unfazed, but I could feel the blood burning through my cheekbones and forehead like acid through litmus paper. I was sure I could feel my yogamates smirking, and probably exchanging amused glances. I'm sure they were loving it. I'm sure they couldn't wait to talk about it over lunch. Honestly, when I think about it, they're all really hateful people.

Indra continued moving through us in her lovely yoga outfit, flowing green pants and matching tank, and I felt disgusting in my own hand-washed black yoga pants, a little crisp at the hem and waist, my black tank top sweaty and stretched out at the neck. I felt revolting.

You know what just occurred to me? Maybe Indra has never had a kundalini experience. Maybe she's the one feeling competitive, because she's afraid I'm going to become a more powerful yogini than she is! Maybe this is all an attempt to keep me under her thumb!

Oh God. No. No, sweet Jesus, that's a ridiculous thought.

OKAY, I'VE DONE some alternate-nostril breathing and I've made myself a cup of tea. I'm looking down at my yogamates who are starting to come up from the pool to get ready for our afternoon class. And you know what? This makes perfect sense. This is how it should be. I get it now.

Here's the thing: I've had a huge spiritual breakthrough. So it's like I've graduated to a whole new level. Like I'm getting my PhD in yoga, now. So of course it's going to get harder. It has to. So if Indra's on my back more than she used to be, it doesn't mean she's a cunty, cunty, Cunty McCunterson.

Ahem.

No. God, no. It just means she's trying to guide me to be a better yogini, and that I NEED TO PUT MY BLAH BLAH EGO ASIDE AND BLAH BLAH DETACHMENT BLAH BLAH.

Ugh. Whatever. I'm going to bed. If anyone bothers to wake me up in time, I'll go to class. If not—I really don't give a damn. I feel like I'm getting an ulcer anyway, so maybe I should just call in sick. Yes, if we had a freaking phone, that's exactly what I would do. I would call in sick.

5. The Prisoner

> Walking the spiritual path properly is a very subtle pro-
> cess; it is not something to jump into naïvely. There
> are numerous sidetracks which lead to a distorted,
> ego-centered version of spirituality; we can deceive our-
> selves into thinking we are developing spiritually when
> instead we are strengthening our egocentricity through
> spiritual techniques.
>
> — CHÖGYAM TRUNGPA, *Cutting Through*
> *Spiritual Materialism*

If you want to learn about your ego, punch it a few times.
It'll swell up nicely, better for proper study.

Not long after my thirtieth birthday, I took a six-month
break from yoga after a woman in an SUV bumped into my
kneecap while I was crossing the street. For months, the
most exercise I got were the lame leg-lifts prescribed by an

indifferent physical therapist. As my muscles atrophied, so did my spiritual discipline. I didn't meditate or chant or read the Sutras. And when I finally decided I was well enough to brave a yoga class, I discovered the meditative aspect of the poses—turning my gaze inward, focusing on my breath—were impossible when I could barely hold a lunge without shaking like a broken-down dog.

Now, to be clear, even after my time in Bali, when I was in the best shape of my life, I've never been one of those yogis who can hold all her weight on one arm or do any of the other fancy-pants variations. The one thing I've always been able to do is concentrate. But with my left leg aching, I couldn't find that place where the movement becomes meditation.

While the rest of the students blissfully extended into their Warriors, I attempted several variations before the shaking and whimpering were too humiliating, too ego bruising in a class with so many lithe and lovely über-yogis. So I gave up and rested in Child's pose, prompting the teacher, a stoner-eyed white boy with short brown dreadlocks, to float over to my mat. He put his hand on my sweaty back, and I lifted my head.

"You know what?" he purred, nodding, smiling. "Guess what? It's just pain."

"Um—"

"Just tell yourself that it's only pain."

"Yeah," I said, "I know, but I have an injury."

"Oh," he said. He looked disappointed, cheated out of his sutra lesson. "Okay, then. You should rest in Child's pose, I guess."

It was all I could do not to tell him that ordinarily I'm pretty good at yoga. No, not just good at it, *great* at it. I had a kundalini experience! Just five . . . years . . . ago.

Oh, ow. Oh, my ego. My poor, sweet, deluded ego. If I thought Indra had bitch-slapped my ego in Bali, my knee injury five years later turned out to be much, much worse.

I decided to take up smoking again. I do that about once a year, and it seemed like the time. I bought a pack at a deli, grinning at the cashier like he was my accomplice. *It's just cancer*, I told myself on the walk home. *Tell yourself that they're only carcinogens.*

It didn't take long for me to come down with a bad chest cold that kept me home, flushing my few remaining cigarettes down the toilet and cursing everything from my knee injury to my prospects for happiness in life. There was no writing I could do, no reading, no cooking or cleaning, nothing that would pull me out of my McGrims. So I gave up and went back to bed. I took three issues of *Yoga Journal* with me, and instead of sleeping, I tortured the cat with affection and leafed through the magazines.

Well.

It took only half an issue for me to remember what was wrong with me: everything. If you believed everything you saw and read in *Yoga Journal*, you'd think every yogi in the world was rich, skinny, and on extremely high doses of antidepressants. How else do these people actually do the things they advise their readers to do? *Por ejemplo*:

Wake Up at Dawn.

That made me laugh. Who does that?

But then I remembered, Indra and Lou did. Real yogis do. I did, once, in Bali, when I was a real yogi.

So, trying not to think about the fact that I wake up closer to the post-meridian than anyone should ever publicly confess, I continued to read about how I should wake up at dawn. This is the time when there's the most energy in the air. Dawn is a spiritual time, the threshold between night and day. I'd often thought as much when I was *going to bed* at dawn. I'd often looked out the window and thought, Hey. *Dawn is nice. But bed is nicer.*

While you're up with the sunrise, the *Journal* suggested, you ought to eat some *agni*-igniting foods like delicious coconut-oat-ghee-farina hot cereal. *Agni* is your digestive fire. In other words, it's your metabolism. But *agni* sounds so much more spiritual than metabolism, right?

It occurred to me that yoga employs Sanskrit for the same purposes that Catholicism used to employ Latin—as a sort of lingua franca for a worldwide religion, but also to imbue certain concepts with mystery, to make them forbidden to those who lack the intellectual complexity to grapple with their profundity.

I didn't think of my metabolism as being so profound a concept that it needed the mystery of Sanskrit, but if mind and body were one, perhaps I was wrong. I turned the page, thinking that so long as yogis didn't start referring to their poop as *dookra* or something, I could stick with my yoga practice. I could just imagine how the yogis at my studio would fling the word *dookra* through the halls like so much monkey shit. "I am working on solidifying my *dookra*, bringing form to my *dookric* shape." "I'll be back, it's time for me to experience my *dookra*." "My *dookra* has golden chunks of corn in it."

The thought made me laugh, but I knew that in the right company, I might refer to my poop as *dookra*. I pictured myself at twenty-five in Bali, sporting a sarong, mala beads twisted around my wrist, trying on this new yoga language as if it were German or French, and felt a pang of longing so profound it brought tears to my eyes. What was so wrong with that, really? Would it have been wrong if I'd used the word *dookra* in Bali? No! I was living in a spiritual culture! Our purpose was to connect every aspect of our lives to the soul, linking matter with energy, the visible with the invisible. If everything is God—if I wanted to believe that—then why not my metabolism? Why not my *dookra*?

Oh, I'll be honest: I wanted a balanced *agni*. I did, I really did. But it wasn't just the perfect yogi's balanced *agni* that I wanted. The *agni* was just the beginning. I wanted the whole picture.

I wanted my practice back. I wanted to show that stoner-eyed yoga teacher what I could really do. "I'm a great fucking yogi," I said. Out loud. To the cat. Which

is funny, really—I never was a great fucking yogi. But I
remembered what it was like to feel like one.

When you get serious about yoga, when you do it every
single day, when you *live* yoga, you start to feel like a god.
You're on a spiritual high all the time. Your body starts
to submit to your will, which makes your brain feel great,
and you start to see how you can change everything about
yourself, from the way you jump from one negative thought
to another, to the way you respond when your mother tells
you what to do. You start to think that you can stop yourself
from sweating, from complaining, that you have the wisdom
to make communism work—and not just in theory.

You feel like a god. You think like a god. People look at
you, as you casually wrap your legs behind your head, not
in a show-offy way, but just, you know, stretching, and they
tell you you're a god. You, who were lost, are now found,
and you begin to believe that your example could lead
others to seek themselves.

That is when you become absolutely insufferable. I
made a quick mental inventory of my yoga studio, which
revealed dozens of them. The gold-star yogis. They make
way too much eye contact, and they've done heart-opening

workshops until they've achieved the personality of a raw oyster. And the egos on them, my God! Always making the right choices, always feeling really good about themselves and waking up at dawn. It's enough to make you sick! When they control their minds and desires, they pat themselves on the backs, you know they do. They must! I certainly would.

Oh shit, I thought. *I certainly did.* I put down my magazine. I was thirty years old, and I finally understood what had happened five years earlier when, for a while, one spiritual breakthrough in Bali turned me into this uniquely exasperating creature, the yogic egomaniac.

After my kundalini experience, I felt so good, so complete, so united with my surroundings, how could I not feel like I had special insight into what yoga was? A weak human mind such as my own easily translates such satisfaction into a conviction that one is more evolved, more aware, more enlightened than those around her.

It was astonishing: The most difficult time to maintain a healthy yogic outlook was when I thought I had a healthy yogic outlook. When it seemed that I really knew what I was doing, that I had it all figured out. That I had a true gift for yoga.

Si comprehendis, non est Deus.

I started collecting gold stars at a young age. In
kindergarten, for reading. In piano lessons, for memorizing.
The whole point of a gold star is to show it off to everybody
else—especially to those who only earned silver stars. So
how do you not become a total asshole if you have the
discipline to get up early, stoke your agni, salute the sun
with your perfect yoga body, and then go about your day
being enlightened? How do you not start to congratulate
yourself on being so expertly yogic, especially when you
look around and see so many others flailing, cigarette in
one hand, mudra in the other, chanting their petty desires
and attachments to anyone who'll listen?

How do you not tell yourself that you are better than the
rest? How do you overcome the urge to polish those gold
stars until the act of polishing them becomes a meditation?

I went back to yoga the next day looking for an answer. I
let my leg shake. I rested a lot. And when it embarrassed
me to be the cripple in the class, I reminded myself that
humiliation was a part of my yoga practice. Or, wait, no.
Humility. Humility was my practice. That's what I told myself,

and it helped, so I practiced it some more, and it helped some more. And soon I began to think that maybe my knee injury had led to a bigger breakthrough than any kundalini awakening ever could have. It might sound cheesy, but that whole notion of being here now? That's what my knee injury taught me. My new mantra was *Wherever my knee is, there I am*. Instead of sending my mind out to compare myself to the über-yogis surrounding me, I trained my mind on my mantra, teaching myself to concentrate again. And when I started to think I was becoming really wise with my mantra, I changed it to *I am a deep asshole*.

These days, at thirty-three, I sometimes practice in beginners' classes, for two reasons. One: because I'm lazy. Two: because beginners' classes are full of people who've never done yoga, people with injuries, and people like me, who have to take breaks from the upper-level classes whenever they start making us feel like we're upper-level yogis.

Not long after my kundalini breakthrough, Indra and Lou began teaching us how to be yoga teachers. Our retreat became less about meditation and more about pedagogy. Soon we would start anatomy classes, philosophy classes, and practice articulating the subtle kinesthesia of the yoga poses. What this meant was that on top of being the recipient of a kundalini breakthrough, I would have the added authority of acting as a teacher, which is but a few steps away from calling myself a guru.

Indra and Lou gave us a talk about ego not long after we began to practice teaching. Since my knee injury, I've found myself thinking about it a lot. Lou told us that there's a simple way to keep your ego in check as a teacher, and that's to remember your own teachers.

If a student comes to you and thanks you for all you've done for her, you must say, "Don't thank me, thank my guru."

So, let's say this student is really serious about finding somebody to thank for her spiritual progress. So she goes looking for your guru and when she finds him, she offers him her thanks. And your guru will listen to your student and respond, "Don't thank me, thank my guru."

Each guru your student finds will say the same thing until she must find a time machine to travel back to the first yogi, meditating in some obscure cave in some ancient corner of India, and thank him. In this way, it is the practice, the teachings, that hold the power. The teacher is only a conduit.

Well, if it were up to me, I would've stayed in my happy place forever, polishing my little gold star of a kundalini experience, bringing it out to show to guests who came to ask me for some wisdom, and when they thanked me for clarifying a yoga sutra or a breathing technique, I would happily receive their thanks and tell them, "Don't thank me. But if you want to? Well, okay, sure. Thank me. Thank me again. Thank you for thanking me." And then I'd send an e-mail to everyone I know, telling them about how I was thanked and that if they want to experience something that will make them thankful, to come and see me soon, the line is long and tickets are selling fast.

Hey, in a competitive yoga world, you've gotta self-promote, right?

Indra seemed to know this about me. That I wanted to be special. That I wanted to be the best. Even now I wonder if she saw it in me because she knew it in herself, or if she saw it in me because she *couldn't* see it in herself.

After that day in the wantilan, all I knew was that Indra was trying to keep me down. I didn't see my ego swelling. I didn't have the perspective of a higher bird. I was down on that low branch, looking at my teacher with

a mind twisted into a yogic pretzel and a nervous worry in
my gut.

I worried and worried, and my stomach churned. I
nursed myself with peppermint tea and still I worried
until I thought I'd be sick. Indra was so cold, so distant,
so critical. But really, she needn't have worked so hard to
punish my poor, swollen ego. She could have just sat back,
relaxed, and allowed the gods to do it for her.

April 7

Until yesterday, I felt like a drop in the ocean of consciousness. As if I were just one cell in the Great Indivisible Self.
Oneness. I was finally starting to get it. Union is real.

But now I feel like I'm about to dip low. Like I need to
defibrillate my kundalini shakti if I'm going to maintain this
wondrous state. God, I can feel it slipping. A minute ago I
was a drop in the ocean of consciousness, but now I can feel
my droplet self swell into more of a pond or a small lake.
Discrete, confined, full of myself. Separate.

Watching Indra smile at Jessica and congratulate Lara
on her beautiful Forward Bends, I feel like a boil on the

backside of the Great and Indivisible Self. HERE I AM, I want to yell at Indra, WHAT ABOUT ME?

Evening

It only gets worse. Indra doesn't compliment me on any poses. She doesn't come by my mat to chat. She's freezing me out. I stopped chanting the kyries again this morning just to see if she would notice and come by, maybe ask me if I'm experiencing a resurgence of Catholic resentment, or if anything's troubling me, but no. Nothing. She doesn't care.

Last night Jessica and I were sitting out on the veranda watching the moon rise when Jason and Lara came back from dinner, so giddy and inspired by their night that we invited them over for tea. They had been out to dinner with Indra and Lou. Just the four of them.

"It was absolutely amazing," Lara said as I poured hot water over her ginger tea. "So nice to get Indra and Lou alone like that."

"I'll bet," I said. I must've sounded less than convincing, however, because Jason patted my back as I sat down and said, "Indra was being hard on you, Suzanne, but I'm sure she meant it with love."

Jessica sat up a little straighter and put her teacup down, her face flushed and indignant. "I think Indra was unfair," she said. "In fact, I think she was projecting."

I swear to God, I could've kissed her. Though I also wanted to ask her if she had hit her head recently, because I never thought I'd hear Jessica say anything negative about our teachers. About any teachers, really.

Lara glanced at me and then back at Jess. "I don't know that she was *projecting*. I mean, she herself isn't competitive. Maybe a little superior, but not competitive. But she did seem to be in a bit of a mood yesterday. So maybe she was just, I don't know—"

Jason leaned his head toward mine. "On her moon cycle?" he said. He raised his eyebrows, nodding mock-gravely, until Lara and I took the bait and punched him from both sides.

"What does your boyfriend think of all this?" Lara asked, changing the subject. "Have you told him all about your kundalini rising?"

I had to admit that I hadn't, yet. "I told him something unexpected and strange happened in class, but I didn't know how to go into it." Lara and Jason exchanged glances, which made me feel worse. Like—tonight they were probably bonding with Indra and Lou about how nice it is to have a spiritual union with your mate, and here I can't even tell my boyfriend about what I'm doing here, because I'm not sure he's going to understand. But I didn't say any of that. Instead, I said, "I'm certainly not going to tell my parents— they would send me to get my brain scanned, no question."

Before they left, Jason told me not to worry. "You're Indra's pet, I'm sure she was just having a rotten day and needed to take it out on somebody."

I shouldn't worry.

That's like telling the sun not to rise.

April 8

It's raining so hard I'm considering building an ark. But I'm only letting Jessica, Jason, Lara, and Baerbel come with me. And Lou, I suppose. And Su and her family. And the chickens.

April 9

I was walking in silent meditation through town today and saw Lou standing around with several men in a pavilion off the main street in Campuhan. I walked slowly, my eyes fixed on my *dhrishti*. *Dhrishti* means "focal point." But when it's a dhrishti, it's more spiritual. Heels, balls of feet, toes. Lou stood in the pavilion watching as a man at the top of a ladder fastened an enormous chicken-wire head atop an equally large chicken-wire body. Su told me that these huge sculptures eventually will be gigantic monsters called ooga-oogas. It's tradition, I guess, to parade them through the town at the Balinese New Year, which is a couple of weeks away.

My walk was going splendidly until I felt my neck grow hot. I turned my eyes back to the pavilion and saw Lou smiling at me. He wore a yellow sarong and a wrinkled linen shirt. I smiled back at him and sent him a message with my mind. *Hello,* I said. *I am sending you this message with my mind.* I could tell he received it, because he nodded with his eyes.

Then my stomach did a few flip-flops. Lou's been making me nervous again lately, God knows why. I thought I was over that.

Later

The thing that is most upsetting about Indra turning on me? I can't concentrate in meditation. I keep wanting to show her how meditative I am, how I am a better student and a better yogini than she's making me out to be. But the more I focus on showing her how well I'm meditating, the harder it is to meditate.

I'm terrified that my kundalini experience was just a temporary high, and that I'll never get it back.

It hardly rained for weeks, but lately it's been raining almost constantly. The sharp, earthy smell of animal dung has pervaded every corner of the grounds, from our house down to the pool. It wafts over from the family compound, where the pigpen floods every other day.

I'm finding myself welcoming the storms and praying for them to stay, because so long as it rains, all I can smell is rain. And maybe dirt. Rain and dirt I can handle. But the minute the sun comes out and the world bakes dry again, a steam of pigshit, garbage, and diesel fumes overwhelms us on our walks to the wantilan or to town. Or just sitting on the veranda. It's sort of an olfactory nightmare. I'm trying to rise above it. Higher bird and all that.

The wantilan is also becoming an epicenter of animal feces. Those beautiful Javanese workers have finished harvesting the rice, and the empty fields around the wantilan have become home to about a million small brown ducks. I look out from my mat and see fields of dry tan bristles, as if each field were a god's personal back scratcher. But when it rains, the fields flood with water and the young ducks get very excited, squawking and swimming in patterns like gulls in the sky, and pretty soon the wantilan smells like a duck's toilet.

Ah, nature. I didn't know what I was missing in Seattle, where rain is just rain.

April 10

Lou's been paying so much attention to me in class. Half the time I feel like I'm going to throw up from the nerves. I want to impress him, maybe that's it. It could also be the dream I have every few nights. In this dream, I'm standing at the foot of my bed, and Lou is in front of me, shirtless and tan. He clasps my face in his hands, then trickles his fingers to my neckline, where he rips my tank top with shelf bra right down the middle. He falls to his knees, slowly lowering my Spandex yoga pants, and then strips them off my body like a matador brandishing a cape. Then he pushes me back on the bed and says, *I see myself . . . in you.*

Later

Indra's on the warpath. She says I'm being competitive or looking outside myself in lots of poses. Not just my Forward Bend, but Downward Dog, Upward Dog, Cat, Cow, Happy Baby pose . . . I mean, Happy Baby pose, are you kidding me? Who the fuck is competitive in Happy Fucking Baby pose?

Whatever. I'm trying not to think about it, because my stomach is so upset and I'm so unhappy. My kundalini experience may as well never have happened, that's how unenlightened I feel. I don't feel like I'm transcending my physical body, I feel like I'm getting trapped in it. My stomach feels like a salted slug. We're leaving soon to go eat dinner, and I'm hoping some rice and leaves will settle me down.

Evening

Oh dear. It sounds like I have a tenant rearranging furniture in my guts. I—hold on.

Later

So, it looks like I—dammit.

Later again

I'm going to try to write this quickly, before I have to—

Oh for the love of Jesus Mary and Joseph, I'll be right back.

Midnight

Um, I have a problem. I've just swallowed about four thousand pounds of neem leaves and a charcoal pill, which should hopefully give me enough time to write this entry. Oh, it's bad. So bad.

JESSICA, LARA, AND I walked to the Bali Buddha tonight for dinner, and about halfway there I became aware of a powerful and alarming sensation in my gut, as if a family of elephants were having kundalini seizures in there.

We were walking in single file, meditating our way through the transport guys and the hair braiders and shop owners, Jessica leading the way, then Lara. I took up the rear, not meditating so much as chanting. *Breathe*, I chanted, *breathe. Please God, please God. Kyrie Eleison, Christe Eleison, Banyan Eleison, ANYONE Eleison.*

"Where is this place?" I called to Jess.

"Just a few more blocks, I swear!" she sang.

I tried to mirror Jessica's beautiful posture, her slightly wobbly feminine head, but the seething in my midsection was impossible to ignore. A waterfall of sweat tumbled down my back—not entirely unusual in this heat, but this sweat was cold. I knew what it was. It had nothing to do with Lou's attention or Indra's disapproval. It had nothing to do with anxiety. It had nothing to do with yoga.

"Jessica, where is it?"

"One more block, I promise!"

"No," I said. I walked as fast as I could to catch up with her. "Where is it? I'm going to run ahead, we're not going fast enough."

I knew exactly what was happening to me and exactly what was *going* to happen to me if I didn't make it to the bathroom in the next minute.

Finally we were on the block. Jessica pointed to the

restaurant. I threw my bag at her and ran. In my agitated state I sort of hopped-ran, actually, like a maimed dog. It wasn't good. Holy Mother Mary, it wasn't good at all.

"There's someone in there," the woman behind the counter at the Bali Buddha said. "You'll have to wait a minute."

I looked at her without really understanding what she had said. "Is there a men's bathroom I could use?" I thought that all she'd have to do is take one look at me and get it, that I was about to cause a health hazard in her restaurant if she didn't work with me.

"That is the men's room!" she replied cheerfully. "Men's and women's!"

I nodded, afraid to use my diaphragm even for speaking. I paced the bottom floor of the restaurant, which is a general store for expatriate vegetarians, from the looks of it. It's where Jessica buys her rice cakes and tahini.

How lovely, I thought, looking around at the boxes of organic pasta and rice cakes. *Don't breathe. Don't breathe and don't think. Rice cakes are lovely. How lovely for Jessica to be able to buy herself some nice rice—don't breathe—cakes.* I kept my thumbs hooked under the elastic waistband of my yoga pants in preparation.

OKAY, I'M BACK. Where was I? Ah, right. So, finally, thank you sweet baby Jesus and all the heavenly saints, finally the door opened and a beautiful white woman in a flowing orange sari emerged. She was touching her lower lip, removing some stray lipstick from the corner of it. I walked straight into her and practically pushed her aside while pulling at my sweat-drenched yoga pants.

Where is my mother? Oh, sigh.

Twenty minutes later I removed myself from the bathroom, shaky and blanched. I took my time climbing the stairs to the open-air restaurant overlooking the street. I felt like I had become an abstraction, just an idea of myself. I had lost my core. I was hyper-aware of my surroundings, of Jessica and Lara on a low couch drinking rosewater lassi, of the coffee table with half-eaten salads and a vase exploding with frangipani flowers in front of them. Everything looked vivid and unreal, like the paintings of jagged red flowers and blank blue faces adorning the low walls.

I sat down across from them in a wicker chair with a silky blue pillow for a seat.

"You were in the bathroom forever," Lara said, looking me up and down.

I sniffed. "They have great lighting in there," I said, attempting to joke.

Jessica wasn't buying it. "The Bali Belly?"

"Mmm," I said. "You bet."

While Jessica and Lara hunted down the waiter and asked him to bring me rice and water, I sank into my chair and tried to relax. And then, after they'd settled back down, I said something utterly stupid, as if I had forgotten where I've been for the past month. I said, "I need to get my hands on some antibiotics."

Jessica made a face. "Antibiotics? Oh, no." She put her drink down to make room for my food, which had arrived. "Do you have any idea what antibiotics do to your body?"

"Cure it of bad bugs?"

"They wreak havoc on your system! No, you can't take antibiotics." She grimaced at Lara, who shrugged, smiling weakly at me as if she hated to break such news. "She can't take antibiotics!"

I quickly surmised where this conversation was headed, and tried to dispense with the inevitable. "I am not engaging in any sort of pissdrinking," I said.

Lara peered at me quizzically. "*Amaroli*, you mean?"

"Pissdrinking."

"It's called *amaroli* in India," she said, watching me sip my water. "And I think that's a much nicer term for something so good for you." She laughed, sitting back. "Drink more of that water and then go try it. You could probably have the Bali Belly licked in no time at all."

I put my water back down.

"Honestly," Jessica said, handing my glass back to me, "everything happens for a reason. Maybe God has given you the Bali Belly so that you'll have a reason to start your urine therapy!"

The words I've feared since the moment I learned the truth about my yogamates, spoken at last. My urine therapy, she called it.

"Jessica" I said. "Lara."

They looked back at me expectantly.

"There is no way I'm drinking pee. It's waste, it's probably toxic, and most important, it's *pee*."

Lara nudged Jessica with her elbow. "That's years of prejudice talking," she said.

Jessica nodded. "Society's taught you that urine is waste, but it isn't, it's pure. It's cleaner than blood!"

"Well, that doesn't exactly make me want to drink it."

"Jason uses it for everything," Lara said. "He snorts it for his hay fever, he gargles it if he has a sort throat. He even washes his eyes with it if he gets a sty."

"And he also drinks it every morning? Like Jess does, every single day?"

She nodded. "Even more when he was getting rid of that parasite."

"And so do you?"

Lara paused, her mouth open as if she were in the middle of a word. She seemed unsure of how to respond, but before she could try, Jessica interrupted her.

"What you don't realize, Suzanne, is that there are people out there who have cured themselves of cancer, of AIDS! With urine! It's the perfect medicine, even the Bible tells us to drink it. *Drink water from your own cistern*, the Bible says. It's ancient, ancient healing!"

"Uh-huh," I said, turning back to Lara. "So, do you drink your pee, Lara? Yes or no?"

She glanced at Jessica. "Well—I don't have a problem using it topically."

Aha! "You don't."

"Well, no. I mean, haven't you ever been told to piss on someone who has a jellyfish sting?"

I vaguely recalled this idea from my childhood. "I think so, but what's the point?"

"Urine neutralizes the poison. The acid in it eats up toxins, that's why it's so good for you."

Jessica nodded vigorously. "Indra told me she used it on a gigantic bug bite the other day, and it totally disappeared!"

"Yeah, I know," I said. "But, Lara, do you drink your pee or don't you?"

Jessica interrupted again. "It's in shampoo, Suzanne. And in moisturizer."

"Lara?"

She squirmed. "I use it in compresses, and if I get a pimple I might put a little urine on it."

"And?"

She sighed. "I'm still trying to get used to the idea of practicing amaroli."

I was as triumphant as a woman with tangled intestines could be. "And please, Lara, enlighten me. How exactly do you get used to it?"

"I smell my pee every morning. I rub a little on my lips."

I shuddered. "God, gross," I said.

"Cigarette smoking is a lot more disgusting," Lara said, "and you used to put that stick of toxins to your lips every day."

Oh, such silliness! I brushed it aside. "But you obviously think amaroli's gross, or else you'd drink it, too, right?"

Lara's neck reddened as she spoke. "I tried to drink it once, but it made me gag. I actually vomited it up. Ever since, I can't bear the thought of swallowing it again."

"Oh, man."

"Yeah." She relaxed a little, sipped her lassi. She cracked a little smile. "It was awful."

My stomach gurgled. "I don't think I can imagine anything worse than vomiting up your own pee."

Jessica was getting impatient. "You guys," she said, "this is beside the point."

"No," I said. "Jessica, this is *exactly* the point."

"You know that people have cured themselves of cancer and still you won't try it?"

"Well, if that's the case, Jess, if people have really cured themselves of diseases that everybody wants to cure, then why don't we know about it?" I knew I had her there.

Jessica leaned back and looked at me as if she'd never realized I was the stupidest person she'd ever known. I'd never seen that look on her face before; it was almost evangelical, as if she were some crazed malarial missionary in the Amazon or something.

"Suzanne," she said slowly, as one speaks to the cognitively challenged, "think about it. What does Lou say? It's a *pharmaceutical conspiracy*, Suzanne. Why would they want us to know about the benefits of urine therapy? It's so obvious why we don't hear about it."

"Well, why then?"

She shook her head, exasperated. "Because, Suzanne. *Pee* is *free!*"

Now, I hate to admit it, but that actually does make some sense to me. I love a good conspiracy theory, especially if it implicates corporate America. It's almost intriguing enough to make me do it.

No, wait. That's a lie. I still don't want to do it.

We walked home, and I only had to stop once to use the restroom at a small hotel in Campuhan, not nearly as bad as I thought the walk home would be. But when we reached the top of the ninety-six stairs, Jessica made me promise her something: I won't take antibiotics.

Was I crazy to promise her that? Well, yeah. I told her I would try her herbal remedies first—neem leaves and grapefruit seed extract. She says it'll take longer to cure me, but that it's still better for me than stripping my body of all its bacteria, good and bad.

I'm trying to stay open to the universe, even if things have been rough lately, even if I feel like a quick antibiotic fix is exactly what I want right now. I will try to flush the bugs out of my system naturally. I will try.

But I told Jessica that if anything starts leaching out my tongue, if I see even the shadow of a gray tinge, all bets are off. We shook on it.

Now, to sleep. My mind will sleep while my body wages war. Go, fight, win.

Later

Sleep? What a joke. I'm up for the fifth time tonight. I hate this. I want to die.

Back when I had my legs waxed, when was that—Easter Sunday?—Reni, the woman doing my waxing for me, kept saying "Ooh, sick, sick," after ripping my pelt off. "Sick, sick," she'd say, blowing on the bald bit, "sensitive, sensitive."

My stomach cramps up badly every few minutes, and I think *sick, sick,* which sort of makes me laugh and sort of makes my stomach hurt worse.

4:00 a.m.

The early-morning roosters and dogs are keeping me company. I'm lying on the futon on the ground floor, next to the bathroom. It just got to be too silly, using the loo and then climbing halfway up the stairs only to turn right back around and run for it again.

I can't help wondering if Indra thinks I'm a lower bird—sitting on my low branch, drinking milkshakes, showing off my "competitive" Happy Baby pose, refusing to drink urine.

But then I think, well, shoot. If the lower bird is Gandhi *and* Hitler, then wouldn't he also be urine and antibiotics? If it's all the same bird, what difference does it make? What difference does *anything* make?

April 12

In the past two days I've swallowed forty neem capsules and an ocean of grapefruit seed extract. I have a bitter taste in my mouth that could be from the extract or from the *flavor of reality.* Because I'm getting the sense that there is no real transcendence so long as one is in a body. There's only this willful, weak flesh, this muck of life.

Yesterday Indra and Lou brought over bowls of soggy rice with bay leaves and some mysterious bowel-solidifying ingredient, and then squinted at me in the blazing midday sun as I lifted spoonful after dribbling spoonful to my mouth, then ran to the loo, then returned to repeat the process until my rice was gone.

Indra was friendly. I think. Honestly, I don't have the strength to try to impress her anymore. The higher bird has deserted me. The higher bird is a total jerk.

Today I haven't bothered to leave the bathroom. I've decided that this is where I live now.

Later

It's actually quite lovely in here. The stone shelves next to the mirror are full of Jessica's aromatherapy beauty products, so it smells like a garden. Or like an expensive boutique. It's my very own jasmine-scented prison cell. When we first got here, Jessica taped some quotations to the wall by the light switch: *If you are patient, your mind will be more settled, and what you do will be more perfect.* Pretty funny quote for a bathroom.

Just beneath that one, *Don't believe everything you think.*

I read somewhere that if you don't worship God, you'll find something else to worship, like money or power or your own reflection in the mirror. Well. I fear I'm starting to get a little nuts. I've been lining Jessica's beauty products up on the counter, and then unscrewing all the lids and smelling them one by one. Indra told me not to forget to pray while I was in here, and I guess I haven't forgotten, exactly. It's just that I am sort of praying to Jessica's products. More idolatry!

When I was a kid I thought that adultery and idolatry

were the same thing. And in a way, they are. I'm cheating on God! Worshiping the promises of wellness and healing on the backs of these glass jars.

The prayers are more like little films running through my head, their colors bold and saturated. I study the labels of arnica oil, calendula cream, rose-hip balm, and it's like I astral-project to the ancient lands where these products originated. Jessica's pantheon of wise women use these in their red tents, rubbing each other down with eucalyptus and almond oils. These products belong to a world that is so much better than the one I live in. It's simpler, it's sweeter, work is honest and no one is cynical.

People barter. If you want some lemon-butter cuticle softener, you trade for it. You give the herbalist something, like a goat. Or an amulet.

I know it's a fantasy, this world. But it's such a beautiful fantasy! I imagine simple farmers gazing at their small crops in the deepening red of sunset, stretching their strong arms; rows of birch trees shimmering in the warm wind; lavender fields flushing purple in waves unbroken for miles. Somewhere nearby there's a small stone house, where a richly seasoned stew simmers in a cast-iron pot. This stew will make me whole. The woman who makes it is a cross between Jessica and Indra, and she will give me herbs and oils to take at night that will make me serene and pure and patient. Sure, everyone in these fantasies has teeth, whereas back in the day they probably didn't. And maybe I ought to remind myself that they wore these lovely-smelling oils to mask the fact that they only bathed after their skins developed a crust.

But I don't want to be a killjoy.

Later

Here's what I'm thinking about: drugstore creams, big-business beauty products? All of them, corrupt. Disgusting. Vile. Fomenters of cancer cells and bad feelings. The back of any such product suggests you use a liberal amount. They practically tell you to use it up as fast as possible so you can go back and buy some more.

But these small-batch hippie products of Jessica's? They suggest a dime-sized dollop, a pinch, a modest, continent helping. They are here to serve but not to exploit. They are saints in the yogic tradition of wellness. So what if Jessica's facial exfoliant costs four times what mine does? Mine was probably made from DDT and the ground-up bones of bald eagles.

Honestly. Can you put a price on wellness?

Later

I can see night falling through the one glassless window in here, as big as a potholder.

Dark out.

Indra was here. She brought me more rice. She watched me eat it, sitting beside me on the futon outside the bathroom. She stroked my hair as I ate, and tucked it behind my ears. And when I said I was finished, she urged me to take just one more bite, like a mother would. So I did.

I'm so tired.

April um. Who knows anymore!

Oh lavender, oh quince, oh calendula, how happy I am to be back in your presence! I left my cell for three hours, three horrible hours. Indra and Lou sent Noadhi here this afternoon to give me a healing massage.

Before he arrived, I climbed the stairs for the first time in ages. Indra and Lou told me he would use the bed as his massage table, and not to bother wearing clothes. "He'll just take them off you," Indra said. I heard him chatting downstairs with Jessica, so I wrapped a red sarong around my naked body, and sat down on the bed to wait for him.

He wore all white, and he was less friendly than normal. He smiled gently at me, but got right down to business. I would have loved a blanket at least to suggest some sort of modesty, but no. Off went the sarong. Noadhi rubbed his hands together and dove in.

An hour into the massage, I was sweating in agony. I haven't had many massages, but from the moment he started, I could tell that Noadhi's isn't typical. His massage is actually a form of torture.

He started on my feet, grinding his finger along each toe, focusing on the joint, where he stripped the cartilage clean. I bit the insides of my cheeks to keep from moaning as he moved upward, digging his fingers into my calf, searching for the hard center of my shin. Once he had found the most sensitive spot, he ran the bony part of his fingers down it, as if to flay the flesh from the bone. In my agony, a surreal movie played in my head, a looping short film of fish being deboned, my grandfather cutting corn off the cob with a paring knife.

This went on for hours. Three hours, to be exact, an eternity of Noadhi psychically removing my intestines and colon through my tailbone and lower ribs. This healing massage is unlike anything I've ever experienced. The pain begins, and begins, and begins again, unceasing and unchanging, never developing into something pleasurable or relaxing, just beginning, and beginning, and beginning some more.

I have a whole new understanding of the idea of eternal damnation.

I must have whimpered at one point, because Noadhi whispered, "Breathe," and rubbed some unction of engine oil and Vicks Vapo-Rub under my nose. It burned. Then he shoved sharp slivers of bamboo under my fingernails and attached electrodes to my nipples.

I haven't spent so much time away from my little cell in days. I'm still wearing nothing but my red sarong—I almost slipped on it as I scuttled down the stairs, trailing oily footprints. I'm never leaving again.

Some day, probably still April

My yogamates have a day off. I've missed so many classes. Weeks of classes, it seems. My body is stiff and sore and my outlook is bleak. It's like I've never done yoga in my life.

Jason, Lara, and Jessica are planning to go with Made to Monkey Forest to play with the macaque monkeys. I plan to stay home and resent them.

I wonder how they would feel if I died today, while they were out carousing with monkeys. I mean, don't they at least want to leave somebody here in case I need a doctor? In case I slip into a coma?

Yogis are selfish. Christianity, Judaism, Islam—these are real religions where people make you soup and pet you when you're sick. Yoga is a self-centered pseudo-religion and I hate it.

I just really want to see some monkeys. It's so unfair. I've wanted to see monkeys in the wild my whole life. It's been my greatest dream, my dearest wish. But do they care? Do they try to hide their excitement? Do they, for once in their lives, think about others, and how they might conceal their excitement out of respect for the fact that I'm stuck here in this shitty cell, basically dying?

No. They do not.

There is no God.

I miss Jonah. He would bring me soup or something. He would say something funny about this so that I kept my will to live. He would entertain me with gossip and stories, seeing as I have no television, no friends, and the boredom is killing me faster than the Bali Belly.

Later

I die a little every day.

Later

Maybe it isn't the Bali Belly. Perhaps this is all a big mistake. I have this pain in my side, and I'm thinking it's cancer of the appendix. Which has probably spread, by now, to my stomach, my intestines, my ovaries. If I don't die, I'll be sterile when this is over.

I've always wanted a child. But I will be barren.

If I live.

Later

They're just about to leave. I can hear Lara and Jason out on the veranda with Jessica, talking about how much fun they're about to have and how happy they are they don't have the Bali Belly. Well—I'm sure that's what they're *thinking*, anyway. Everybody loves being alive when they're not the one dying!

Holy shit.

I just looked in the mirror for the first time in God knows how long. The skin beneath my eyes is a silvery purple, the color of the inside of an oyster shell. This color bleeds into a gray mask that is the rest of my face. That discovery was disconcerting enough. But then I stuck my tongue out, and—oh my God. It's not black, but it isn't pink. It's sort of greenish gray. Something's happening to me. I feel like I'm transforming into another life-form, like Kafka's cockroach or the Fly. Do metamorphoses start in the tongue?

I'M IN A pickle.

They left maybe an hour ago. Before they did, I showed Jessica my tongue. I was a little panicked. I just can't take a black tongue, it's too much for me to bear on top of everything else, the cancer, the barren womb, etc.

She came in close, her hands on my shoulders, and peered into my mouth. "Oh, *Suzanne*," she sighed. "You have to use urine."

"No," I said. "No! We made a deal, and I'm going to find a way to get some antibiotics." I could hear Jason's and Lara's voices on the veranda. I stood up. Jason would help me, he'd have to help me. I was like Winona Ryder in *Dracula*, mouth bitten and bleeding: *Take me away from all this death*.

Jessica caught my hand. "Wait, how are you going to find antibiotics today? By the time you actually get a prescription from a doctor, your tongue could be black."

"Oh, hell," I said. I suddenly became very still. It occurred to me that this was not my fault. This was Jessica's fault, Lara's fault. I felt as if I weighed a thousand dense pounds, I was a block of cement. "What am I supposed to do?" It wasn't a question; it was an accusation.

Jessica paused, biting her lip. "You know what will help?" she said. "It will help if you think of urine therapy as a ritual."

I stared her down, unmoved. She looked back at me,

kindly. "Before I have my first morning treatment, I like to say a prayer."

I refused even to nod. I wanted her to suffer for this.

She cleared her throat and then sang, her voice ethereal and sibilant, *"Bless me, Golden Tonic, as you cleanse my system and purify my soul."*

I became a little less steely. This is all a dream, I thought. Soon Jessica will start juggling swordfish and I'll eat my shoe. Then I'll know I'm asleep. As I stared at my roommate, taking in her priceless little prayer, Jason popped his head in the front door.

"Suzanne," he said, "just drink a little urine and get on with your life! You can do it, love."

I heard Lara laughing and turned back to Jessica. My voice floated from my throat like a bit of dandelion fluff. "How?"

So Jessica gave me some pointers. She said to remember to collect only the midstream. When I asked why, she shrugged. "The first bit of urine cleans your yoni," she said. "It sterilizes you, so the midstream is pure. And the last bit"—she giggled and absently twisted a lock of her hair—"well, it's crunchy."

"Excuse me?" I said.

"You know," she said, waving her hand in front of her face. "It's got a sort of sediment to it. You don't need the crunchy bits."

There was absolutely nothing I could say in response to that, so I said good-bye and told her to give my love to the monkeys.

Now I'm sitting on the futon, debating. I can't believe I'm even entertaining the idea of doing this. Am I? Am I capable of doing it?

God. I don't know.

.   .   .

I'VE SPENT THE past half hour or so contemplating my tongue. I've studied it in all lights, from every possible angle. I tried scraping it with the side of a fork. I've visualized a pink tongue. I've made a mantra out of telling myself that I am feeling better. But I'm not.

What's the worst that could happen?

The worst is that I will throw up. That would be bad, but it wouldn't be the end of the world. And it's not so different from what I've been doing the past few days, anyway.

No one at home will ever have to know.

I JUST PEED into a glass.

It proved trickier than I thought it would be. I've only peed in this fashion—collecting the midstream—at the doctor's office, and then into short little plastic cups. I used a tall glass from the kitchen, just as Indra told us to.

To say that it was unwieldy would be an understatement. It was a mess. I had to wipe up each side of the glass with toilet paper, then the seat of the toilet, and then my thighs. It looks like I have about two shots' worth of urine in my glass. I can't do the full eight ounces Indra and everybody recommend. A double shot of urine will have to suffice.

Oh. Wait. Hold on. When did I go crazy?

I'm not drinking this. No way, no how.

HOLY GROSS. I just lifted the glass to my mouth to try and do it, and I felt a caress of warm steam on my nose. I put the glass down instantly: there's no way in hell I'm drinking warm pee.

Ah yes, I am crazy. I say *no warm pee* as if it'll be

deliciously refreshing cold. As if I should blend it with ice, make a daiquiri.

I'VE BEEN LEANING against the door frame, studying my glass of tonic for crunchy bits. I don't see any. Now the glass is sitting on the back of the toilet, waiting for me to do something.

Here's what I keep telling myself: I'm going to do a yellow Jaeger shot. Down the hatch, one fell swoop, like a double shot of Jaeger. I've made a big pot of tea and it's sitting on the bathroom counter. That'll be my chaser. I've never been good at shots, but I will channel every twenty-first-birthday party I've ever attended to get me through this.

Down the hatch, one fell swoop, like a double shot of Jaeger with a ginger-tea chaser. Here we go, Suzie-Q, here we go…

BLARF.

HOLY MOTHERMARYJESUSJOSEPH. Oh my Christ. Oh my

Sunset
I'm sitting on the veranda.

Oh, wait. Who's sitting on the veranda?

A *pissdrinker* is sitting on the veranda.

Honestly? Can I be honest with myself? Well, Self, it was delicious. Rich yet refreshing, nutty yet sweet, with a dazzle of tannins that sparkled on the tongue before somersaulting into a long, smooth finish. Next time I'm going to pair it with cheese and wear high heels. Make a real party out of it.

Okay.

So maybe it wasn't quite like that.

My God, I wish my sister were here. She would die. This might be the point at which she has to force-feed me steak and make me smoke cigarettes to bring me back to myself. Too late, though, dear sister. Too late. The Kool-Aid's been drunk.

I've never blacked out from drinking liquor, but I very nearly did from drinking pee.

I did exactly what I said I would do. I chanted *pharmaceutical conspiracy, pharmaceutical conspiracy*, then I picked that glass up off the back of the toilet and downed it in one fell swoop. Down the hatch, like a shot of Jaeger. And then my vision went spotty, and I weaved a little, clutching the countertop with my free hand to steady myself.

When my eyes adjusted, I caught my reflection in the mirror and cracked up until I started to gag. *Oh no*, I thought, clutching the countertop, *you are not throwing this up*. I grabbed my cup of tea and drank it as quickly as I could before pouring myself another cup. This was difficult, because I couldn't stop laughing and sputtering and talking to myself.

You foul, disgusting pissdrinker! Jonah will never kiss you again!

It's the strangest taste. Buttery and metallic, as if I'd stuck my head under the fake-butter dispenser at the movie theater and filled it all the way up, then gone over to the cash register and grabbed a bunch of pennies, added them to my butter-filled mouth, and gargled the whole concoction. It tastes like verdigris.

Oh, who am I kidding? It tastes like *pee*.

When I finished all the tea in the pot, I moved on to bananas. I ate a whole banana, the most fruit I've eaten in days. But the taste would not be washed out. Like a buttered nickel sitting on my tongue. I have been branded, and I don't think there's a revirginization ritual to give me back who I once was.

I curled up on the futon, trying to think of what else I could eat to clean out my mouth. It's baffling that I didn't think to just brush my teeth. I bet that would've helped. Maybe I had Bali Belly of the brain. Anyway, I curled up on the futon in the heat of midday, and when I woke up, the sun was going down. That's more than I've slept in one stretch in days. And now I'm sitting here, listening to the evening gamelan, and I have to say—I feel pretty good. I checked out my tongue in the mirror after I woke up, and it's a bit better, too. I was afraid I'd look in the mirror and it would be as black as sin, as if I'd been drinking shoe polish. But there it was, not some gleaming new perfectly pink tongue, but maybe a little less green.

I really am feeling better. It was probably the nap that did it. Or, I don't know—a miracle.

April 14

It is a miracle. The Bali Belly is gone. I mean, it's really, truly, one-hundred-percent gone. I'm cured. I haven't returned to my garden cell in hours. I may never go back.

I can't believe it. Last night I thought I was just feeling more rested. But then I went to bed and slept through the night, and I ate a regular breakfast of bananas and rice and then went to class and I am fine. I am cured!

I keep thinking about what this could mean for me. If I

could do this every day, like my yogamates do, what would my life be like? I mean, besides the social ostracism?

The flu, cramps, migraines: gone forever. No need to worry ever again about cancer or meningitis or osteoporosis or any of the conditions and diseases I worry about constantly. The hair on my legs will grow at a slower, *healthier* speed. My cheekbones will be higher and I'll never, ever break out on my chin or have PMS again.

My days of cowardice are over. I have done the one thing that has terrified me since I arrived here. Show me a cliff face, and I will scale it. Show me a shark-filled sea, and I will swim it.

The only thing is, I don't know if I can start doing it every day. Not yet. I didn't drink any today, and I kind of just want to enjoy being well again. So I'll start up regularly tomorrow.

Tomorrow. Tomorrow I begin!

April 15

I plan to send an e-mail to my sister and to Jonah:

> *If they could see me now, that little gang of mine*
> *I'm eating greens and rice and drinking my u-rine.*

I really can't wait to read their responses.

That said, I must confess that this morning I forgot all about my new morning routine until I went out onto the veranda and saw Jessica there with her Starbucks mug.

I'm going to have to be very disciplined about this, because I can tell I'm losing my resolve to actually become a practicing pissdrinker. I keep wondering if just doing it once will suffice—if I've coated my organs in uriney protection, like a sealant or a topcoat. That would be nice.

. . .

It was a bit shocking to get back to class yesterday. Turns out I missed only three days. Felt like an eternity. But three days was enough to find myself in a new world order.

Two women have arrived to take part in the final stretch of our teacher training. One is a student, Marianne, and the other, SuZen, is here to teach us anatomy.

Indra clearly adores them. They've both studied with her before, and when she introduced them as "my dear, dear friends, Marianne and SuZen," she sounded positively giddy. Marianne is my age and she looks like she should be on the cover of *Yoga Journal*. Small-boned but strong, with glossy red hair and polished skin. She is the epitome of the placid yogini—she speaks as if she once did a lot of acid and is still enjoying the flashbacks. "It's so...*wow*. Yeah. It's so good, you know?" she said in check-in. She shivered her thick hair down her back and flashed a surprised smile at all of us, as if she'd just noticed where she was. "So good. To be...*here*."

SuZen is actually one of Indra's oldest and best friends. She looks like some of the white women I once took African dance classes with at home. Short, shaggy blond hair, Native American tattoos on her lower back and ankles. But where those women earnestly carried handwoven bags from Guatemala or Nepal, SuZen carried on her shoulder a yoga bag that cost hundreds of dollars—the one I saw Christy Turlington model in a magazine Lara was reading—out of which she pulled a matching yoga mat. We eyed her as she unfurled her designer mat and proceeded to spray it down with some sort of aromatherapy antibacterial mat spray. Tea tree and eucalyptus oils from the spray spread through the thick wantilan air, mingling with the lavender from her scented savasana eye pillows. She and Marianne had fancy towels, blankets, and a collection of other yoga toys that accumulated by their mats as they prepared for class.

Jason and I exchanged looks. I caught Lara raising an eyebrow at the display of yoga accoutrements. Only Baerbel spoke out loud, "It seems as if you have brought an entire toy store with you to Bali," she said, her dimples showing. "I never knew yoga required so many toys!"

My yogamates and I look a little shabby by comparison. Our mats have been through nearly eight hours of yoga a day for weeks, so they're all a bit dingy and pockmarked from dirt and sweat and friction. We've been hand-washing our yoga clothes, so they're always a little funky looking, and none of us brought anything like the clothes these women wear. Their clothes look like money.

I thought of the higher and lower birds, and what Indra said about how indulging in those things that give us pleasure, like milkshakes, means that we will also have to feel pain or disgust. I was considering this—how much pain I'd be willing to experience in exchange for a pair of Marianne's yoga pants—when we did our final three Oms for the day.

Later

I'm at Casa Luna for dinner with Jess, Jason, and Lara. We're creating our own classes. We're supposed to give our class a name—it can be anything we want to call it, even a made-up name—and then think of an image that represents our class, and a few words to describe it.

SuZen says we should be thinking about creating our own brand of yoga. She says that, for instance, right now there's a lot of marketing out there for something called doga, which is yoga for your dog. She said the types of yoga are going to keep proliferating until you can find a yoga class for any need you can come up with. She says we should get in the game early.

Over dinner we spent a long time talking about this doga thing. Lara hated it, and her hatred seemed to extend to SuZen for suggesting it. "That is just too much," she said. "I'm sure she's a lovely person, but it's people like SuZen who are ruining this practice. I mean, doga? Really? It's exactly what everybody's doing in London, taking their expensive dogs in for expensive yoga classes as if they need yoga in addition to their doggie antidepressants. What's next? Parakeet yoga? Yogakeet?"

Jason kept his eyes on his plate as he used a piece of bread to nudge brown rice onto his fork. "I don't think there's anything wrong with teaching your dog yoga."

"Depends on your definition of *wrong*," I said.

"Jason, it's people cashing in."

"Well, but what if the little doggies like it?"

Lara shook her head and pulled out her notebook.

Now we're all writing away about our classes. I've decided to call my yoga Complete Yoga. It's yoga that makes you complete. We're all walking around in our lives with parts of us missing, either because we live away from our friends or our families, or because we've lost our ability to be both a mind and a body at the same time. That's my pitch, anyway. So, Complete Yoga.

Words to describe it? Wholeness. Oneness. Complete... ness.

And an image. Huh. I don't know. Something complete looking.

Maybe I'll be the image. Me, standing in Mountain pose, which is a pretty complete sort of pose. I'm wearing long, slim black trousers. Very slimming. Nice pointy-toed black leather boots. A black shirt with a great collar. And tucked beneath my arm, just sort of taunting you with a little splash of color, is a vision of pistachio-green leather Prada, the real deal. No fake bag in my yoga image! That little splash of color is just what the image needs. It completes the outfit! Get it? Complete Yoga?

I just told everybody about it, and they think it's ingenious...but that maybe I should come up with another idea to present to class tomorrow.

"Though I'm sure SuZen would love it," Lara added. "If she hasn't already branded a handbag-based yoga practice herself. Or a doggie-bag yoga?"

You know, I didn't say as much to Lara just now, but maybe it's a good thing to teach our dogs yoga. I mean, I would definitely like it if the scary dogs on Bali were a little more yogified. But really, it comes down to this: we have to take good care of our dogs if the yogis are right, and we're all going to be reincarnated. I mean, we don't know for sure if reincarnation is real, but let's say it is—then don't we want to take care of our dogs because someday we could, you know, be them?

Maybe doga is just enlightened self-interest.

April 16

Indra showed up for class today transformed. Her blonde hair has been braided into teensy-tiny cornrows, and she's put Bo Derek beads at the bottom of each braid. They clicked and clacked every time she moved her head. I could see the white scalp between her braids.

When she arrives in the wantilan these days, she goes straight over to Marianne or SuZen to check in and say hi, and then they chat for a while as the rest of us finish moving the gamelan instruments to the side and placing our mats in a circle for check-in.

We've been gossiping a little bit. About Marianne and SuZen. It's really yogic gossiping, though, because they do this thing that, as Marcy puts it, "is really harshing our mellow." See, Marianne and SuZen have a really annoying way of chanting Om.

As a group, we have found our Om. Seriously, we're like the freaking St. Olaf's Choir with our Oms. For many weeks now, we have opened and closed every class with three Oms. In that time we have learned to listen to one another, blending our voices together so that our gorgeously round and full Om rises up to the rafters like the voice of Indivisible Unity itself. We chant an Om so rich in vibrations, it could create a universe. An Om that sounds like the word that began it all.

We never even had to speak of it, we just created this Om together every day. Then Marianne and SuZen arrived. As Marcy put it at lunch today, "I don't think they get it. I don't mean to be elitist or anything, because everybody has their own way of doing it, but I think they've misunderstood the seed sounds."

I don't know about the seed sounds, all I can say is it sounds like they are trying to chant and clear out their sinuses at the same time. It's a very harsh, nasal sound they make at the beginning and end of each class. But Marcy insists that what they are doing is overemphasizing the seed sounds. The seed sounds are the three sounds of Om. If you say Om slowly, you'll notice that it breaks down into an *ah* that leads to an *ooh* that leads to the *oh…m*. Marcy says that some people spell it *Aum* for this reason.

But the idea is that these vowels are present in the Om already. One need not exaggerate the seed sounds because they're already there. But Marianne and SuZen chant AAAAAAAHHHHHHH in those thin, nasal voices, and then they switch to OOOOOOOHHHHH, their mouths puckered like blow-up dolls. And then they land it with a short and sharp MMM. Sitting next to one of them while trying to recapture our group's lost Om is like trying to sink into a deliciously comfortable bed while a hornet buzzes in your ear.

"Yeah, they're really crap with the Oms, aren't they?" Jason agreed.

Worst of all? I think their Om is contagious. Indra seems to be catching it.

THE COUNTDOWN TO teaching has begun. Our afternoon classes are now devoted to learning about every single muscle in the human body and then palpating our neighbors to see if they've got them. SuZen's our teacher, and she doesn't seem to be all that interested in anatomy. I think she'd rather be teaching a business seminar on how to start your own yoga brand.

I spent most of today's class crafting an e-mail to Jonah in my head. I think he would find SuZen terribly pretentious.

Later

I've been trying to meditate, but our days are so active now, there's hardly any time for it. I was hoping to fit in a few minutes on the veranda, but Jessica came home flustered and upset—she had a run-in with Indra over SuZen's anatomy class. She doesn't want to take it. Jessica has taken countless courses in anatomy to become a massage thera-pist/bodyworker person. She could probably teach the class.

The thing is, we're paying SuZen a separate fee for anatomy classes, so it's rather like a bill's just come due, and Jessica doesn't want to pay it. She told Indra as much, but Indra is insistent that she take this class. My guess is that she and Lou promised SuZen a certain income for coming out here, and if Jessica doesn't participate, it'll cause busi-ness problems.

Here's what's weird: Indra told Jessica that she has at-tachment issues with money, and that paying for the anat-omy class will help her to overcome those issues. I've never seen Jessica indignant before, but that's exactly what she is. Her face turned bright red when she told me about it, and she didn't make eye contact when she spoke. She looked just beyond me, her voice flat and colorless.

Seeing Jessica like this, I was furious. I can't help but think that Indra's taking advantage of her. I said as much, but then Jessica started fingering the spiral binding on her journal and said, "But maybe Indra's right? I do have money issues. I grew up poor and I don't like to give up my money, even if it might be good for my soul if I did."

I don't know. My soul feels a little squirmy thinking about it. Anytime you have to fork over money to better your soul, it's a little fishy, right?

I mean, except for paying to be here. And paying for my yoga classes. That's different, I think. I mean, yoga teachers have to eat, too.

Anyway, people are pissed. Lara and Jason both think that Indra was out of line and manipulating Jessica. But maybe that has more to do with the fact that we all hate our hour of anatomy every day—really, SuZen is an excruciatingly boring teacher until she starts talking about branding or marketing. As far as anatomy goes, we'd get more out of "the knee bone's connected to the leg bone" than we're getting out of this class.

"I don't think Indra gets it," Lara said. "It is unacceptable to manipulate Jessica like this, and for what? So that SuZen can get more money? Is that what this retreat is all about, for Indra?"

April 18

Watching Jessica correct SuZen in anatomy class is quite possibly the most entertaining thing about that otherwise tedious class. Today SuZen said that the cranium doesn't move, and Jessica freaked out!

"I don't want to be disrespectful," she said, her face turning red, "but you are so wrong!"

"Excuse me?" SuZen said, lifting her eyes from the textbook she was reading from. I think she was really surprised that anyone would contradict her.

"You are so, so wrong. The bones of the cranium move. If you knew about craniosacral work, you would experience it yourself and never teach that again!" She looked around at the rest of us. "It moves, you guys, and if any of you want to see for yourself, ask me to show you later."

I told everybody then about how Jessica had given me one of her head rubs and that it was true, my skull moved and so did the earth. Take that!

INDRA AND LOU call our names out in class a lot, telling us to adjust our knees or our sacrums or whatever, and every time they call out my name, SuZen adjusts herself, and when they speak to SuZen, I do. It's pretty funny. Or no. Wait. Actually, it's annoying.

April 19

I'm staring at a woodcarving that's been wrapped in newspapers and bound with rubber bands. It belongs to Jason and Lara, but they left it on our table after stopping by for tea just now.

We had our usual morning class today. Eight million Sun Salutations. Meditation. The usual. But when it was done, Indra asked us to sit in a circle, and then she retrieved a thick blue duffel bag from one side of the wantilan. She told us she had offerings to share with us. She reached into the bag, her Bo Derek beads clicking and clacking, and then gently placed a wooden carving in front of us.

It was a figurine on a foot-wide base, standing about a foot high. Its subject matter was a long-haired woman in Warrior Two pose. The wood had been stained dark brown, but I could make out where the chisel had been—it had that rough-hewn quality that a lot of Balinese folk art has. She told us that she had commissioned a woodworker here to carve the statues for her. "It was so much fun modeling the poses for him," she said, holding the statue up with both hands for all of us to admire. "And I want you to have something to remember our experience by. I hope these will continue to inspire you in your practice wherever you go from here!"

A statue of Indra to take home with me. I immediately found it both exciting and weird. It could help me to remember all of the good things Indra's taught me, I thought. But then I looked at her more closely. I saw the way she held the statue of herself up to the light, like a precious, priceless offering, and I felt so strange; like I was retreating from her, as if she had something catching. Something like hypocrisy. She has pointed out every flush of ego she detects in me, and yet there she was, worshiping her own effigy?

I knew I didn't want the one of Indra in a Forward Bend.

She held the statue out for all of us to get a better look. "Now, back home, these would go for fifty, sixty dollars apiece. Balinese crafts are in high demand! But since we're in Bali"—she looked at Lou and smiled, and her voice was all business, like SuZen's—"I'm not going to name a price for them. Instead, we'll do it the way the Balinese do. We'll haggle!"

A few muted chuckles broke out around the circle. Jason leaned in to take the statue from Indra. He ran his fingers over it. "These are brilliant," he said.

Indra pushed the duffel bag to the center of the circle. "There's enough here for everyone to get one and even buy a few gifts for family and friends. Who knows, maybe it'll inspire them to start their own yoga practice!"

Most of my yogamates got up and offered her thirty, forty dollars for their statues. I didn't. I don't know if Indra noticed it or not. I just couldn't do it. I felt like the wantilan had suddenly become an open-air market, and even if a part of me wanted a statue to bring home and place on my shelf, an object that I could point out to friends as proof of my spiritual journey, I didn't want it like this. The last thing I want to do with my yoga teacher is haggle.

I just asked Jessica if she bought one—she's listening to her Walkman on the edge of the veranda—and she said no. "But I have money issues, remember?" she said.

I think it's the first time I've heard Jessica be sarcastic. And I gotta say—I kind of liked it.

Later

I forgot to mention something Jessica told me last night. Apparently, while I was trapped in my bathroom cell and sleeping on the futon downstairs, Jessica woke up in the middle of the night to find a mop levitating in our open window! It hung in the air for a while, and then started thrusting in and out of the house, rattling the windowpane. I asked her if it was just a surreal sex dream or something, but she swore on Saraswati that it wasn't. She said it really happened. We have a ghost. Supposedly. A Mop Ghost. Forgive me if I'm not terribly frightened.

Anyway, she didn't tell me about it until last night, because she didn't want to worry me when I was sick. I think that was a wise decision. I love ghost stories, but not if I'm sleeping by myself in a bathroom. I guess Noadhi's going to come by tomorrow to purify the house, so we have to spend the day in town. Maybe tomorrow's a good day to see some monkeys.

April 20

Eating fruit before class. I forgot to drink pee again this morning. Bad! Oh, well. Maybe tomorrow I'll be inspired. Yeah. Maybe. Or maybe I won't be.

I'm tired, I'm sore, my brain is exploding with the names of ligaments and tendons and ideas for yogic "brands," and the idea of going to class and listening to Indra laugh it up with SuZen and Marianne just isn't sounding that good.

Today's date is trying to tell me something. Is it somebody's birthday? Shoot, I really can't recall, but I know that there is something I'm supposed to remember about today. It's been so long since I've even checked my e-mail—I keep thinking of these e-mails to send people, but then I don't get around to it. I'm completely out of touch with the outside world. It's hard to imagine ever going back.

Later

When we sat in our check-in circle this morning, Indra looked at me and smiled. I wanted to be wary and guarded and say something about how uncomfortable I was with the haggling yesterday, but I couldn't help myself, I grinned right back at her, like a trained monkey. Then she said, "So, Suzanne and SuZen, I think we have a little problem with your names." Everybody laughed. Then she turned to me. "Suzanne, how would you feel if we changed your name? What if we called you Suzie from here on out?"

Um. Suzie is not the name of my higher self. Her name is Suzanne. Or, you know—*Suzananda*. But I knew what I was supposed to say. I've been here long enough. I was supposed to say something like *Of course you may call me Suzie. One string of syllables is the same as any other in this capacious ocean that is existence.*

Honestly, though, I didn't think it would be a big deal. Most of my family members call me Suzie, I went by Suzie until high school. I didn't see any reason not to go for it. So I said sure, no problem.

Holy cannoli, it was a problem.

Class started out just fine. As we moved through the first few slow rounds of Sun Salutations, I felt like I was clawing my way out of the mood I woke up in. I felt my body wake up with the stretches and lunges. I wondered if I might not clear my head of all those nagging, grumpy voices and get back my post-kundalini high.

Then something happened. We were halfway through our fifth round when Indra spoke to me. "Tuck your pelvis, Suzie," she said.

I was startled out of my meditation by the name. Suzie. I tried to keep my mind focused on my breath, but inexplicably I felt a little knot of fear in my throat.

I did what she said, and tucked my pelvis, but at the same time I felt my heart tighten into a fist, and my eyes became wet with something like indignation, or resentment. I tried to wrestle these feelings to the ground: Why fear? Why indignation? Why now? I thought I'd moved past the fears that brought me here. I thought my breakthrough had purged me, liberated me. So why were they coming back?

I glanced at Indra, her braids swinging around her face, and became aware of a sort of rage gathering around my sudden and unbidden understanding: Indra could do nothing for me anymore. I felt SuZen somewhere in the room, enjoying her own name as well as Indra's friendship and attentions. And I hated my nickname, the way it reduced me to Little Suzie, to Suzie-Q, to Thister Thuzie Thittin' on a Thithle.

"That's right, Suzie, there you go," she said.

I could feel the tendons in my throat. My windpipe burned with each inhalation. I thrust my arms toward the ceiling in the next pose in the series, and then dove downward to Standing Forward Bend, my throat aching. My teeth clamped down on the smooth flesh of my cheeks, my jaw slid forward and froze.

I pushed my left leg back, then my right, in Plank Pose. We held that push-up for longer than any human need ever hold a push-up. The longer we stayed there, the hotter and tighter my heart felt, as if it were on fire. As if it were creeping up my throat. I imagined my heart flying from my mouth and exploding like a firebomb, igniting the wantilan, consuming all of us.

In Downward Dog, my arms shook.

"Strength, Suzie!"

Adrenaline coursed through me like it did when I was a kid, playing tag, my older brother chasing me, yelling my name, *Suzie*. I imagined the fire blowing the roof off the wantilan in a great explosion of sparks and black smoke. I wanted to fly up in a plume of that black smoke, retrieve the roof as it blew away, and then bring it back down to earth to break over SuZen's head. Or perhaps I could simply kick my legs up into handstand and walk across the burning wood on my hands, weaving a path around charred yogis in Upward Dog, circling back to SuZen's precious designer mat and there I would kick, kick, kick my legs in the air, knocking her into a ball, rolling her around the circumference of the wantilan until she cried out for mercy.

Suzananda Eleison, she would cry, *Suzanne have mercy!*

Give me my name, I would growl, kick-kick-kicking. *Give me my name, SuZen, give me my real name, you Sue-One-Hand-Clapping.*

And then Lou made a mistake. "Pelvis down, Suzanne," he said. "I mean—Suzie."

We lifted our arms to the ceiling, our heads back, and I felt water running into my ears and down my jaw and neck. We lowered our arms in a swan dive and folded our bodies in Forward Bends. Water ran like fingertips up my forehead and into my hair, tickling my scalp. I held the backs of my legs, wiping my wet cheeks on my calves.

Right leg back in Warrior One, eyes straight ahead, I was drowning, I was sick, my rib cage rising and falling in choppy waves.

I didn't know what was happening to me. I was over-whelmed. I hated myself for crying, for being so stupid and emotional over a name, but hating myself only made me cry more.

An hour passed. Each time I caught my breath and thought I was back in control, Indra or Lou would call me Suzie and I was consumed again by a dark ache. I relived twenty-five years of that name, images of my parents and brothers and sister flashing in front of me, my grandparents, great-grandparents, my friends, all of them calling me Suzie, their own. The place where I am Suzie is the place I will be leaving soon, maybe forever. Home.

When I lay down on my mat to rest, I caught my breath for a moment before the quaking began again. And then, I swear to God, I split in two.

I rose up to the woven ceiling of the wantilan, and I hovered with the geckos in the rafters. I looked down at myself. I was the brunette on the pink mat. I saw her crying. And then I was next to her, on the wooden floor beside her mat. I slid my arm under her waist, where I could feel her breath starting and stopping. I pressed my body into hers until she became still, and I could feel her heart beating in my chest. And then, without saying a word, I reminded her that today is the day Jonah moves to New York.

6. *Nobody's Child*

> Indeed, we bitched nearly everybody at the seminar. We
> decided that...these professionally religious people
> were hypocrites, posers, windbags. From our decision, a
> convenient conclusion could be drawn: if they weren't
> acting up to their professed principles, then we needn't
> act up to ours.
>
> — CHRISTOPHER ISHERWOOD,
> *My Guru and His Disciple*

At twenty-eight, I took to drinking a tea I bought at a
popular yoga studio in Manhattan. After sneezing my way
through a class, the teacher—a stunning, raven-haired
actress—guided me into the studio boutique and advised
me to purchase her favorite brand of neti pot, a tub of
eucalyptus salts for my bath, and a box of tea that tasted
like a roomful of hippies. I don't know if it boosted my

immune system or not, but I enjoyed the tea because each tea bag came with a spiritual aphorism printed on its white paper tag. My favorite was this one:

What is yoga? When you open yourself up and let the universe come in you.

Now, forgive my filthy mind, but doesn't that seem just a little bit slutty?

That's how I felt the day Jonah moved to New York and I lost my shit in the wantilan. I felt like a spiritual slut. Like I had spent many weeks becoming one of those wet-eyed, overly emotional seekers who are forever riding a spiritual roller coaster that, from another angle, could look like emotional masturbation. I looked back at the weeks before and couldn't believe myself: Where was my skepticism? Where was my reason? Would I become one of those New Age wanderers who traveled from workshop to ashram to sweat lodge, always looking for the next spiritual fix, the next kundalini awakening, the next catharsis?

If I needed to live in a constant state of epiphany, I would never be strong enough for life outside the retreat.

Life outside the retreat. I hadn't thought about my real life, or the very real changes ahead of me, in weeks.

It was astonishing to hear my home name and feel pushed out of the safe nest of my retreat and back into the real world—or, rather, the illusory world of the lower bird, where my attachments and ego and desires lived and breathed and expected things of me. How bewildering, to look back at so many weeks of retreat behind me, only to turn forward and see the same visions of loss and death that made me retreat from the world in the first place.

Indra thought it was good for me. After class she sat with me and hugged and petted me while I cried some more. She was so kind. Her eyes were so concerned. By the time I stopped crying, she'd come up with an idea: She wanted to keep going with this line of therapy. She wanted to keep calling me Suzie in order to help me work through my fears about leaving home.

I knew that if I agreed, we'd have lots of conversations in the remaining weeks, that she'd check in with me to see how I was doing—if, by using my nickname, she eroded its power over me. This would be a chance to have Indra all to myself. To win her attention, her approval, her love. This would give me the right to request time alone with her to really talk about our lives, our paths, our beliefs. And who knows? Maybe it could lead me to that God I was sensing, to overcoming my brain's need to disprove everything.

She could help me prepare for my future with Jonah.

I considered all of this very quickly, with Indra's warm brown eyes looking at me as sweetly and expectantly as they did when I first came to her for advice. And then, as kindly as I possibly could, I quoted Whitney Houston: *Hell to the No.*

She was disappointed. I could see it in her face. Disappointed and surprised. She nodded, saying, "It's up to you, of course, but…" The funny thing was, I didn't mind her disappointment. I almost liked it.

This was inevitable, you see. We had been on retreat for weeks. When you're doing yoga eight hours a day, days are like weeks, and weeks are like months. So basically I had been on retreat for like fifteen years. I was a teenager in retreat land. I was ready to rebel. Somehow, along the winding path from one week to the next, Indra and Lou had changed from idols to surrogate parents insisting that I see everything the way they did, that I eat the foods they eat, drink the bodily fluids they drink, and go to church, or the wantilan, whenever they said I was supposed to be there.

It's always the mother who gets it worst from her teenage daughters. Lou was beyond reproach, I thought, but when I looked at Indra I saw a woman who wanted me to grow up and be like her. And for the first time in months, I wanted to be myself again. I yearned for a good cup of coffee and a gray day. I wanted to wear a sweater and be around people who swear.

All teenagers question the way they've been raised, how their parents might have done things differently. With Indra, I started to question her integrity, looking for holes. Between the haggling in the wantilan and her conversation with Jessica about paying for anatomy, I wondered if maybe Indra saw us as customers as much as students. I didn't understand why money should ever come up on a spiritual retreat. Was she manipulating us into forking over more cash? With Jessica, was she trying to control her, or just protecting SuZen's interests? Or both?

I looked at my own financial sins—how I'd cheated Lou's studio because I wanted to practice yoga and it cost more money than I thought I could afford. I knew that was the wrong thing to do, but maybe Karlee had been right, maybe money corrupted all spiritual practices. Maybe yoga studios should be like churches, where everybody tithes to keep the place running, but no more than that. Or like gyms, where you don't need God or philosophy to properly experience the elliptical machine, and nobody cares if you have an ego.

A few months after I returned from Bali, my sister flew with me to New York to help me move. By the time she left, I had a lead on a job, a yoga studio, and a futon big enough for both Jonah and me.

Jonah and I found a group of friends who quickly became our urban family. These were the friends who met every cousin, aunt, and sibling who came to visit me in New York, and several of them caught on to the fact that no one in my family called me Suzanne. The only friends who called me Suzie were those I'd known since elementary school, so to hear these new friends call me by such an intimate term was strange, but also delightful. In Bali, my name filled me with terror. In New York, it made me feel loved.

I have never been so homesick as I was that first year in
New York. I missed my family the way I would miss my legs
if they were amputated. I longed for the green and the gray
of Seattle, for the lakes and the mountains. I remember a
day that first August, wading through the thick summer
air on my way to Penn Station to pick up a visiting friend,
when, for a second, I caught a sliver of a glimpse of the
Hudson River. Just the sight of that silvery water, and I felt
my lungs expand with air, as if I hadn't taken a full breath
in months.

I tried every yoga studio in the city. I was desperate for
those ninety-minute opportunities to really breathe, but
far too often I found myself distracted by the shiny objects
for sale in the gift shops, which were tantalizingly situated
so that you had to walk through them to get anywhere. I
wanted to breathe, but the classes were as crowded as the
subway platform at rush hour. In the subway, I quickly grew
accustomed to the inevitability of inhaling my neighbor's
breath, but in yoga classes it made my heart race and my
chest constrict—the exact opposite of what I was there to
achieve. And what was worse, when my fellow students
complained, loudly—I didn't, I'm from Seattle—it quickly

became apparent that the most important consideration for studio owners was the bottom line.

Which made sense, up to a point. Yoga teachers have to pay rent, too. And I had to admit that it was probably good on some level that so many people were willing to pack themselves into an oversold yoga class. Maybe studio owners simply wanted to give the greatest number of people a chance to practice yoga. But even so, I began to understand how early Protestants might have felt regarding the excesses of the Vatican. Every studio I visited had commercial tie-ins, endorsements, plans for expansion. And one day, leaving an enormous gym-like studio in Union Square after the owner invited me to the launch party for her latest line of yoga-pose flash cards, it dawned on me that my time in Bali might have been the end of yoga as I knew it. The spiritual practice I had known was undergoing a transformation as profound as any I'd ever sought for myself. It was becoming an industry.

For most of my second year in New York, I stopped bothering with yoga studios and tried to keep up my practice at home. Jonah was out most nights, so I had a quiet place to meditate, even if there wasn't enough room for a proper asana practice. On the nights he was home, he'd lock himself in the bedroom so that I could meditate. Separated from Jonah by a thin partition, I chanted quietly, knowing we'd both start laughing if I did too many *lang-vang-rang-yang-hang-ang-Oms*.

I managed in this way for a while, but then, one evening in mid-November, a friend took me to a studio downtown that I actually liked. Sure, there was a huge boutique right in the entrance that sold everything from magnets with yogic aphorisms emblazoned on them to T-shirts that read BODY BY YOGA. But I liked it anyway. I needed to.

Jonah and I had been fighting about Christmas. I wanted to go home; he wanted to stay and have a real New York Christmas, just the two of us. Neither of us would budge, and that afternoon I went ahead and booked my own flight home, telling Jonah that there was no Christmas for me in New York.

Somehow, in the moment we began our breathing exercises at the start of class, I knew that Jonah and I would work it out. Maybe by next Christmas I'd be ready to stay in New York. Or maybe he'd be willing to come home. I didn't think about the eighty-dollar tanks in the gift shop or the fact that the yoga teacher had cultivated her teaching voice to sound like butterfly kisses. I even told myself that I could use the claustrophobia of the overcrowded class to teach myself to relax under strain.

I left feeling expansive, invigorated, at home in my adopted city.

I resumed my asana practice with zeal. It was such a relief to breathe and stretch and clear my mind. I wanted to feel that way all the time. I wanted to live in my yoga studio. Soon, even the boutique felt like an extension of my practice. Each time I went to class, those expensive yoga tanks called to me. Those après-yoga sweater wraps whistled at me. Books and CDs and DVDs made declarations. The sirens of oils and neti pots and candles lured me over to the rocks—or, rather, to the smooth river stones on sale for sixteen dollars, just the kind of feng-shui "texture" to place around your home to improve the flow of ch'i!

I wanted to improve the flow of my ch'i.

As the prodigal daughter returning to her practice, how could I not give in to my inner spiritual slut? She wanted to be loved, and the things these yogic toys said to her! The promises they made!

I read *Yoga Journal* like it was the Bible and the QVC network rolled into one. Its articles made me think about the way I could employ yogic concepts in my life and in my relationship with Jonah, and the shopping section filled me with lust. I wanted those objects, those expensive, natural-fiber and essential-oil-filled objects, because I was told, and I believed, that they would make me feel holy, reverent, sacred. That in lieu of any specific God, they would satisfy my need for ritual and serenity.

The thing is? They did. Sometimes the candles, the images of Ganesha, the river stones, the endlessly reinterpreted bum-hugging yoga pants, sometimes they reminded me of a state of mind that I wanted to go back to, the same way the crucifixes in every room of my aunt's house remind her to be Christlike. I'd sit in our apartment, counting the days till I could go home for a visit, and those objects would help me remember to breathe. But then, one night after an evening with my lovely friends, I opened the latest issue of *Yoga Journal* to find an advertisement for a credit card called the "Visa Enlightenment" card. One of the most famous yoga teachers in the country was its spokesyogini, posing beatifically among silvery birch trees.

Having recently bought one of her yoga DVDs, I considered, briefly, the merits of such a credit card.

For twenty-percent interest on my purchases, I could get discounts on sacred vacations and earn points toward massage, yoga clothes, organic beauty products, and decorative Buddhas. The idea was that this card would help me to consume *mindfully*. And the more mindful things I consumed, the more points I'd earn toward even more mindful consumption.

My God, I thought. *I am such a chump.*

In another issue of *Yoga Journal* I found a long apologia for the yoga industry. It suggested that I shouldn't feel bad that American yoga had become so venal. So what, it said, if a prominent yoga teacher preaches austerity and yet enjoys expensive cars and country houses? So what if the most famous yoga teachers employ agents and publicists and think about marketing and branding as much as they think about the path?

The point, the writer argued, was that if these same yoga teachers lived in India, they would be sadhus, wandering monks, exchanging their wisdom and yogic knowledge for bowls of rice and berries. They would wear rags and be happy to do so, because they were in it for the wisdom. But in America, that's not how it's done. And let's face it, you can only be as enlightened as the economy in which you live!

The spokesyogini in the Visa ad was one of the most admired yoga teachers in the country. The curl of my lip as I regarded her meditative posture reminded me of the Annual Appeal at my church when I was growing up. I hated it when the priest I despised told everyone in the pews to open their pocketbooks. But what if instead of reminding us to tithe in support of the church's school and charity programs, he had invited us to apply for the Visa Catholicism Card? How would my fellow parishioners have reacted then? If, when the ushers did the collection at Mass, you could swipe your Visa Catholicism Card for points toward decorative crosses and designer rosaries and five-star vacation packages to Lourdes?

If I bought in to this, I would be the biggest fool ever to be duped by an oligarchy of yogic charlatans. And as if roused by the snap of a hypnotist, I woke up from my yogic spending spree and realized that this brand of yoga, this American yoga, was just a business, pure and simple. And it was ingenious.

Here's a combination of exercise and practical philosophy that can make us healthier, happier, more relaxed and beautiful. You can get your yoga with or without God. Yoga memberships are already insanely expensive, so that self-selects for a certain class of woman. And that class of woman—middle class, upper middle class—likes to shop. She gets a spiritual hit off of shopping. So, in this yoga, she gets two spiritual practices in one. An astonishing commercial success story! Create a need? No need. The need is an eternal one. It's been filled by countless religions, and they've often asked us for money in exchange for our serenity. But yoga's got them all beat, and they don't even try to hide it. They put those boutiques right out front.

I thought of Lara, back in Bali, when she complained about her London studio being full of pretentious, designer-clad yogis, and felt a pang. I missed my yogamates. I missed the simplicity of our practice, the earnestness of it. The thought nearly made my eyes cross, but I longed to go back to practicing yoga with people who drink pee.

I decided I needed my practice to mean something. I needed it to be something more than just a commercial transaction or a self-help program for the privileged.

I wouldn't do yoga anymore unless it was free or by donation. I wouldn't buy yoga toys I didn't need. And for the first time I found myself right at the intersection of orthodoxy and cynicism: the more yoga studios confirmed for me that this yuppie feel-good catchall commercial spiritual practice was cynical to its core, the more I told myself that only the purists really got it. None of these famous yoga teachers got it, none of them understood what yoga was about. In fact, it would appear that nobody got it but me. And so I decided I would ascend the mountain alone, the last living yogi—but I couldn't sit to meditate without dwelling on how much money I was saving by not going to a studio, without congratulating myself on being so much more enlightened than the yoga industry, and soon it occurred to me that maybe I didn't get it either. In fact, maybe this spiritual practice was too open to interpretation not to be easily corrupted. A spiritual practice for people like me, who sometimes like the idea of God and sometimes don't, who can't seem to tell the difference between a spiritual epiphany and a shopping high? What the hell kind of spirituality is that?

So I stopped practicing. And though I thought about

it, dreamed about it, wrote about it, and complained about it, I had no intention of ever going back. After all, why on earth would I want to be a part of any spirituality that would have me as its practitioner?

April 21

It's past dawn. Roosters and dogs are competing with fireworks that sound like gunshots. Like the Japanese are back to reclaim the island.

Just reliving class yesterday makes me want to weep. But I won't let myself, because I want to get the rest of the day down. The day was epic. I lived a thousand lives in one day, and I'm still awake enough to live one more.

After class I wanted to go home and go back to bed. I wanted to sleep the day away, wanted nothing more to do with it. I had forgotten that Noadhi was at the house, carving ginger amulets to place over all the doorways and windows to protect us from our Mop Ghost. He didn't want us to come back to the house till sunset.

To say that I was displeased when Jessica reminded me of this would be an understatement. I was furious. And ready to call bullshit on this whole "spirits" phenomenon. It was fun to think of spirits when they weren't inconveniencing, but I had cried my face off through class, and then again with Indra afterwards, and now I had to entertain myself in town all day because of a possessed mop? My eyes were swollen and red and my head hurt. I was humiliated. I was pissed. I hate crying in public. Hate it.

Jessica took one look at me and pulled me away from our yogamates. As we walked, she spoke hurriedly, as if in a race against our worst impulses.

"Suzanne," she said, pulling me along by the arm, "I know you're in a really bad mood right now, and I know we can't go home, but we really shouldn't go and have a coconut vanilla milkshake." She pulled me along the trail through the forest and down the four million stairs to Campuhan. "We should be focused on the path," she said, pushing us through the transport guys and shopkeepers on the main road into Ubud, leading with her shoulder, like a quarterback heading for a touchdown. "We should keep our eyes on the prize," she said as we walked past the bar and into the restaurant at Casa Luna. We sat down at a table, and when the waitress came by we spoke in unison, without a moment's hesitation.

The milkshakes were just as delicious as we remembered them.

But there was a small problem. One minute we were enjoying our milkshakes, giddy as schoolchildren, and the next, we were staring at two empty glasses.

It was a problem.

But don't worry! We solved it very quickly.

We were on the verge of ordering another round when one of us noticed something in the menu. I don't remember who noticed it first. Well—maybe I do. Okay, it was me. I discovered a brownie. By "discovered" I mean that I notice this brownie on the menu every single time we eat at Casa

Luna and occasionally have dreams about it in which I am rubbing it all over my body.

But, really, it isn't just a brownie. No mere brownie would inspire such dreams. It's a brownie the size of a brick, and when you stab it with your fork, molten chocolate comes pouring out of it. In the interest of avoiding chocolate overload, they've kindly added an offering of three scoops of vanilla ice cream. And then, just because they can, they pour a pint of hot fudge over the entire thing.

This sinful concoction is called the Killer Brownie, and according to the menu, it is *THE BEST DESSERT IN UBUD!!!!!!!*

"We will have it," I said to the waitress, who nodded and started to write it down.

"Wait!" Jessica said. She was worried. "That's going a little too far, isn't it? Oh no, I don't think so. We shouldn't, right? We should be thinking about the path! We should be thinking about the higher bird, right?"

I looked into her blue eyes and smiled. "You know what, hon? *Fuck* the higher bird."

She was stunned. Then she started to giggle. "Oh, you are bad," she said. Her voice was hushed, awestruck. "*Fuck the higher bird!*"

I turned back to the waitress, ashamed of nothing but the fact that we were making her wait. "One Killer Brownie," I said. "Two spoons."

Jessica couldn't stop laughing. "Fuck the higher bird!" she cried, lifting her empty milkshake glass. She sounded like a kid who was just learning how to swear.

"Fuck the higher bird!" I cried, clinking my glass against hers.

"Bring me a slingshot," she sang.

"Jess," I said, "you rock."

Can you imagine what happens when you have that much sugar in one sitting, after virtually none for almost two months? I'll tell you what happens: *you blow your mind.* Soon we were so spazzed out, it was like every single one of our nerve endings was having its own private kundalini experience. I told Jessica she was the greatest. She told me I was the greatest.

"No, you're the greatest."

"No, you're the greatest."

"You're greatester."

"No you're greatester."

"You great!"

"You greater!"

Hmmm. We thought this was the funniest thing ever, but I don't think it translates well to paper. Anyway, we needed something to cut the sweet or soon we were going to start flashing people. Jessica suggested we order coffees. Just two teensy little cappuccinos, just enough to bring us back down to earth.

Voulez-vous Fuck Zat Higher Bird avec moi ce soir?

From there it was a very short leap to a bottle of red wine, and then tiny glasses of port, and then we were telling each other how much we loved each other and how this was a friendship that would last forever, and that we should order another bottle of wine so that we could toast our friendship! We can't toast our friendship with empty glasses!

"You know what?" Jessica said, eyeing the sweet and alcoholic carnage strewn across our table. "I think wine is the secret for living in the moment."

"Our inebriation *is* profound."

"Yes! It gives everything a certain…moment…quality, you know?"

"Moment-ness."

"We're here now."

"Totally. I'm totally here. Now."

The restaurant was closing as we raised our glasses one last time. Even as we toasted I felt that near-weepy, clingy sensation in my throat and chest, that impatient desire to stretch the evening a little longer, to not let it end, this drink, this conversation, this shade of light, these open hours at the restaurant. Must we go home?

"Fuck the higher bird!" Jessica said, like a resolution.

"Amen, sister," I replied.

We paid our bill and stepped out into the night. A left turn would have brought us home quickly. A right turn was what we made, toward Monkey Forest Road. Soon our noses were pressed against the glass door of the Prada boutique.

"There she is," I said. "Still there. Waiting."

"She is pretty," Jessica admitted.

"Does she look lonely to you?"

"Maybe a little."

"Don't be lonely," we crooned through the glass.

"I'll come for you soon, little one," I said. "If you are who you say you are."

Jessica giggled, her eyes half closed, and tried to take my hand, but missed. She tried again, grabbing at it as if it were a piece of paper caught in the wind. She patted it with her other hand and we started to walk.

We agreed that tomorrow we would rededicate ourselves to becoming yoga teachers, but that tonight the higher bird needed to be fucked by the lower bird. We agreed that it doesn't bother the higher bird to be so utterly fucked by the lower bird, because the higher bird is, you know, higher up. In the branches.

The walk home sobered us up a bit, and we sat on the veranda for a while, drinking gallons of water. When we finally came up to bed, we lay on our sides in the darkness, our feet resting in a pool of moonlight. As we talked I sensed something rare: happiness. For a few minutes, talking with my roommate after a cathartic night of wine and chocolate, I felt that I was happy. It made my life seem possible.

"You'll go to New York," Jessica said, "and I'll come and visit you. We can go to all the hip yoga studios and go shopping for beautiful clothes and we'll drink wine!"

"Maybe...," I said. "And maybe Jonah and I will be happy, living together. Maybe it will make us stronger. Do you think it will?"

"It could, who knows? Why not just go and have an adventure? You have no idea what it'll be like. What's your gut telling you?"

"That I love Jonah. I can't imagine living without him. And if we got married it would make so many people happy. He's already a part of my family." I looked at Jessica's face in the dark and felt that I could be more like her, if I let myself be. She's open, she's unafraid. She doesn't seem to worry about losing time, or losing connections with people she loves. I asked her if she was ever scared when she thought about the future.

"I'm scared all the time," she said. "But I don't think God put me here just to die. God put me here to find myself and to find love." Then she rolled onto her back and sighed. "I can't wait to find love," she said. "You're so lucky to have it."

. . .

JESSICA FELL ASLEEP hours ago. I should join her. But I keep replaying the last twenty-four hours from beginning to end, and then I can't help thinking about the last few weeks, the last few months, the last few years... Jessica's right. I'm lucky.

Jonah is best friends with my siblings. He loves my grandparents. Grandpa asks me on a daily basis when I'm going to marry Jonah. When I move to New York, Jonah will be my family there. I should stop worrying, and stop looking for answers from a woman who has never seen me outside of this yoga world. She's never even seen me in jeans—how can she know me well enough to advise me? I should be like Jessica, and give myself over, wholeheartedly, to whatever the future holds.

And I should go to sleep. Now.

April 21

Omigolly.

We have the day off. Thank God. We both slept in later than usual, and when we got up, Jessica didn't bring her Starbucks mug with her to the bathroom, and she's not sitting on the edge of the veranda drinking from it as she usually would be. We've been at the table for over an hour, reading, or writing in our journals, not really talking. It's a little uncomfortable. Jessica's not her usual self, and neither am I. I know what it is. There's a sin at the table with us, a transgression neither of us knows exactly how to process.

Fuck the higher bird.

In one night, with one phrase, we pissed on something sacred. It reminds me of people who tried to make jokes in the month after 9/11. It's just wrong.

Jessica wants to go into town to do a walking meditation. I think I'd better. I feel like we're in trouble. Like her mom is going to call my mom or something. Penance.

Evening

I was thinking about something. No, make that some*one*. The Sailor, actually. I've had beers and a drink with an umbrella in it. And it's making me think about how sometimes I want to throw myself on the Sailor but I don't. Because of boyfriend. Cheating? Is WRONG.

It's wrong in all its parts. Will NOT be a Jezzebel. Jezebelle. JezebWHATEVER.

But if everything's an illusion, does it matter? And also, hello, unattachment?

I had a point. But tired now. Jonah is love.

It's bed.

April 22

Well, gosh.

Something is happening to my yoga retreat. I've gone from being a monkish seeker of truth and wisdom to a drunk and randy Bridget Jones. Probably not a step up, spiritually speaking.

Yesterday I thought Jessica and I were going into town for a walking meditation. Our penance for fucking the higher bird so thoroughly the night before. Well. I was wrong. And maybe I should've been prepared, considering that we've spent all this time learning that our perceptions of the world and other people are flawed. That sometimes we believe other people are thinking or feeling things that are really *our* thoughts or *our* feelings. Jessica wasn't interested in penance. She was interested in *shoes*.

Our walking meditation was a beeline to Jessica's beaded

white wedding shoes. I followed her straight into town and watched her walk into that boutique, ignoring the way the saleswoman tried to wave her off. She offered a respectable sum and walked out with her future on her feet. She said she would wear them only once, but then they would be saved for the day she gets married.

Once that was done, we walked through the market, where we ran into Marianne, her auburn hair pulled back in a pink scarf. She'd been shopping. We stood on the sidewalk, chatting for a while, and Marianne said that she and Indra had been talking and discovered that they both came to yoga in the same way, because the poses, "you know, felt like...coming home." She spaced out for a minute, nodding, her brown eyes glassy and vacant. Then she smiled. "Wow," she said.

Apparently she and Indra have a deep spiritual bond. Which kind of makes me want to barf, but whatever.

What's funny is that this I'm-slipping-into-another-dimension thing Marianne does halted the moment we introduced her to the Prada store. She became very focused, suddenly, going purse-by-purse through the store before declaring, in a full, unambiguous voice, that they were lovely. She said she couldn't be absolutely sure, but that she had read about stores like this, which sold real bags at international prices. Her whole flakey, spaced-out vibe was gone. She was all business, forking over her credit card to buy one of the larger handbags and three different wallets. I almost caved in and bought my purse, but at the last minute I couldn't bring myself to do it.

Don't want to be a chump. Even if my bag sang to me from its shelf, inviting me, like Marianne, to *come on home*.

We met Jason and Lara at Casa Luna, and the five of us

went to this walk-in reflexology place Marianne had read about. That's when the sex thoughts started. My reflexologist was a man, a very nice-looking man with a shaggy haircut and beautiful, high cheekbones. I was fully clothed for the massage, but fully clothed meant I was wearing a short sarong and a tank top. Not so fully clothed. He started on one foot, and then worked up to my ankle, grabbing my leg with both hands as if to strangle it, and working in this strangling sort of way up to my inner thigh. There, he continued to make this rotating motion with his hands, even though it was very clear—to me at least—that he wasn't just massaging my leg anymore. Holy Christ, I was so embarrassed. But I also didn't want him to stop.

He did, of course, and before I had anything to be really embarrassed about. Afterwards Marianne excused herself, saying she wanted to prepare for her class tomorrow. Or, as she put it, "I just want to, you know, get my bliss on." The rest of us went back to Casa Luna for dinner, and I couldn't help but announce that I had just had the most erotically charged massage of my life. I felt giddy and slightly perverted, telling my celibate yogamates about it. But thankfully I was not alone—Jason chimed in with stories from his travels throughout Southeast Asia, and one massage in Thailand that had an unexpected happy ending.

"I didn't know what to do," he said sheepishly. "The woman just grabbed hold of me before I could say no. And once she started, it was really hard to stop."

"*Hard* being the operative word, ladies," Lara said. "Now, Jason, when a masseuse asks you if you *want special massage*, you know what she means!"

Soon Baerbel and Marcy showed up, and they were only too happy to join in the conversation. Marcy told us that she and her husband practice tantric sex. Jessica and Lara and I listened, enthralled, as she described the workshops they attend every year to learn how to slow his orgasm and multiply hers. Our greens and rice went untouched.

"God," Lara said. "Don't you think Indra and Lou must be practicing tantric sex? Like Sting and Trudy Styler?"

Marcy pointed her fork at Baerbel. "Baerbel would know," she said. Baerbel started to deny it, but Marcy interrupted her. "Oh, come on. You've known Lou for years."

Baerbel tittered. "Well, yes, but this is not the sort of question I make a habit of asking." She made a lascivious face, which on her looked very innocent and goofy, her eyes half-closed and her lips pursed. " '*Do you and your lover practice tantra?*' Yeah, okay, this is a very familiar question even among friends, don't you think? And besides," she added, lifting her water glass and drinking from it, "I don't know Indra that well. I knew Lou's first wife much better."

"His first wife?" Jessica said.

"Yeah," Baerbel said. "She was a good teacher. Very smart. I studied with them here, in the wantilan. And then, one time, Indra comes here to be their student, and the next thing you know, Lou is divorcing his wife and teaching with Indra."

I'm not exactly sure what happened next, except that everybody freaked the fuck out. There have always been stories about yoga teachers and gurus having sex with their disciples, and I guess my yogamates took Baerbel's story to be one of those. Marcy was incensed; she had studied with someone in California who was known for sleeping with his students, and she had vowed never to fall for a guru like that again. "But I wonder if Indra charmed him into leaving his wife," she said. "That might sound sexist, but she's beautiful and charismatic, and maybe Lou wasn't a match for that?"

It sounds sort of nuts, but everyone seems to agree that Indra was at fault. If my yogamates were pissed at Indra for making Jessica feel like she has money issues, this was a whole new ballgame. Suddenly, Indra, the woman who only six weeks earlier was considered practically enlightened, was nothing but Lou's mistress, just another Jezebel homewrecker.

And then Baerbel said the magic words that transformed our little table of yogamates into yoga heretics. "Do you know what I would like to try?" she said. "I would like to try this coconut-vanilla milkshake you girls have been going on about."

A hush went around the table. And then all hell broke loose. Milkshakes for everyone! Bitching about our teachers on a sugar high! Treason! Mutiny!

Jessica and I split off as soon as our milkshakes were drained, and found a quiet little bar where we could talk. And drink beer. I think we needed to check in with each other; I don't know why, but Jessica and I sort of have this private connection over Indra and Lou. It's almost like we own their love story, and hearing our yogamates talk about Indra as this temptress, this homewrecker, was disturbing. It messes with the legend we've created around our teachers, this myth that inspires us and gives us both so much hope for our own love lives.

We talked it out over our beers, and at the end of the night, over cocktails with umbrellas in them, we decided that it didn't matter, any of it, because what truly mattered was that the little god who lived at the bottom of the martini glass kept telling us to order another one. And when a god speaks, you must listen.

Today, I can't help wondering if maybe Lou's story was

similar to Indra's. Maybe he couldn't be himself with his ex-wife, or couldn't grow the way he wanted to grow until he found Indra. Maybe Indra needed solitude to find herself, those years she spent alone between her first marriage and meeting Lou—and maybe Lou needed Indra to find himself.

I don't know. Or maybe they're a coupla homewreckers.

Class is going to suck today. I can just feel it.

April 24

Jessica and I were hanging out on the veranda last night, still talking about Indra and Lou, when a man in an expensive-looking business suit showed up from behind the house. He loitered around the temple, looking down at the pool, poking around the grounds, until Jessica and I asked him what he was doing. Turns out he's Su's uncle, in town from Jakarta. He owns the property we're on.

He was chubby and sweating in his dark suit. The rectangular lenses of his glasses were smudged.

"You're here to do yoga, right?" he said, smiling, resting one foot on our bottom step, a hand in his pocket. He spoke with an Australian accent. "You westerners love yoga."

Jessica nodded and I said, "Sometimes."

Jessica scowled at me. "Suzanne! Stop that. You're on the path."

"I think I'm sitting on the path," I said. I looked at Su's uncle. "I need a break from yoga."

He laughed. "When I needed a break from the hocus-pocus of Bali, I moved to Jakarta." He gestured at Jessica's blue mat, laid out across the tiled veranda. "What you do is athletic, at least, so it's good for your body. There's a *there* there. But we Balinese, our yoga is just bells and incense and offerings to spirits," he said. "We're like children, playing an imaginary game. Though it is good for the economy—so long as you love the Balinese for our superstitions, we will all eat! But some of us have moved on."

Jessica gave me a look like this conversation was my fault. But I wanted to know what he meant by that. I like the bells and incense. I like the feeling of playacting. I could do that all day, just don't talk to me about God, or money. I can't take it anymore. So I asked him what he meant, and next thing, Su's uncle is giving us a lecture on the cyclical nature of humankind. When she heard the word *cycle*, Jessica perked right up. But I don't think he gave her what she wanted.

He said that human desire is cyclical. He drew a clock in the air with his finger and pointed to the top of the circle, where the 12 would be on a clock. "This is the beginning of a civilized people," he said, slowly moving his finger past one o'clock and two o'clock, and so on. "As you move forward, you accumulate comforts. You struggle for possessions and power and money and land. Your people have been there already." He landed on the 6. "Now you are here, moving up and away from the material world." He moved his hand clockwise toward the 12. "You have everything you could possibly ever need, and you have it because you've been taking it from the rest of us for hundreds of years. And you are unhappy still!"

He pointed to one o'clock. "This is where the rest of us are. We want what you have, and we have the one thing you want."

"What's that?" I asked.

"God," he said. "We have God, but we would rather have your big cars and houses and your women who will make lots of money while I stay at home!" He laughed.

Jessica rolled her eyes at me. "I'm going upstairs," she said.

"You don't want to hear more about the cycle?"

She snorted in reply. Su's uncle left shortly after that, off to poke around Baerbel and Marcy's place.

GOD. SOMETIMES I think there might be a god out there, and that every once in a while he tunes in to see what we're up to, and have a good laugh at how we like to dress him up in various costumes. Robes, thorny crowns, yarmulkes and curls, saris and butt-hugging yoga pants. Male, female, a genderless reincarnation factory; a Mother Earth or a withholding Father Christmas. I would think it would amuse the hell out of him. That we're all idolaters, worshiping figments of our own creation who bear no resemblance to him.

Maybe he's sitting in some alternate dimension somewhere, saying, "Shit, I didn't even create the world! I was just cooking my dinner, not paying attention to the heat, and suddenly there was this big bang and a few hours later, a bunch of dinosaurs..."

April 25

Indra was very sweet to me today, checking in throughout class, calling me Suzanne M. instead of Suzie. But then Lou asked me to demonstrate my Wheel for the class so that he could talk about how to teach backbends. So I did, and afterwards SuZen said that it looked as if my spine was made out of rubber. Which was very nice of her to say, really.

But Indra swiftly jumped in to say that while I have a flexible spine, it's by no means *extraordinarily* flexible. There's really nothing *special* about my spine.

Which is true, but Jesus! I wouldn't have been surprised if Indra had followed that up with "And also, Suzanne has fat thighs and ugly hair."

I kind of hate her today.

She showed us her Wheel just for good measure, and it was breathtaking. The woman has nothing to prove. She is superior to us all. So why must she remind me so frequently?

Every time Lou adjusts my hips in class, I think of Indra attending this very same retreat, like me, and Lou's wife where Indra is now. I wonder if Lou adjusted Indra's hips with his wife looking on, or if he knew his intentions weren't yogic and left Indra alone. I wonder if Indra dreamed of Lou at night, and if in her dreams he would occasionally show up with his nose grown into a long elephant trunk, like Ganesha, and if that long trunk would find its way under her sarong from time to time. Not that I've had a dream like that. I mean—not yet, but given my propensity for filthy-mindedness, I'm sure it's just a matter of time.

IT'S PRETTY FREAKING hard to think about the yoga class I have to teach when there are fireworks exploding every five minutes.

Next week is Nyepi, the Balinese New Year, and the fireworks are a part of the preparation. I think they're supposed to scare bad spirits away or something.

It's certainly working on our Mop Ghost. So that's good.

The Balinese calendar is ridiculously complicated, but according to Jessica, the year renews itself approximately every nine or ten months. One year is about the length of the gestation of a human baby. Jessica delivered an exultant vagina monologue in response to this piece of information. The wisdom of the Ancient Yoni!

All over the village and in town there are monsters in various stages of production. These are the ooga-oogas. I love that name so much, I want to find every opportunity to say it. *Ooga-ooga*. Some of these monsters are enormous, at least fifteen feet tall, and trapped in bamboo scaffolding the men climb over to build their chicken-wire heads, or to place huge strips of papier-mâché over their faces.

The ooga-oogas are supposed to be scary enough to frighten away bad spirits camping out on the island. They are the main attraction on New Year's. At one time, after they paraded the ooga-oogas through town, they burned them in the cemetery. Now, Lou said, they parade them through town and then sell them to German tourists.

April 26

We are so obnoxious in anatomy. SuZen has completely lost control of us. We pass notes and talk out of turn. We crack up and tickle each other when we're supposed to be feeling our partner's iliopsoas and adductors.

We're engaging in just the sort of behavior that would have had my mother shrieking from the front seat of the car, "I don't want to police you! Don't make me be a policewoman!"

In class this morning, Jessica kicked me in the occipital while I spotted her in handstand. We both cried. I blame Indra.

Everything Indra does bugs me now. I mean, I love her, I guess, but I'm sick of being told what to do. I'm sick of her calling me Sister Suzanne. I'm sick of clinging to her apron strings. It's time to cut the freakin' cord, already.

Later

Solipsism is boring.

I am boring.

My navel is boring.

Today I wonder: Is this all just ritualized narcissism dolled up to look like a system of virtues, an inner science, a path to God?

Also, would Jessica like to step out into the night in search of dessert?

She would!

That is the opposite of boring.

April 27

Baerbel and I just had a great laugh about her unabridged Upanishads.

Wow, that sounds so lame, doesn't it?

Well, anyway, we were talking about how Baerbel showed Indra a lesson in the Upanishads about how to woo a woman, and Indra was *not* amused. The lesson goes something like this:

Step one: Tell the woman you want to go to bed with her. If she says yes, then go to! If she says no, proceed to step two.

Step two: Bring the woman presents. If she now says yes, then go to! If she says no, proceed to step three.

Step three: Bring her a big stick. Beat her with this stick until she says yes, and then, go to!

Ah, *religion*. It's the greatest.

Baerbel says that Indra didn't even want to talk about this lesson. She said that Indra seemed uncomfortable and unwilling to consider that there might be something *wrong* in the Upanishads.

I love it. Makes me think of Lot's wife—both before she's turned into a pillar of salt, when Lot offers up his daughters to the angel-raping men of Sodom and Gomorrah, and after her salt-self has commingled with the sands, when her daughters get Lot drunk and have sex with him. As Baerbel put it, it's good to have these stories in our holy books, to remind us that they were written by humans. Filthy-minded, morally ambiguous humans.

Evening

Baerbel and I went out for lunch, and she forced me to eat some green leaves and rice before ordering dessert. I told her that I was making up for lost time. She told me I was practicing jalayoga, which is union with food.

I told her that jalayoga sounded very romantic, and that she was more than welcome to share my killer brownie with me. She thanked me and we asked for another spoon.

April 29
Nyepi, the Balinese New Year

We'll be let out of class early today in order to prepare for the holiday. We have tomorrow off. The entire island has the day off, in fact, because after the New Year's celebration tonight, the island, by custom, becomes as still and silent as a ghost town. Which means that you can't make any loud noises or use any electricity, and you can't leave your house all day. Apparently you will be fined if you're caught out of your house or turning your lights on.

It's all part of the plan. Tonight the parade will scare all the bad spirits off the island. The ooga-oogas are sort of like Bali's nuclear weapons in their ongoing war against the spirits—the ooga-oogas will rid the island of every spirit, from the small, pesky ones who inhabit blenders and animate mops, to the cruel, angry devils who break our minds and sicken our loved ones, who engender violence and worry and heartache.

The ooga-oogas must be noisy and awful-looking, capable of inspiring such terror that the spirits will flee the island en masse so as not to piss themselves from fright. At midnight, the lights must be out and everyone at home, and then you huddle down for twenty-four hours so that the spirits think that everybody has deserted the island. If there's nobody here, then there's no point in possessing our "abandoned" blenders and mops, so the spirits don't come back until they start to figure out that they've been duped.

I love it. Tricking the tricksters!

After Midnight

I'm still digesting the night, both literally and figuratively.

The parade of ooga-oogas wasn't like a parade at home, where people line the streets and are held to the curb by barriers and policemen on horseback. In my American imagination, the ooga-oogas were on floats, maybe with Junior Miss Ubud waving at us in her offering crown of gold-boxed chicken and fruit. But such a sterile, safe parade is not for the Balinese. By the time the moon rose in the sky, downtown Ubud looked like someone had dropped a twelve-ton bag of rats in the center of it. People swarmed the shadowy streets, standing around as if to block the parade from passing through, perching on fenceposts and ledges: thousands of Balinese people and the tourists who love them.

Jessica and I pushed our way through the crowd until we found a relatively empty spot in the middle of the street. Soon, through the half-lit gloom at the end of the road we could make out the first collection of gamelan musicians approaching.

Each ooga-ooga was preceded by its very own gamelan marching band. The musicians were all male, in matching shirts of orange, red, or blue; they almost looked like soccer jerseys, as if eventually they would be setting aside their instruments to play a match. The sound was deafening. These pieces of music weren't the whimsical, transcendent sounds we often hear floating out of the wantilan in the evening. They were battle sounds, armor rattling, steel being sharpened. I was surprised to feel the music throbbing anxiously in my chest; I was nervous and wanted to run away from it.

But when the first ooga-oogas came marching into view, I relaxed. They were adorable. Baby monsters built into bamboo palanquins carried by young boys in blue jerseys, each with a swath of black fabric tied around his forehead. The scariest of the boys' monsters looked like a school project, papier-mâché painted a matte emerald green with black scales drawn on, its head like Puff the Magic Dragon, but with giant teardrops of tomato-red blood dribbling down its neck.

We turned to watch the boys continue down the street, until an explosion of fireworks behind us jolted us to attention. The little boys were done. Now it was the men's turn.

At the end of the street, a creature seemed to be called up from the shadows by the din of its own orchestra. Enormous, at least fifteen feet tall, with the body of a dog and the face of Rangda, a creature with a tongue of fire and black thatch hair. Its front legs moved as if to swipe the crowd with its razor claws. Its jaws opened and closed, each time setting off an explosion of firecrackers. It sat atop a giant bamboo grid, in which at least a dozen men in orange jerseys stood, acting as the monster's many-legged throne. They gave the monster its dance, running it into the crowd, dipping and bowing as a group to make the monster do the same.

The parade became interactive. The monsters and the men in their grids moved so quickly, in a sweeping motion, that they were upon us before we realized that we needed to run. They shuddered, pitching forward suddenly only to halt, shake, and twitch into their next thrust onward. I'm still not sure what would have happened if we had failed to get out of the way. It seemed certain that we would be trampled, and so we ran.

After that first rush of adrenaline, I caught my breath and looked at Jessica. "Forget the Macy's Day Parade," I said. "This is the Macy's Day Parade on acid."

The final monster loomed from halfway down the street, a female form rising above the one-story buildings from the largest grid full of men. She swept through the crowd, painted red, her shapely legs squatting in a menacing sort of Horse pose, her breasts pointing straight ahead between her flying arms, the blood-red nipples standing out like bullets. Her hair was orange straw and red rope, and it flew around her face as she dipped and swerved and shuddered toward us like a bloodsucking Raggedy Ann doll. She pinched her black talons together in sharp, bloody mudras. This one would scare the worst of the spirits away.

She was mesmerizing, perched atop her grid, dipping and running and swooping forward, threatening to trample anyone who failed to get out of her way. Her long hair swept the street as if to lash the faces in the crowd with knotted red ropes that looked like barbed wire. Beneath her, her minions sweated and wailed as her hair flew about her face, as she smiled through her fangs. Her orchestra played for her, and the men made her dance.

In the space of a breath, before she was on top of us, I thought of what I was going home to. I noticed how that world has fallen away from me, but now seems to be creeping in, the way the spirits must creep back to the island when they start to notice they've been duped, that nothing has really changed. But then the monster's hair whipped across our faces and there was no more time for thought. So we ran, at first laughing as we ran, but when we looked back she was on our heels, so we ran faster.

We ran until we had lost the parade and recovered our senses. We slowed as we approached the Bali Buddha and turned to look at each other, giggling sheepishly. We were kids so caught up in a scary game we'd forgotten it wasn't real.

Jess and I had decided to celebrate New Year's on our own, at the Bali Buddha, over wine and desserts. But when we got there I looked up and saw Jason and Lara leaning over the balcony, trying to yell something down at us, but they were laughing so hard they couldn't speak.

When we stepped onto the balcony, Jason threw his arms around us. "You looked terrified, like you were being chased by monsters, not puppets!" he said. "Silly girls."

Jessica and I were so busy making excuses for ourselves that it took me a minute to look around and notice that Jason was leading us toward a round table overflowing with dessert plates, shot glasses, and candy wrappers. Littered with beer cans and bottles of wine both empty and full. And seated around this table were all of our yogamates: Baerbel offering a hunk of chocolate cake to Marcy, Marcy pouring herself a fresh glass of red wine; Lara gesturing to the waiter to pass round the Sambuca shots he had brought on his tray; Jason borrowing said waiter's lighter in order to set each shot on fire.

My yogamates were going to have to do a lot of karma yoga to make up for this night.

I don't normally like doing shots, but tonight I drank sugary liqueurs with my yogamates as if to drain an ocean's worth with a thimble. We toasted everything we could think of to toast, but mainly we drank to fuel the gossip. Somehow we started referring to each other as Brother Jason and Sister Jessica, as in, "Brother Jason, will you please light my shot on fire?" Or "Sister Marcy, will you please elaborate on your theory that Indra has secret conversations with crystals, and that they tell her she's enlightened?"

Jason complained that it's hard for him to concentrate in anatomy class when SuZen asks Indra to take her clothes off. We did a shot to ease his pain, and then another after dissecting her conversation with Jessica about paying for anatomy class, and another when we fell into hysterics over how horrible anatomy class is, and then someone got going about how Indra said that we, like, always have to keep our hips facing forward like headlights in Pigeon pose, and how she seriously doesn't understand that when she criticizes us for not having our hips facing forward like headlights, she's a serious hypocrite, because in Pigeon pose her hips *do not face forward like headlights* and it's just so annoying and frustrating and...

Okay, so we got a little petty.

There was one revelation, though. Lara had brought her statue of Indra to show everybody. "Did you notice anything wrong with the woodcarvings Indra sold us?" she asked. She reached into her canvas Ganesha tote bag and pulled out her statue, still partially wrapped in newspaper.

She handed it to me. "Do you see anything wrong with this woodcarving?

I looked at it, turning it over in my hands. It was exactly the same as the one Indra had offered us in the wantilan; a wooden portrait of Indra, her arms outstretched in Warrior Two. "Yeah, it doesn't look anything like her," I said.

Lara and Jason started to laugh.

"Look more closely, love," Jason said. "Pay attention."

I ran my hands over the rough wood. And then I noticed something. Tiny holes. There were tiny holes all over the carving, as if someone had used a pin-sized drill to puncture every inch of the statue. "Oh," I said. "Is this—"

"Woodworm!" Jason cried. "Every single statue that woman sold us is infested. This little Indra is being eaten from the inside out by worms."

Baerbel laughed, tapping her hand on the lip of the table. "By the time we get them home, they will be nothing but inspiring piles of dust."

"Woodworm, Lord!" Lara said. "I mean, for God's sake, she should know better."

"Well, I plan to keep mine," Baerbel said, leaning back in her chair and folding her hands at her midsection. She was enjoying herself. "I have a wedding to go to next month, and I do not like the bride. So I am going to give it to her and tell her that it would look very nice on her grand piano!" She beamed happily around the table.

"Nice, Baerbel," I said. "Very enlightened."

"So, what are we going to do?" Jessica said quietly. She looked around the table at all of us, bewildered. "I just don't understand what's happened with Indra. I thought she was enlightened."

We fell silent. I didn't know what to say. Jason and Lara

exchanged glances. Baerbel shrugged. Marcy started to say something about how maybe we were being sexist to blame Indra for everything when Lou left his wife for her, but by then it didn't matter; the restaurant was closing, and we had to get home before silent day began.

We were running late. The streets were already empty of people and motorbikes. Streams of multicolored crepe paper floated in the wind, collecting in the gutters and drains on either side of the street. They caught in the vines hanging along Campuhan, as if we had stumbled upon a wild party whose guests had simply dissolved into the air after the last dance. It was so quiet, and the streets were still so festive. We were the last to leave. It wasn't even our party.

We walked in the middle of the street, a small army of drunken, shit-talking future yoga teachers. We were a mutinous lot, rolling through the streets on a Sambuca buzz, chanting slurred mantras and skipping past collapsing scaffolding that used to cage in the ooga-oogas.

Jason pointed to twelve feet of derelict scaffolding in the pavilion just before the turn to the ninety-six stairs. He whistled at it. "The monsters have been released!" he cried.

NOW I'M SITTING up, listening to the fireworks and the dogs and trying to digest all the food and drink. I feel revolting, like I just ate a drugstore's worth of junk food. I can't help but wonder what happened to my retreat, exactly? Is this just an inevitable equal and opposite reaction to a puritanical seven weeks?

All this talk of spirits has got me thinking about the night of the blender exorcism. I keep picturing Indra that night, leaning into Lou. And the story she told me about driving cross-country to get away from her life.

Isn't that what I've done, essentially? I've crossed the world to get away from my life. And now my life is hurtling toward me. Seven days. Seven days till we leave.

Was there any point to this retreat? I mean, sure, I'll end up with a certificate to teach yoga, but I've never really given a rat's ass about certificates. I'd much rather know that the experience meant something than to have a piece of paper assuring me that it did.

April 30
Silent Day

I dreamed a girl I knew was going to kill herself. I stole her poison so she couldn't do it, but someone had to die, so I drank it myself. Didn't even give it a second thought, just down the hatch, one fell swoop. Next thing I know, I'm reincarnated. I'm in a different home, and I don't yet realize that I have a different body. Soon I find out that Jonah, my sister, and the rest of my family are learning that I've died. I panic, thinking that maybe I can e-mail Jonah and tell him I'm okay, but I can't figure out whether I'm a ghost or a new person. I try to call, to write, I try telepathy. I manage to reach my sister by telepathy, and she's relieved to know I'm alive, but the panic to reach Jonah is overwhelming.

I'm devastated, in the dream, to think of what I've done. This horrible mistake I've made.

Suddenly I'm in one of my lit classes in college, with the Sailor's sister, and I see my mother outside the classroom. I follow her up to her bathroom in our old house, the house I grew up in, where she's pruning a large ficus plant. I try to tell her that I'm me, but she just cries and says she must be going out of her mind. Then I remember I've committed suicide. I see myself walking into the ocean, holding two black plastic film containers full of poison, drinking from them as the waves rise around me.

The most important thing for me to do was to find my people and tell them that I didn't do it because of them. Once they had accepted me in my new body, I wanted everything to go back to normal. I rehearsed this speech over and over in the dream, telling Jonah and my family that everything would be exactly the way it had always been, that I hadn't changed so much, even if I seemed different. I told Jonah everything I could tell him that only the two of us would know so that he would believe me. I was still his.

And the whole time I kept thinking, *My God. What have I done?*

I got out of bed just now and looked at my naked body in the mirror on the armoire. I am different. I look sort of thinner, or more sculpted, as if I've been subtly remodeled. And I keep thinking, if my body is changed, what about my mind, my heart? What about them?

7. To Keep My Love Alive

I've always wanted to have an experience like the ones
you read about in spiritual memoirs. All spiritual memoirs
follow the same path, from *I was lost* to *Now I'm found.*
Failure leads to soul searching, suffering, and setbacks,
but toward the end of the story, something happens: an
epiphany, a catharsis, a near-death experience, an encounter
with a wise native or homeless person. No matter what
the particulars are, spiritual memoirs always suggest that
there is a butterfly emerging from the cocoon at the end of
the journey, and that was what I wanted. I wanted Saint

Augustine's enlightenment in the garden, I wanted miracles and transformation. My story wasn't exactly like that.

I left Bali all too aware that I most certainly was not a butterfly. I did not feel transformed or enlightened. I felt exhausted and disillusioned. But eight years later I can see that I was changed. Simply meditating on the promise of transformation changes a person. But of course I wasn't a butterfly winging it home—I was simply a girl who had planted a few seeds that would sprout in their own time, whether I asked them to or not.

I noticed right away that it was harder for me to go back to mocking organized religion with my atheist friends. I was more willing to accept embarrassing things about myself, like that I might yearn for some sort of God or faith till the day I die, or that maybe I did want to join in the drum circle. (I haven't yet, don't worry.) The more I was willing to accept such embarrassing, unsophisticated truths, the easier it became to hear the lies I told myself.

I had wanted to leave Bali basically enlightened, with my whole life figured out. But by the end of the retreat, I was no clearer, so I opted to do what I thought I *should* do: *Don't look back, don't look around, just march forward on the path laid out in front of you. Stick to the plan.* I told myself that I would move to New York, and Jonah and I would love each other in a new, healthy, mature way, not like college kids playing at adulthood. I would let my family go, knowing that we loved each other and would see each other at the holidays. I would do what I thought I was supposed to do.

But somewhere in my mind or soul, a seed or two was burgeoning, and soon I began to see that entire scenario as a sweet, sad lie I had told myself for the most honest of reasons: because I didn't know how to do what my heart secretly wanted.

My story in Bali ended with a wedding, generally considered to be a sign of optimism and faith, a restoring of order. Which makes me think of Jessica.

Seven years after Jessica and I returned from Bali, I traveled an hour south of Seattle to sit in a beautiful garden between a purple Craftsman house and a matching outbuilding remodeled for massage therapy and yoga classes. The garden was Jessica's, and the event was her wedding. She wore her wedding shoes from Bali, the white beaded sandals. They were pristine.

If you met Jessica's husband, you would seriously consider engaging in some of the shamanistic rituals Jessica used to attract him. He's a great dancer, just like Jessica; he's tall and handsome and smart and...how do I put this? He's *normal*. Not even remotely woo-woo. He told me that the first time he tried to take antibiotics around Jessica, she said, "You know, you can't just take a pill to solve all your problems!"

To which he replied, "Well, can I take two?"

After the ceremony, I found him catching his breath beneath an enormous lilac tree in their backyard.

"Did you notice Jessica's mark on the ceremony?" he said, which was hilarious considering the ceremony consisted of a group meditation accompanied by Tibetan singing bowls, a gong ritual in which masculine and feminine gongs were played together to symbolize the union of yoni and lingam, an invitation to the four seasons and their attendant animal spirits to bear witness to the ceremony, a feather dusting with love and gratitude incense, a ritual thanking of the stone head Jessica used to bring her love to her ("and it worked!"), and a lot of talk about ecstatic coupling and evanescing and rippling their love outward.

I laughed and told him yes, I had noticed Jessica's mark on the ceremony. He shrugged happily and said, "I would have done even weirder things to marry Jessica."

I used to think that sort of sentiment was corny, but isn't that exactly what we're all looking for? Someone who loves how weird you are? A lover, a mentor, a God who looks at you with all your peculiarities and contradictions and sees not a design flaw, but a perfectly, uniquely lovable soul?

I was twenty-eight when I finally got it. I began to sense something real and weird in me that wanted to be known and loved. A part of me that wanted to believe in something, to be loved unconditionally, for exactly who I am. The need felt like a weakness. I was a child of the feminist movement, I shouldn't need anything but my ideals and my ambitions! I shouldn't need to lean on a man or a guru, and especially not on a God. So why did I want to so badly? I tried to tell Jonah about it, but I was too proud. Jonah thought I was strong. I couldn't disappoint him. Instead, I flew home to the embrace of family every chance I got, for long weekends and longer holidays, but none of my visits were long enough.

Both of my grandparents died while I lived in New York. I got the call about Gram not long after I moved, and I flew home at once, telling my new employer at a big consulting firm that they'd have to do without me for a while. When I got the call about my grandfather, I did the same. They could have threatened to fire me, and I wouldn't have cared. I needed to be there to say good-bye. I arrived the same day that Gabe flew in from Lake Tahoe, cutting short his vacation to attend to my Protestant grandfather, who had been a surrogate grandparent to my Catholic cousins. We were all there, flooding the hospital's waiting rooms and driving the nurses batty if Grandpa had to wait a second too long for his next dose of morphine. We sat with him for hours as his lungs filled with fluid, nursing and telling jokes, and occasionally, in the space between night and day, we would pray.

Gabe arrived at the hospital near dawn. We barely said hello before he began performing the last rites. My brothers and sister and I had waited up for him, and now we held

hands around my grandfather's bed and prayed. I couldn't
have told you who or what I prayed to—my acoustic skull?
the thrum in my chest?—but I prayed he wouldn't be in
pain much longer. I had the feeling that he was going to an
eternal sleep, that after this he would be no more, and we
wouldn't be seeing each other again. And yet...and yet!
I also felt that I could be wrong, that I couldn't know for
sure.

He died while my sister and I were out getting lunch.
We rushed back to the hospital, and when we got there
my father told us we could still say good-bye, that "we
stick around for a little while" after dying. So we hovered
over his bed while my aunts placed photographs around
his body. Images of him at every stage of life, as a grinning
toddler, a newlywed, a father with his four children, a
picture taken in the hospital a few days before Gram
died, of my red-eyed grandpa holding one of his great-
grandchildren. As my aunts decorated his body with
pictures of his life, we told him how much we would miss
him, how much he had meant to us all. And all at once,
my chest corseted with sorrow, I felt myself get back to
work, tending an invisible garden.

. . .

Not long after I returned to New York from my grandfather's funeral, Jonah and I traveled upstate to attend the wedding of two members of our little urban family. The bride had asked me to teach a yoga class the morning of the wedding, and I agreed to do so, though the prospect terrified me.

To this day, it is the only yoga class I've ever taught outside of Bali. Technically, I'm not even certified to teach yoga. Those three days I was sick with the Bali Belly meant I was short a few hours for certification. Once I realized I wanted to be a yoga student, not a yoga teacher, I forgot about making them up. (Of course, if you come over and we drink a lot of wine, I might end up teaching a spontaneous yoga class. I've even branded this style. It's called *Drunkoffassana*. Pranayama, the breathing exercises, consists of my bumming cigarettes from you. You don't need a certificate to teach it.)

It was a beautiful fall weekend in upstate New York. All of our friends from Seattle and New York were there. Many of them had gotten married recently, and they looked like I wanted to feel. Jonah and I weren't fighting—we didn't do that much. We simply weren't interacting. We moved around each other. I glumly plotted ways to make us better, stronger, happier, but it was hard to reconnect when I kept leaving Jonah in New York to fly home to my family, and now my plans for our transformation only made me feel exhausted.

I held class in an old barn with a river running nearby. Half of the wedding party attended. I got there early to stretch and think about what I would do. I was stiff. I hadn't been to a yoga class in months, not since I decided the whole practice was a sham. Would I teach the yogaerobics everyone was doing in New York? Or something more peaceful and spiritual, like the class Jessica taught in Bali?

I taught a class Indra or Lou would have taught. I was nervous, but a few minutes in I almost felt as if they were teaching the class for me. Guiding my friends through the poses with Indra's voice in my ear, I remembered something about yoga that was easy to forget in the world of celebriyogis and sacred schwag. At its best, it nourishes something real in me. Something vulnerable and authentic, where I am most myself. Whether that's my soul or my nervous system, I don't know. But I watched it nourish the people in my class. I saw how being in a room

in which all were engaged in a ritual designed to improve
their hearts—their physical and metaphysical hearts—was,
in itself, nourishing. And that was the word—*nourish*—
that stuck with me that fall, as I prepared myself to inflict
pain on someone I loved. I was beyond being embarrassed
by the softness of the word, the self-help of it. It was the
correct word, that was all that mattered. It was a word that
made pain worthwhile, if at the end of my pain I would be
free to look for a life that nourished me.

You see, I didn't want to waste any more time.

May 2

Today is a day for monkeys. We graduate in two days and
this might be my last chance.

I was going to spend the day with my yogamates, but I
need to be alone. We had breakfast together at Casa Luna
this morning and I joked about ordering a brownie for
breakfast. Okay, so maybe I was seriously considering it. But
I didn't, because of something Baerbel said. I told her that
I needed the killer brownie because chocolate had become

my sex substitute. She said, "No, Suzanne. You are ordering the killer brownie because you have no self-discipline."

Everybody laughed, including me, but I can't stop thinking about it. I'm so embarrassed. Here I've been dreaming about this transformation, flattering myself that I've become someone new, someone bendier and more enlightened, and I haven't changed a bit. I'm sitting on a bench at the entrance to Monkey Forest, and I am myself, the same slob I've always been, just with slightly more upper body strength and an inflamed ego. On my walk here from Casa Luna, I noticed that Ubud didn't sparkle with exotic people and strange sounds the way it used to. It isn't a refuge or a getaway; it's just where I am. Still around people, still walking streets, still in my body; still me, watching me.

I can hear monkeys in there, screaming.

When I was seven years old, my father and I were part of an organization at the YMCA called Indian Princesses. Every month we met with other fathers ("guides") and their daughters ("princesses") and wore leather headbands with feathers dyed in primary colors sticking out of them. We wore leather vests with beaded fringe dangling from the hem. The big wooden beads meant something, each one a gold star for some sort of Indian-ish accomplishment like archery or learning how to smoke salmon. As Indian princesses, we would learn to be like Pocahontas, who painted with all the colors of the wind, and wasn't a pussy like suburban girls. We would have cool, nature-based names that sound sort of stilted when you say them, like you're a real Indian. I was Snow Star. My father was Thunder Frog.

It was the greatest: I had my father all to myself, and I got to dress up like an Indian, and once a year we went on a campout, which was a chance to learn how to row a boat and dig for clams and be Indianlike.

It was on one of these campouts that I got lost. We were on Orcas Island, only a few hours from Seattle, but at seven Orcas Island seemed as far from home as Bali. My dad had stayed back at the cabin while I went for a walk through the woods to the beach with one of the guides and a clutch of princesses. I must have drifted off to look for shells because when I looked up, the beach was empty. I had lost my tribe.

I had recently seen *Greystoke: The Legend of Tarzan* at my aunt's house, so I knew that if you got lost in the wild you turned into a monkey. I sat down on a rock and looked out at the sea, then back up at the wooded cliffs above the beach, and the yellow fruits in the trees weren't pinecones anymore, but bunches of bananas. I would either become a monkey-human, or I would drown when the tide came in. I remember looking out at the waves and deciding that I would just wait there until the tide came in for me. I tried to fall asleep, thinking death would come faster that way. Then I tried yelling, hoping that somebody would hear me and save me from my fate. But no one did.

What I remember most clearly is that even with all the rosaries and bedtime prayers and masses of my childhood years, it didn't occur to me in that moment to pray. My yogamates are always talking about this natural impulse we have to meditate, to pray to God or to a higher power, and I get it—I talk to the God in my head all the time—and yet at this crucial moment when I was as close to being an innocent child as I'd ever get, I didn't talk to God.

What does that mean?

God only knows. Ha.

So, I didn't pray. Instead, I got up off the rock and tipped it over. Hermit crabs darted in all directions and most of them were too fast for me, but one I could pick up. I cupped my hands around the tiny brown-red shell and little legs and found another rock, brushed its seat of sand with one awkward forearm, and sat down to focus on the little pincers nipping at the fleshy parts of my hands. It was comforting. I was small and the ocean in front of me was vast and indifferent.

Maybe that's it. Maybe I knew the truth when I was a kid, that the skies are empty, and the ocean proves the existence of nothing but the ocean. Maybe the natural world is all we get. I suppose it's possible I knew in some inchoate way that my religion was only my culture, something my people did to express the mystery that linked us, that made us witnesses to the absurd accident of each others' lives. Maybe I knew praying together was our way of eyeing one another as if to say, *You feel it, too, this strangeness? This bewilderment? You wonder, too?*

Enough. No more thinking. I'm going in to spend time with some distant relatives.

Later

The monkeys in Monkey Forest are as tame as house pets— tamer, even, than the dogs that roam the streets of Ubud. I mean, sure, they're still completely spazzy, but in an endearing way. But maybe that's just because watching them dart here and there, now grooming themselves, now screaming at a mate, now sitting and spacing out in a papaya coma, I do feel a certain kinship.

The forest itself is stunning. The stone path that leads to the center of the forest is wide, with a waist-high wall along either side that is coated in a velvety green moss.

I spent a long time sitting on that wall and watching as tourists cooed at the mother macaques with their doll-like babies. They sat on their haunches and ate their bananas and papayas almost elegantly, not so much tossing the peels aside as dismissing them, like a fop in a Molière play. They might have been casually dropping a perfumed handkerchief on a settee, knowing an obliging servant would soon be by to pick it up. And there he was, their servant: a small man in a yellow sarong and black T-shirt, feeding the monkeys from a basket full of papayas.

A bit farther down the wall, I noticed two mother macaques sitting together on the ground, facing each other with their babies in their laps as if they were discussing the tribulations of modern motherhood, the importance of work/life balance. I moved toward them and crouched a foot away to get a better look. They ignored me. The babies clung to their mothers' hairy chests and stared at me. Jesus, they were cute. It occurred to me that I would like to have a monkey for a pet. Also, that I would like to be Jane Goodall, go to Africa and live with chimps. Embrace science, for a change. Abandon all this hocus-pocus in exchange for empirical proofs!

Just as I was thinking this, a sudden weight landed on my shoulder and tiny fingers clung to my hair. I turned my head to look into the funny face of a young macaque. He grinned at me and proceeded to rub a banana peel on my arm. At the same time, a tall, bearded white guy approached with a grin.

"Cheeky monkey!" he cried, laughing. The monkey posed happily as fanny-packed tourists rushed over to capture the moment with their digital cameras. I sat still as long as I could, smiling at my new friend as if I were Jane Goodall posing for her latest book. But I was still me, worrying less about Jane Goodall things like monkey habitats and chimp behaviors than about the possibility that this cheeky little bugger was going to pee on my shoulder or give me lice. My new friend was grooming my hair as if he had already passed his own critters over to my head. His little fingers at the nape of my neck tickled. I stood up, trying to stay poised for the photo op, but as I did so, my new friend jumped off my shoulder onto the ledge and hopped away, screaming.

As I sat back down on the mossy wall, brushing slimy bits of banana off my arm and shoulder, I noticed that the white guy was still hanging around, watching me. He was long and gaunt, at least six foot two, and skinny, as if he'd been five foot five before he was put in a taffy pull. He wore his white button-down shirt untucked, and it was stained with sweat under each arm. His hair and beard were short and inky black. And he was tipsy, maybe drunk.

"Can I join you?" he asked, smiling broadly. He had an Australian accent.

I really would have preferred to be alone. "I'm just watching the monkeys," I said.

"I wasn't asking about monkeys," he said. "I asked if I could join you."

I shrugged. "Whatever," I said.

"You don't have to beg," he said happily, sitting down on the wall next to me and extracting a pack of cigarettes from his breast pocket. For a minute or two we were silent. He smoked, and I did nothing but focus on not asking him for one. I wished Baerbel were there to see me being so disciplined.

"So, what is it, then?" he finally asked.

"What is what?"

"What is it you're doing here in Ubud, classic traveling

question." He looked me up and down, his gray-blue eyes a little foggy, but mostly curious.

I told him, and he jumped off the ledge to the ground. "Yoga!" he said. "I do it, too." He sat on the cobblestones in lotus. Then he winked at me before bending forward at the waist in order to slide his arms through his legs and lift himself up off the ground.

All this with a cigarette clenched between his teeth. He beamed at me and spoke like a yogic Humphrey Bogart: "I learned it in India."

I was speechless. And annoyed; I still can't do that pose. "What were you doing in India?" I asked.

"I was in jail there for eighteen months."

"Oh."

"My cellmate taught it to me."

"Ah." I made a mental note not to go deeper into the forest with this man.

"But, you know, asana really isn't where it's at. You've got to meditate. Asana is the easy part. Meditation is where you'll find true liberation. And then you'll be able to recognize the real beauty of life."

This tan, hairy drunk was telling me about the real beauty of life. I laughed. "I think I'm looking at it right now," I said, gesturing at the trees and the monkeys.

He looked puzzled. "So, what are you learning in this yoga camp of yours? Wait, let me introduce myself. I'm Carl."

"Suzanne."

"Okay."

"Well," I began. "I'm learning about…" I looked at Carl, then straight ahead. My brain hurt. I couldn't think of a single thing to say. I've fried my brain with pranayama and Sambuca shots. "I'm learning about yoga, and—well, shit. I don't know."

"You'll find your true self in meditation," he said. "If you keep doing it. Most people think meditation is a bus you take to your destination. But no." He shook his head as if to second himself. "It's a struggle. A struggle every minute, but it's the most worthwhile activity there is."

This was when I decided I was too old to think that bums were wise. "I'm going to walk a little farther in and see some more of the forest," I said, standing. "It was nice to meet you."

"That's cool," he said, standing to join me, and the next thing I knew, we were walking deeper into the forest.

That's me. Sticking to my guns.

"Look at us," Carl said, skipping along beside me. "Two yogis on the path, walking down a path." He grinned at me, rolling his eyes a little, which made me laugh in spite of myself.

"I'm not sure if I'm on the path or not," I said. "I think I may have fallen off the path."

"You just don't want to struggle," he said, and just hearing the word *struggle* made me want to lie down right there in the middle of the forest. I took a deep breath and sighed.

"Okay," I said, "so why is meditation such a struggle?"

"The mountain."

"Okay?"

"You're eventually going to discover the mountain you have to climb. You look ahead of you and see that enormous mountain, you look behind you and, just having tasted a bit of the serenity of meditation, all's become misery. You see too clearly. So which do you choose?"

"I choose . . ." I stopped. "Hell, I don't know."

"Listen," he said, "do you want to be free from mental suffering?"

I nodded.

Carl began to shake, and then he started shouting like a preacher. "Do you want to be free…from pain?"

Suddenly my drunk companion went berserk, lifting his arms up and thrusting them repeatedly higher; he looked like Atlas trying to swat the world off his neck. He launched into a sort of drunken sermon, delivered in a twitchy caricature of a Southern Baptist. "Do you want to be free from confusion?" he asked me, "From lust, from resentment, from jealousy?"

I stood back and watched, shrinking slightly as tourists walking by were jolted from their monkey watching by my companion's performance. "Do you want to be free from anger? Do you want to be free from despair? Do you want to be free of politics and the raging abuses we heap on one another every day? Do you want to be free from fear?" His eyes opened, but they didn't focus on anything in particular. He blinked a few times and then lowered his chin so that he could look at me. He was waiting for an answer. I grabbed him by the arm and guided him back onto the path, away from the gawkers. "Seriously," he said. "Do you?"

"Yeah," I said.

He giggled and glanced over his shoulder at the scene he'd left behind. He turned to me and grinned. "Me too."

I am a lightning rod for the insane.

We walked along the path, aimless now. Carl pulled a flask out of the back pocket of his trousers.

"So, what did you do in India to land in jail?" I asked.

"I killed a pimp. Several, actually, but I was only caught for the one."

I looked at him. "Are you serious?"

"Yeah. Child-hustlers. I've never lost any sleep over it."

I nodded. "Well, good, I guess." I wasn't sure if I believed him or not. But something was distracting me from Carl's story of pimp killing. Each time I turned my head to the right, I couldn't help but sense that the macaque that had befriended my shoulder for a few minutes had left something of himself behind.

"Hey, Carl?" I said, interrupting him, "do you smell something on me?"

He leaned in and smelled my neck. He hummed. "Delicious," he said.

I laughed. "No," I said, "I think it's my shoulder."

He sniffed my right shoulder. "Ohh," he said. "Monkey ass."

"Gross," I said, pulling back. "I've got to do something about this."

Carl took on a more scientific tone. He smelled it a few more times, then wrinkled his nose. His whiskers twitched. "Tangy," he commented. "There's a distinct tang to it, isn't there?"

I had to laugh, but I wished I could take my arm off at the shoulder and chuck it into the ravine. I don't think I've ever wanted to transcend my physical body more profoundly.

Just then, Carl cried out. "Lookie!" he said. "Look at that!"

I followed his arm to where a large macaque was screaming and clawing in the direction of a smaller female. Another female rushed at the male, scaring him off for a moment or two before he came charging back at them, baring his teeth and hunching his shoulders to look larger.

"What is he doing?"

"Look, there," Carl said, "the one on the left."

The female in question was holding a calico kitten in her arms. Its tiny body bristled with fear as it clawed at the female macaque, who only held on to it more tightly. Once or twice the kitten managed to writhe free from the monkey's arms and crawl around her neck, but each time the mother patiently ripped it off like a piece of Velcro and cuddled it again. She appeared completely unfazed by the male macaque, as if she had absolute faith in the diplomatic powers of her female friend, who continued to bark and spit at the male.

Carl's face was reverent. "I love the animal kingdom," he breathed.

"You love the animal kingdom now," I said. "Wait till you can smell its ass on your shoulder."

We made our way back to the central monkey-watching spot, where we said good-bye. As I turned to leave, Carl wished me luck on the path. Then he pulled his flask out of his pocket and gestured with it, saying, "As you can see, it's done a lot for me." With that, our brief acquaintance ended. Carl drifted toward a group of French tourists, and I hauled ass to Casa Luna, where I've spent the past twenty minutes scrubbing my shoulder clean.

Later

I certainly believed in the wisdom of the Drunken Bum when I was a teenager. Just as I probably believed in the archetype of the Wise Native forever cropping up in westerners' spiritual narratives to dispense their simple, profound, native truths. College delivered me of that evil, I think. But perhaps not; my brief encounter with Carl has, strangely, obliquely clarified something for me:

The strongest among us are atheists. The weakest are those of us who would believe, if only we could. We are the most susceptible to despair. We want to believe, we sense there might be something out there, but we can't find it, can't feel it, or can't believe in it. And calling ourselves agnostics doesn't do a damned bit of good.

My head wants to be an atheist. I want to commit to this life, this world, this plane of being, a finite world of milkshakes and monkey asses. But I can't accept that science has excluded the possibility of a God. I don't buy it. Atheism would be as big a leap of faith as accepting Christ as my Lord and Savior. But I would love to be able to wake up and make choices knowing that I get one shot at life and that when I die, I'm dead.

I belong to the camp of wishers, dreamers, wouldn't it-be-nicers. I yearn for order, for sense. For God. That's why I'm here, I think. Because I'm too much of a pussy to just suck it up and make my own meaning.

My heart wants to believe. I want to be someone who wakes up every day and meditates, or prays, or goes to Mass or temple or the mosque. The atheist might say these folks are weak, that they need a crutch, but, my God, what I wouldn't give for that crutch! Life is hard and full of opportunities for strains and breaks. Good to have a crutch on hand, just in case.

I just wish that I could find a spiritual leader who didn't disappoint me. Or an idea of God that held water. Gosh, they're basically the same, aren't they? Indra, God, religion. All flawed. All disappointing, in the end, no matter how promising they once seemed.

But, Christ. Who am I kidding? I'm the disappointing one. I'm the one who doesn't want to struggle, like Carl said. Because I am a coddled American who still acts like a spoiled teenager. Poor me, my yoga retreat has disappointed me! Poor me!

You know what? Fuck it. Fuck that higher bird!

I'm going to go buy myself a purse. Isn't that my cultural religion? Weren't we all told after 9/11 to pray to God and go shopping?

Perhaps one learns to have faith from taking smaller leaps first.

Ah, yes. My precious. My dearest, my darling.

One small step for my inner doubter, one giant step for my outer wardrobe.

Perhaps I should think of it this way: my handbag could have come from the mind of a great designer, or from the chaos of an anonymous assembly line. But if everything is an illusion, then real or fake doesn't mean a thing. It just *is*. It is me, I am it. And, honestly, in this moment, I don't give a rat's ass if it's real or not. Go practice your cultural religion, Suzie-Q. Don't question it, just give in, indulge yourself. Isn't that what faith is all about?

May 4

I'm so happy about today. I woke up early, and I wasn't hung-over because Jessica and I actually stayed home last night and drank water and tea. Sure, we ate about five pounds of sugary black rice pudding apiece, but that's as bad as we let ourselves be. And we didn't gossip, either. We practiced teaching each other our classes, because today was our day to teach.

I was up early, and I meditated for an hour. I felt that familiar sinking sensation again. It occurs to me now that buying my handbag was the best thing I could do for my spiritual well-being, because now that I possess it, I don't have to meditate on it anymore. It's no wonder, really, that rich people can commit to spiritual quests. They're not consumed by lust for things because they already have them!

Maybe Su's uncle was right.

After meditating, I felt refreshed and ready to embrace the world again. And then we walked single file to class. En route, we passed three naked men who were bathing in the river, and they smiled at us and we smiled back, hello there, *selamat pagi*, wishing the men and their privates a good day.

I was shocked, at the end of my class, to discover that I loved teaching yoga. I loved it. The view from above is so different from the view on the mat. I could see everybody working so hard to improve themselves, some of them struggling. I could see Marcy looking around the room to compare her Standing Forward Bend to her neighbor's. I saw frustration on Jessica's face in Camel pose; she's been worrying that her heart isn't open enough, so chest openers give her a lot of anxiety. I saw six people walk in with tight hamstrings and sand in their eyes, and walk out a brighter, more fluid bunch. Teaching this class felt like an act of love. How strange.

I always thought I hated teaching. Probably because I've only ever taught kids. The last time I taught a class, it was to elementary school kids, and during an acting exercise I turned my ankle and, in front of a dozen eight-to-ten-year-olds, I said, "Oh, FUCK."

Yeah. Not so gifted with the children.

Later

I've packed up my things. How strange to see my suitcase so plump and the armoire so bare. Oh, but I am looking forward to being home. To laundry and tap water and lipstick and movies with my sister.

While I was packing, I found the Sailor's novel. Funny, I've hardly thought of it in the last few weeks. All of my dreams have been of Jonah. I'm so excited to get home and book my flight to New York. The Sailor is just a friend. It's nice to have friends you're attracted to, I suppose. Makes you feel alive. Especially when you've created this idea that their soul is like yours, that you both yearn for some kind of truth. I'd bet if we got too close, we'd be disappointed. Better to leave it unfulfilled.

We're off to the Jazz Café for one last night of debauchery before we graduate. Sweet Jesus, it's almost over. If that isn't an excuse for a little wildness, I don't know what is.

May 5

My yogamates and I have graduated, and Indra and Lou are married.

I feel like I've gone cross-eyed. Let's see, what's the tally for today?

Last class, last two milkshakes (not in the same sitting, I'm trying to be good after all), one graduation, one wedding, and one NARROW ESCAPE.

The trouble began last night, at the Jazz Café, when I tried to befriend SuZen and Marianne. I wanted to end our retreat as friends. Also, they were smoking, and I wanted to be near smoking if I couldn't enjoy it myself. (It was shocking to two yogis with cigarettes in their hands. Shocking in a good way.)

Anyway, the singer last night was a woman who sang like she was Ella Fitzgerald reincarnated. This led us to talk about jazz music and our favorite singers, and I told them about a Rodgers and Hart song I've always loved.

SuZen is pushy. The instant I mentioned the song, she started harassing me to ask the band to play backup so I could perform it for the entire club. Um, no. That was the last thing I wanted to do. She wouldn't let it go until I told them I'd sing it for them on the way home.

The song goes like this:

> *I've married many men, a ton of them*
> *Because I was untrue to none of them*
> *Because I bumped off every one of them*
> *To keep my love alive!*

The singer goes on to describe how she murders each of her husbands when they start to bother her. It's a great song. What women had to do before feminism, right?

So I sang it for them as we walked home, and SuZen went crazy. She thought it was the most hilarious song she'd heard in her entire life. "You should sing it tomorrow for Indra's wedding." she said. "She'll laugh her ass off!"

"I don't know," I said. I didn't think it was appropriate. A wedding is kind of a serious thing—I would think my teachers wouldn't want me to make a joke of it.

I told SuZen that I could teach it to her so that she could perform it, if she thought Indra would like it so much. That made more sense—SuZen is one of Indra's oldest friends, someone who could get away with an irreverent wedding offering.

"No," she said, "you have to do it, you've got it nailed! She's going to love it."

She went on like this all the way home, and by the time we parted ways, I had agreed to think about it.

"Then it's done," SuZen said. "You're going to be great." She waved good-bye. "It's going to be amazing. It's too perfect!"

I was still debating it with Lara, Jason, and Jessica this morning, when Marianne stopped by our house. She sat down at the table on our veranda, looking concerned. "I don't know what SuZen's thinking," she said. "I hope you aren't planning to sing that song today?"

I told her I didn't think I should, and she breathed a sigh of relief. "Thank God," she said. "I think it would be very rude, considering how many times Indra's been married."

I found this a little annoying, to be honest. Marianne acting like she was Indra's protector. "Well, a second marriage isn't anything to be ashamed of," I said.

Marianne shook her head. "No," she said. "I'm pretty sure this is her sixth."

!

!

!

Holy Hell in a Handbasket!

So I was about to sing a song about a woman who kills off her husbands in order to remarry at the wedding of a MANEATER.

At first we were all sort of stunned. "Oh," I said. "*Oh.*"

"Six times, she's married?" Jason said.

"But...but..." Jessica looked from Marianne to me and shook her head.

"We'd better get ready," I said to Marianne. I hope it wasn't too obvious that I was trying to get rid of her, but we couldn't respond as fully as any of us wanted to, so long as she was there.

As soon as we saw her head disappear beyond the pool, we freaked out.

Jason looked dazed. "SuZen set you up," he said. "What exactly was she trying to do, telling you to sing that song?"

Lara was *pissed*. She said she never really thought Indra was enlightened, that now that she thought about it, there had been so many signs...Jason and Lara started comparing notes to see who could have guessed it based on anything Indra had said over the last two months. Everyone agreed that this was the proof we'd all been suspecting, in one way or another: Indra was no god, no avatar, no prophet. She was no better than any of the rest of us, apart from her extraordinarily flexible spine.

"But she's made us think that she's so much better than us," Lara said seriously, "more enlightened, more evolved. And when you make yourself superior to others even though you're not enlightened, not truly superior, well, then—I think that makes you a worse person."

"A fraud," I agreed.

"A false prophet," Jason said.

Perhaps we were being unfair. I don't know. All I know is that our words made Jessica tear up. "You guys," she said, sniffing, "that's not the point. Indra is perfect as she is."

"Perfect?" I said. Now, writing this, I can hear how bitter I must have sounded. "Perfect, are you kidding?" I didn't want to listen to her. I was too angry. And if I'm honest with myself, it felt amazing, this anger. It felt righteous and invigorating, like I was pumping twice as much blood as normal. How liberating to kick Indra off her pedestal, and then kick her! And kick her! And stomp on her head!

I mean, my God. This woman had me believing that I should change everything. Drop my life off a cliff and go looking for something like her relationship with Lou. That if I took the kind of chance she once took, I might discover for myself the authentic life I thought she was living.

But how many lives does one have to drop off a cliff to get to that authentic life? How many Jonahs are left behind as she drives away? What's bothering me now is that I can't remember the exact words she used to tell me that story. Did she lie to me about her first husband, making it sound as if he was the only man she'd ever been married to? Or did I just edit out other statements because I loved this one narrative so much? I only have my own accounting of this story written down. Not hers.

But, even so. The tone she imparted was always that Lou was The One—not The Sixth. Good Lord, how did I fall for this woman? How did I lose my skepticism? I know that one must jettison skepticism in order to have faith, but it's my skepticism that protects me from these self-elected spiritual charlatans roaming this earth, ensnaring young and old when we are most lost, when we are searching.

Maybe this is Indra's final lesson for me. Jessica says that Indra is perfect as she is. That's what she kept trying to say, even though Jason and Lara and I ignore her. She said that the role Indra has been sent to play in our lives has been to disillusion us, to remind us that we must listen to our own hearts and souls, that we must walk our own paths to find God and love. She said Indra's on her own winding path, too, and that we should be grateful to her.

"Grateful?" Jason said. "What a lot of crap, Jessica. I'm sorry, love, but I'm not buying it."

"Think of the prayer we say at the end of every class," Jessica said, her eyes wet and full of conviction. "We say, *Om bolo sad-Guru maharaj ji ki.* 'We bow to the Guru of our own heart and soul.' That's the whole point, you guys." She looked at us, desperate, it seemed, for us to understand and agree with her. Her voice broke. "That's what this is all about."

I don't know. Sounds pretty Pollyanna to me. Here's what I think: I think I'm going to go home the same person

I've always been. Maybe that's not such a bad thing. Maybe I've always been fine, apart from this urge to transform myself, this urge to worship something beyond myself. Who knows? Maybe it's in disillusionment that we find ourselves.

May 6

Everybody's downstairs packing up Made's car to leave Penestanan. We head out in just a few minutes. But I want to write one last entry before I go.

Yesterday's ceremonies took place in the wantilan, of course, and we all wore special sarongs and sashes for the occasion. Indra and Lou looked beautiful, both of them dressed in white and gold sarongs, Lou with a white linen shirt over his, Indra with the traditional Balinese camisole and lacy blouse. She had taken her braids out so that her blonde hair fell down her back again.

Noadhi lit the candles on the altar, which overflowed with offerings. And then, just as he had done at the blender purification ritual, he took a bowl of water in one hand and a lotus flower in the other, and splashed each of us in turn. He pressed rice kernels on our foreheads and temples, and at the base of our throats. I tried not to laugh as Baerbel turned to me, blinking earnestly at the rice kernels stuck in her eyelashes.

I would have liked to hear the women's gamelan play, but it was several men from the village who played the women's instruments for the ceremony. The music began with a hoarse wooden flute, then six mallets struck a deep, broad chord. One by one we stood to go to the altar and collect our diplomas from our teachers. When we were all seated once more, clutching our certificates in our sweaty hands, Indra and Lou turned toward the altar, gesturing to

Baerbel, SuZen, and Jason to come and stand up with them. They formed a protective crescent around our teachers, looking on as Noadhi sprayed them with water, pressed rice on their foreheads and throats, and spoke his prayers in a low, muted voice.

As Indra and Lou followed the balian, I was struck by their attitude of deference toward him. Noadhi stands almost a foot shorter than my teachers, but his bearing made him seem larger, somehow. Powerful. He blessed them and bound them to one another, wrapping their wrists together in a white cloth stitched with gold. He chanted and they responded. With their chins bowed and their hands gathered in prayer, Indra and Lou looked like supplicants.

I knew so much more than I wanted to know about Indra, and I willed myself to see her wedding with my mind, not my heart. But the ritual overwhelmed everything my mind was screaming at me. It snickered, thinking *Maybe the sixth time's the charm*. It lamented, telling me I'd been betrayed by a false idol. But seeing them bound together, their heads bowed, I couldn't help but cry. We all did. We cried as if we were saying goodbye to teachers we loved, who loved each other. As if all of this had meant something.

Good-bye, Bali. I'm homeward bound.

Epilogue: The Healer

Could a greater miracle take place than for us to look
through each other's eyes for an instant?
— HENRY DAVID THOREAU, *Walden*

Lou once said that your injuries can be your greatest
teachers. An injury can teach you compassion for your own
mind and body, and if you suffer well, it might endow you
with compassion for others. Eight years after leaving Bali, I
know he's right.

A friend and I were having drinks a while back and
got to talking about what, precisely, makes breaking up
with someone you love but can't be with so agonizing. We
weren't talking about those breakups where the love is dead,
or was never there to begin with, or where one partner has

so injured the other that there can be no future. We were talking about the saddest kind of breakup, the one where you simply aren't right for each other, no matter how much love there is between you.

The trouble, as we saw it, was that the moment you break up, the entire relationship distills down to that first essence you fell in love with. Gone are the irritations, pressures, anxieties. You don't fixate on their hypocrisies or failures, or how they didn't understand you. You've broken up—there's nothing left to rail against. All that remains is the memory of that first, purest love you felt for the other person, and that, we decided, sucks balls. It hurts. When all that's left is that first love, the loss is so much greater— you didn't lose the person who, late in the relationship, made you feel trapped or duped or diminished. You lost the person you first fell in love with, who you went to bed dreaming about and woke up dying to see, the one who felt like the kind of home you'd always wanted to make.

You try to make sense of the end, but it makes no sense. For every moment that pointed toward our demise, I could name another that said we were soul mates, the stuff of forever, till death do us part. Trying to understand how such a pure, sweet love could become polluted and confused is an exercise in futility, like trying to understand the Trinity, or why so many people bought *The Secret*.

It took a long time and several journals' worth of agonizing before I understood the meaning of the word *futility*, and tried to move on.

The funny thing? I'm not sure who I'm talking about— Jonah? Or Indra?

Maybe both.

I wasn't in New York long. Less than three years. Long enough to make things work beautifully with Jonah and then for it all to fall apart when I finally admitted I didn't want to marry him, or live in New York, or live a life I wouldn't choose on my own. We parted as friends, sweetly, sadly, wishing each other well.

I flew home to Seattle to live with my aunt for a while, and soon found myself doing the same things every day: I read books about failed love affairs (*Anna Karenina, Madame Bovary, The Awakening*, all of which seemed to suggest that I should be considering suicide) and at night I did penance. All of those unsaid Our Fathers and Glory Be's poured from

my pen as I tried to understand what went wrong, what
I failed to do, how I could make things feel right again. I
replayed over and over again the morning Jonah and I said
good-bye, how we told each other *good-bye, good luck, I love
you.* I watched him in my mind, again and again, his posture
strangely stiff as he walked out the door that day.

I told myself I was being narcissistic, thinking I was the
pole on which Jonah's happiness turned. I told myself he
would be fine, I would be fine, that we were both allowed
to seek our own happiness. That was what we had promised
each other.

But one night, on my aunt's deck, I looked out at the
fresh, clean rain and the green trees of home. I smoked
cigarettes and remembered how, in Bali, I had wanted to
drop my life off a cliff and watch it break into a million
pieces. Now I had done just that, and what kind of person
would wish for such a thing? Had I really believed I could
get away without regrets? I thought of my family of friends
in New York, of the way my parents and siblings tiptoed
around me and tried not to mention Jonah. Oh, I was so
flawed. I was so fucked. I smoked as if to punish myself
for still breathing, drank enough coffee to give an ox

insomnia, and then stayed up all night writing journal
entries like this:

I suck.

I suck.

I am a Sucky McSuckerson.

Not as flowery as a Hail Mary, perhaps, but to my eyes
there was nothing truer.

After I'd finished reading yet another book in which order
is restored when a woman kills herself, my sister told
me she'd had enough. "Read something else," she said.
"Women don't have to kill themselves over men anymore!"

So I stopped reading entirely, to better focus on
my penance. I didn't read for weeks, just wound myself
around the same spool every day. But then, one misty gray
afternoon, looking out at the mountains from my aunt's
back deck, I heard the young voice from Sáint Augustine's
memoir in my head, the voice that changed everything for
him, that brought him to Christ. *Pick it up and read,* it said.

And so I did. I read the book the Sailor gave me. Three
years had passed since it lay in my suitcase in the armoire
in Bali. It still smelled a little like mothballs. Emaciated by

sadness, unemployed, living in my aunt's basement, I read it in small doses, like medicine. Or like messages from a man I was almost ready for.

The book was a collection of novellas about the misadventures of a character named Maqroll el Gaviero, or Maqroll the Lookout. The first story is Maqroll's journal of an ill-fated journey upriver through an unnamed jungle in South America. Early on, he distracts himself from the madness on ship by establishing precepts. "Remnants of life at the Jesuit academy, they do no good, lead nowhere, but they have that quality of benign magic I always turn to when I feel the foundations giving way."

I loved that. I read on:

"Is it true we forget most of what has happened to us? Isn't it more likely that a portion of the past serves as a seed, an unnamed incentive for setting out again toward a destiny we had foolishly abandoned?"

I put the book down and listened, for once, to my heart. And then, three years after he'd given me *Maqroll*, I called the Sailor to tell him I was reading it.

Soon my journal was full of his name—his real name, Kurt, which for so many years had felt too real, or maybe too sacred, to put into writing. I met him for a drink while my heart was still raw, and soon found myself telling him everything, absolutely everything, about my heartbreak, the years of writing about him in my journal in code, about how I dreamed of him all through my time in Bali.

One day we got to talking about God. We were in Kurt's bedroom, where we'd been living for most of that week, listening to Bob Dylan and eating cheese and crackers in bed. Kurt told me he was an atheist. "Always have been, always will be. I remember being fourteen and knowing there wasn't a God."

I told him that was how I wanted to be. To live this one life without postponing my happiness to the next one. "Kurt," I said, inspired. "Let's *not* transcend."

He laughed. "Why would we?" he said.

"No, I mean it. Let's not transcend. Let's just live together on this plane. Fuck all this transcending and questioning and yearning for God. Let's just do this. Be together. Read books. Maybe I can finally start living if I let go of this idea of God."

We were sitting face to face, our knees touching. "But you know," he said. "I don't think you would be yourself if you stopped looking. And besides, last I checked, being on the hunt for something real counted as living."

"So you're an atheist but you don't think people who yearn for some kind of God or spiritual practice are weird? Or dumb?"

He laughed. "Weird, yes. Dumb, no."

"So what if we had some children and I suddenly went all Saint Augustine and found Christ. Would you be willing to raise our kids Catholic? I mean, not that I will, but what if I did?"

"Of course," he said. "Or we could do the opposite of your parents: raise them with no faith, but send them to Catholic schools. See how *that* experiment pans out."

"Nice," I said. "Pawn 'em off on the Church to get their religion." I thought about it for a moment. "Or I could just teach them yoga."

"I am not raising a bunch of pissdrinkers," Kurt said. "My kids won't drink pee."

"Your wife won't either," I said. "Once was enough for me."

His eyes brightened, and I heard what I had said. "Oh shit."

His cheeks flushed red, and he pulled me closer. I clasped his face in my hands. "I didn't know you were possible," I said.

I left his house that evening in the strangest state. I
felt convinced that I had just said good night to the man
I wanted to spend my life with, and yet I couldn't help
looking over my shoulder like an adulterer. I went home to
write up a euphoric account of the day, and then followed
that with a night's worth of Hail Marys.

I kept up my penance for many months. And when I
wasn't luxuriating in my nightly penance on my aunt's deck,
I was with Kurt—and I was happier than I'd ever been in my
life. At times it seemed that there had to be something wrong.
A man isn't supposed to make you *happy*, especially when you
have no business being happy. I was being duped. The happier
I felt with Kurt, the less I trusted it and the more severe my
penance was later. Happiness? I thought. That's not for me,
not anymore. It's hair shirts and mea culpas from here on out.

But eventually my sadness gave way to a sort of
wonderment: waking up in Kurt's bed, I'd watch him sleep
and let the tiniest glimmer of hope warm me. Maybe this was
real. This love I'd heard about, the love I thought I'd seen
in Indra and Lou, the love I'd yearned for, might actually be
possible. It might actually be lying right next to me.

Sometimes I even found myself wondering: if a love

like this, the kind that jackknifes you open like an oyster shell, if that isn't a myth, what else might be real?

I was still having attacks of guilty penance several months into my relationship with Kurt, like aftershocks from the earthquake I'd been through. And once again I thought that a change of scenery might be the trick. So, one year after leaving New York, Kurt and I went to South America in search of Incan ruins and giant glasses of Malbec.

In Lima, our friend Kathi told us about the healer. A few times a year, Kathi and her family visit this healer, this *curandera*, in northern Peru for purification rituals. Kurt says that the second he heard the words *healer* and *rituals*, he looked at my face and knew he was screwed—I needed to see this healer. Six hours back from Machu Picchu, heads still soggy with the altitude change, we were on a plane north, to Chiclayo.

"We're off to see the wizard!" Kurt sang when our alarm went off at dawn.

We spent the day wandering around Chiclayo, visiting the hot, dusty pyramids of Túcume, and poking around the witches' market, where a man tried to sell me shrunken heads and Moche artifacts. At midnight we took a taxi to a lonely corner of town, where there were stray dogs, garbage in the streets, and one dim yellow street lamp that was nearly swallowed up by the dark night.

We were there to see Ysabel, the healer. Her assistant, Yolanda, greeted us at the door, and we gave her an envelope of cash, which she folded in half and pocketed before guiding us through the house. It was almost as dusty inside as it was in the street. Even the low ceilings had sandy cobwebs hanging from them.

Ysabel's husband and children were gathered around a small, dented television set. The house smelled of fish and frying oil.

Yolanda led us to a side door that opened onto a small courtyard. The night was clear, and we all instinctively looked up at the web of constellations above us. Soon we were arranged, squatting or sitting in lotus, around a small altar that Ysabel called her *mesa*. It was crowded with potions and colognes, prayer cards, rocks, sticks, figurines, pieces of ribbon, a half-dozen crucifixes, and a shallow gray-white Tupperware bowl filled with a greenish liquid. It looked like liquid Jell-O, but it was actually the juice of a mildly hallucinogenic cactus called San Pedro.

I've never been one to experiment with drugs, really, but tonight I drank the San Pedro up like it was going to cure me of some awful disease. As if it wasn't a drug, but a gate; as if Saint Peter himself were welcoming me into heaven with each cupful. I would walk through his gate tonight, and wake up tomorrow in heaven with God and the angels and the man I loved. We drank as Ysabel chanted the rosary in Spanish. We drank, and we drank again. It tasted thin and bittergreen, like biting into a dandelion stem.

After the drug kicked in, Ysabel asked us to stand in the courtyard. She gave each of us a smooth wooden baton and told us to rub our bodies with it. Our faces, our arms, our chests, legs, and feet. Throughout this scrubbing we were told to flick the baton away from our bodies, as if it had collected a sludge of bad spirits like the skim from hot milk.

We must've done this for hours. We scrubbed, and Ysabel and Yolanda prayed over us, walking between us as we worked, baptizing us with cologne and holy water and grain alcohol, which they blew from their mouths. I got to thinking that I was undergoing a massive spiritual exfoliation, scrubbing layers of penitence and regret and grief off of my body so that I could be new, so that I could step forward into my new life with Kurt, happy, free, liberated from my past. And it must have been the San Pedro, but I could actually see some of those bad memories and guilty feelings on my skin, like evil fairies that needed to be squashed with my powerful, magical healing baton!

They collected in a broken heap at my feet. The mound grew larger, and I felt lighter.

Every few minutes Ysabel or Yolanda would scrape my silhouette with metal or wood batons and then spit at me a few times. And I was rubbing my aura off, rubbing my skin off, rubbing out my past, and the lighter I felt, the more I thought, *It's working! It's working!* I released myself from Jonah, from New York, from my disappointed friends and worried family. I forgave myself and Jonah and even God—and I didn't add, as I almost always do, the words "if you exist."

I felt Kurt by my side, this tall, broad, bearded sailorman allowing himself to be spat upon by two women with rosaries in their hands and cactus juice in their teeth. This man could have dismissed such a ritual as impossibly airy-fairy, as the sort of thing he would never have done in

his life, but because he loved me, he was here. I could feel
him scrubbing his skin with the same seriousness of purpose
I had, and I wanted to tell him that having him there
made me understand the faithful; how they find a home in
their faith, a truth beyond doubt, a comfort never known.
I hadn't found that faith in God, not yet, but I had found
love, which was a kind of faith. I felt Kurt beside me and
allowed myself, finally, to surrender to my heart, to make
my heart a sanctuary for his. That ridiculous, embarrassing,
irrational organ had led me here, to a place my mind never
could have taken me.

Afterwards, we went out for beers. I hadn't felt so free,
so connected to the world around me, since my kundalini
breakthrough years before. I kept turning to Kurt and
saying, "Seriously, sweetie? We need to do more drugs."

The next morning I woke up with myself again. Not
ecstatic, not as liberated as I'd felt the night before. I could
still feel a little glow from last night's epiphany, but mostly
I was just me, a little tired, a little hungover, happy to see
the man on the pillow next to mine. And my thoughts
ran to Indra. For the first time, I imagined what her life

must have been like. Not the mythical life I had created

for her, but the life she had lived. I remembered her saying

something like, "You think my chest is open in backbends?

Have your heart broken as many times as mine has been,

and you'll find there's a lot more room in there!" At the

time, in Bali, I laughed, because it was sort of a funny thing

to say, but the truth behind her words didn't sink in. How

could it have? I wasn't thinking about Indra, not really. In

Bali I told myself I was thinking about Indra when I was

actually thinking about me. Now I imagined Indra leaving

that first husband of hers, driving cross-country in search

of God and transformation, and tears sprang to my eyes. I

understood now. Indra had suffered.

I thought of how many times she had been disappointed,

how many times she had started over, and it struck me

that the most extraordinary thing was that she still had

hope and faith. Suddenly that seemed more impressive and

inspiring than anything else she'd ever taught me.

Not long after we got back to Seattle, I visited Indra and Lou's

studio one more time. I signed in, I brought my checkbook.

The studio was the same as it had been years before, bright, sweet, simple. Still no boutique, though I did see two of Indra's woodcarvings perched on a windowsill.

Lou was teaching, but Indra was there, acting as his assistant. It had been four years since I'd seen them. Lou said hello, but his eyes were distant, and I felt that I had let him down somehow, that my absence had been an insult. But maybe that was me. Maybe I've always projected my fears onto Lou. Indra didn't notice me at first, and I wondered if the woman I had so wanted to emulate would recognize the woman I had become. It wasn't until I was folded in a standing forward bend that she saw me. She came over to my mat and bent herself in half to look me in the eye. Her hair was shorter and darker, and she was still as beautiful as I remembered her being. "Hello, you," she said. Her eyes were warm, and they knew me.

I smiled my hello. She looked younger, and happier, than I remembered her. When the class ended, she sat behind Lou, one hand on his back as they bent forward in namaste. I put my hands at my heart, as one does at the end of a class, and without reservation, I bowed to my teachers.

Acknowledgments

Nearly a decade has passed since I left Bali, and it wasn't long after I returned home that I started thinking about this story. Which is to say that I have nearly ten years' worth of advice, support, and favors to repay. I hate to think I may have forgotten someone, but if you are that someone, e-mail me, and I'll take you out for ice cream.

I am deeply grateful to Danielle Svetcov, my awe-inspiring agent, who believed in this book even when I didn't, and to Elizabeth Fisher, Monika Verma, Kerry Sparks, and all the good folks at Levine Greenberg for years of enthusiasm and faith.

Thank you to the magnificent team at Three Rivers Press: Domenica Alioto, Annie Chagnot, Tina Pohlman, Catherine Pollock, Caroline Sill, and Campbell Wharton. I'm particularly grateful for my editor, Christine Pride, whose insight, intuition, and sense of humor run through this book, and for Hallie Falquet, for stepping in to bring the *Bitch* home.

Thank you to my wonderful parents, Frank and Kathy Morrison, who have been almost absurdly supportive of a daughter who uses cuss words in her titles. And the existence of my siblings, Frank and Jessica Morrison, David and Jill

Jackson, Jimmy Morrison and Elizabeth Kennedy, suggests that there is indeed a benevolent God looking out for me.

I have an enormous extended family, the type of clan that inspires ushers at my shows to say, "Wait—all thirty want to sit *together*?!" Thanks for a lifetime of support to the Andersons, Bassetts, Dreschers, Gulacsiks, Hintons, Iversons, Jacksons, Morrisons, Mountjoys, Quarders, Schusters, Spieldenners, Thurtles, and Woods.

A thousand salutations in honor of Marlice Gulacsik for editing, advice, and lodging when it was most needed. And Virginia Schuster—thank you, Gini, for always upping the ante. If I've ever said *short story*, you've said *book*. If I've said *song*, you've demanded an *opera*. It has helped.

Thanks to Kathleen Jeffs, Lizzy Brown, Jamie and Lorna Brown, Rebekah Anderson, Claire Dederer, Brian McGuigan, and Keira McDonald. Thank you, Theatre Off-Jackson, Debut Lit, the Hugo House, 4Culture, and Artist Trust.

Thank you, Mary Ashley, Brad Wieners, and Kristin Kimball, for getting me started in New York.

Thank you, Status, Jay and Cheri Causey, Erin and Debbie Brindley, Kit and Tawny Case, Laurel Anderson and Cal Jackson. Thank you, Kim Namba, Brian Castellani, and Lia Aprile.

Thank you to my sounding boards and defibrillators over the past decade: Pace Ebbesen, Joby Emmons, Kathi Huber, Dan Humphries, Jessica Jory, Keisha Knight, Whitney Lawless, Tiffany Parks, Ryan and Maggie Rogers, Francesca Severini, Katy Sewall, Judah and Sarah Stevenson, Daniel Werner, and Amy, Michael, and David Zager. Thank you for the conversations, the coffees, the drinks, and the smokes. And for occasionally accompanying me to the yoga studio.

That goes double for Kate Hess and Andy Secunda, who gave me exactly the advice I needed at exactly the right time. I hope someday to return the favor.

Thanks to Josh Baran for his generosity and wisdom.

Thank you, Jessica Ryan, for many a milkshake, and my teachers, for introducing me to everything I love about yoga.

Thanks to the marvelous S. P. Miskowski, who repeatedly inspires me to keep working; Veronica D'Orazio for keeping me off the Planet Clare; and Crystal Gandrud, for being the kind of writer and friend I want to talk to all day.

Thank you to Mike Daisey, who has been a port in many storms, an ark in many a deluge, and a wise, dear heart I have often relied upon. Thank you most especially to Jean-Michele Gregory, who has been with me on this trip since I first came home from Bali and told her I might have a story to tell, who has read every draft, staged every performance, and whose mark is on every page of this book. JM, I quite literally could not have done it without you.

Finally, I give thanks to any and all gods that I get to share my life with Kurt Peter Anderson, who daily gives me courage and faith, and more joy than I ever would have believed possible.

SUZANNE MORRISON is a writer and solo performer whose one-woman shows *Yoga Bitch* and *Optimism* have played in New York, London, and around the world. She lives in Seattle with her husband and a delightfully inbred cat named Riley. You can find Suzanne blogging at the Huffington Post Books Section and at suzannemorrison.blogspot.com, where she writes about absolutely everything she's reading, writing, and rehearsing.